P9-BIX-060

The
THRACIANS

R. F. Hoddinott

The
THRACIANS

WITH 168 ILLUSTRATIONS

THAMES AND HUDSON

Ancient Peoples and Places
GENERAL EDITOR: GLYN DANIEL

To Barbara

© 1981 R. F. Hoddinott

First published in the USA in 1981 by Thames and Hudson, Inc., 500 Fifth Avenue, New York, New York 10110

Library of Congress Catalog Card Number 80–51906

Printed and bound in Spain

D.L. TO: 724-80

Contents

Acknowledgments

To list the archaeologists and others in Bulgaria, Czechoslovakia, Greece, Hungary, Romania, Turkey, USSR, the Ukrainian SSR and Yugoslavia who have helped my wife and myself in the research for this book would need another long chapter. I am sorry there is insufficient space for this, but I hope they will accept individually this overall expression of our gratitude for the time and trouble so freely given on journeys, at archaeological sites and in museums, for information, photographs and publications, and for aid in my own photography. The memory of this cooperation and the friendships thus made are a lasting pleasure to us both, undiminished by the fact that I have sometimes reached conclusions other than theirs and have not always been able to include mention of their valuable contributions. Exceptionally, I would like to record our debt to two who have died during the preparation of this book, Professor D. P. Dimitrov and Dr N. Fıratlı.

My thanks for generous gifts of photographs, and other help, are due to: in Bulgaria, the Committees for Art and Culture and for Friendship and Cultural Relations with Foreign Countries, Professor A. Fol, Director of the Institute of Thracology, Professor V. Velkov and colleagues of the Institute of Archaeology, Dr H. Djambov, Director of the Plovdiv Archaeological Museum, Dr D. I. Dimitrov and the Varna Archaeological Museum; in Romania, Dr R. Florescu and the Committee for Socialist Culture and Education, Professor D. M. Pippidi, Director of the Archaeological Institute and his colleagues, Dr H. Daicoviciu, Director of the Historical Museum, Cluj, and Professor M. Petrescu-Dîmboviţa, Director of the Institute of Archaeology, Iaşi.

Both at home and abroad my wife's contribution and support have been invaluable and indispensable. With pleasure I record my appreciation of the patience and meticulous care which Miss Sheila Gibson has given to her drawings. To Miss Nancy Sandars and Professor T. Sulimirski I am especially indebted for their willingness to share their wisdom and knowledge.

I am most grateful to the Hugh Last Fund of the Society for the Promotion of Roman Studies for a generous grant towards the expenses involved in the book's completion. I would like to thank the Great Britain/East Europe Centre and the British Council for help in making overseas contacts, and the Librarians and their colleagues of the Institutes of Archaeology and Classical Studies, the Warburg Institute and the School of Slavonic and East European Studies of the

University of London for aid with research material. In conclusion I would like to thank Professor Glyn Daniel, General Editor of the Ancient Peoples and Places series, for inviting me to join its many distinguished authors by contributing a book on the Thracians.

Foreword

Who were the Thracians and what was their place in European prehistory and history? The purpose of this book is to try to assemble the available evidence for an answer to these questions, even though tentative and often controversial.

Until recent years only a few scholars knew the Thracians as other than barbarian neighbours of the Greeks and, briefly, Romans. The written sources vary greatly in reliability and are usually applicable only to the fringe of Thracian lands. Relatively few Thracian monuments great or small have survived and many have been attributed to other peoples. The Thracians had no written language; their longest inscription, in Greek letters on the bezel of a finger-ring, has still to be satisfactorily deciphered. They are best known, perhaps, through their burials, and it has been much harder to discover how, even where, they lived.

Now archaeology, unevenly but with growing momentum, and aided by a reappraisal of the written sources, especially Herodotos, and by other disciplines, notably linguistics, is rapidly changing the picture. The Thracians are beginning to emerge as a people of great antiquity, who contributed substantially to the foundation and growth of Troy, who in the Later Bronze Age appear as a power to rank with Mycenaean Greece and Hittite Anatolia. Still important in decline, especially in relation to Celts and Scyths, they virtually disappear early in the Christian era.

This quest for the Thracians covers a wide geographical area with variable and uncertain boundaries, and a span of several millennia. I have tried to trace the ancestry, continuity and limits of certain traditions reflected in artefacts of everyday life which, even if some are shared with other peoples, taken together constitute a Thracian identity. Research has made me abandon many preconceived ideas and reach unexpected conclusions which I could only slowly accept. Others may disagree, but at this stage almost all conclusions are tentative and controversy essential to progress.

The present occupiers of Thracian lands have naturally brought different archaeological approaches and priorities. As far as possible, except for ease of geographical location, I have used natural ancient divisions, calling them North, Danubian, South and East Thracian. Moldavia encompasses Romanian and Soviet territories and Aegean Thrace Greek and Turkish ones.

Although often not directed specifically to the Thracians, the relevant multilingual literature is vast. My wife, who has worked equally with me on the research and writing of this book, and I have read and assimilated as much as time, capacity and availability would allow. The bibliographical references, which represent only a very small amount of this, are intended both as source material and a select bibliography, which their own bibliographies will amplify. We have supplemented our reading by extensive travel over many years in the regions concerned, visiting sites and museums and everywhere receiving generous help from archaeologists and other scholars for which we are truly grateful.

In a relatively short book personal fallibility is compounded by the need for compression, inevitably leading to oversimplification and also accounting for the omission of important material, *inter alia* the history of the Phrygians and of other expatriate groups and individuals.

Note on chronology

Thracian studies have been hampered by the use of widely differing chronologies. Until the 1960s it was customary to use the central European short chronology except in Greece and Turkey where an historical basis was available. During the 1960s Bulgaria and the USSR began to accept uncalibrated C_{14} dates based on a 5568 years half-life, although revision of earlier established dates has been a slower process. In the main, archaeological works published in the other countries concerned, although frequently avoiding absolute dating, continued to observe variations of the central European short chronology. Thus in the Early Bronze Age an apparent difference of a thousand years or more existed between the two banks of the lower Danube. Recently there has been a general and growing tendency to use C_{14} dates calibrated according to the Californian bristle-cone pine.

It has thus been necessary to try to formulate, however tentatively, a uniform chronological framework for the Thracian lands within which common internal and external developments could be related and harmonized with established historical dates. Carbon dating, appropriately calibrated (explaining the occasional use of higher dates than those appearing in quoted source material) has provided dates for certain key prehistoric sites, although the number with sufficient C_{14} samples still leaves large gaps. For most of the prehistoric period I have approximated major cultural and other changes to quarter or half millennia; even so, there may be a considerable margin of error. The consequent stretching of the short chronology Neolithic, Chalcolithic and Bronze Ages has, as others have already pointed out, sometimes necessitated reconsideration of south-east European, that is to say proto-Thracian and Thracian relationships with the Aegean region and Anatolia.

Today modern communications and other factors have established a common 'culture' over south-east Europe to a degree which was inconceivable during my first visits there in 1938 and 1939. Even now remnants of earlier cultures linger in remote, especially mountainous areas. The valuable comment of a Bulgarian archaeologist, excavating a Roman period cemetery, that if the pottery had not been found *in situ* it would confidently have been dated some six centuries earlier (p. 160) is a warning that all dating must be treated with caution.

I have kept the chronological divisions of the Neolithic, Chalcolithic, Bronze and Early Iron Ages as prehistoric eras begun and ended by periods of significant change, often long drawn-out and geographically variable. The terms Hallstatt and La Tène have been avoided as essentially central European. Their application to Thracian territories, common as it is, is often misleading.

R. F. H. August 1979

Key to Map of Thracian Lands *(overleaf)*

Bulgaria

1 Ahtopol
2 Ardino
3 Blagoevgrad
4 Botevgrad
5 Bourgas
6 Branichevo
7 Chertigrad
8 Chirpan
9 Devetaki
10 *Dionysopolis* (Balchik)
11 Dobrina
12 Douvanli
13 Endje
14 Ezero
15 Ezerovo
16 Galata
17 Galiche
18 Glava Panega
19 Gradeshnitsa
20 Haskovo
21 Kabyle
22 Kaliakra
23 Karanovo
24 Kazanluk
25 Krushovitsa
26 Kurdjali
27 Letnitsa
28 Lovech
29 Madara
30 Magoura
31 Malko Kale
32 Merichleri
33 Mezek
34 Mihalich
35 Nesebur (*Mesambria Pontica*)
36 Nova Zagora
37 Oryahovo
38 Panagyurishte
39 Pazardjik
40 Pernik
41 Pleven
42 Plovdiv (*Philippopolis*)
43 Polyanitsa
44 Pshenichevo
45 Ravna
46 Razgrad
47 Razlog
48 Rousse
49 Salmanovo (Denev)
50 *Seuthopolis*
51 Sevlievo
52 Shoumen
53 Silistra (*Durostorum*)
54 Sliven
55 Smolyan
56 Sofia (*Serdica*)
57 Sofronievo
58 Sozopol (*Apollonia Pontica*)
59 Stara Zagora
60 Svilengrad
61 Tolbukhin
62 Turgovishte
63 Turnava
64 Turnovo, Veliko
65 Varna (*Odessos*)
66 Velingrad
67 Vinitsa
68 Vratsa
69 Yakimovo
70 Yambol
71 Yunatsite

Czechoslovakia

1 Barca
2 Blatnica
3 Bratislava
4 Čaka
5 Chotín
6 Čierna nad Tisou
7 Ducové
8 Gánovce
9 Mad'arovce
10 Malé Kosihy
11 Nitriansky Hrádok
12 Spišský Štvrtok
13 Streda nad Bodrogom
14 Tibava
15 Zemplín

Greece

1 *Abdera*
2 *Amphipolis*
3 Axiochorion
4 Chauchitsa
5 Dikili Tash
6 Dimeni
7 *Dodona*
8 Kalambaka
9 Kavalla
10 Komotini
11 Krannon
12 Kritsana
13 *Maroneia*
14 *Olynthos*
15 Paradimi
16 Pateli
17 *Philippi*
18 Poliochni
19 Rakhmani
20 Servia
21 Sesklo
22 Sitagroi
23 Thermi
24 Thessalonica
25 Tsangli
26 Tsani Magoula
27 Vergina
28 Verria

Hungary

1 Bodrogkeresztúr
2 Budapest
3 Füszesabony
4 Gáva
5 Hajdúsámson
6 Hatvan
7 Kosziderpadlás
8 Nagyrév
9 Sopron
10 Szöny

POLAND

Volhynia

(CZECHO-)SLOVAKIA

TATRA

NORTH CARPATHIANS

Carpatho-Ukraine

Galicia

Podolia

Moldavia

HUNGARY

ROMANIA

Transylvania

APUSENI

EAST CARPATHIANS

Moldova

Banat

Voivodina

ORASTIE

SOUTH CARPATHIANS

Muntenia

Dobroudja

YUGOSLAVIA

IRON GATES

Oltenia

Jiu

Olt

BULGARIA

STARA PLANINA

SREDNA GORA

SAKAR

RILA

PIRIN

RHODOPES

Thracian Plain

STRANDJA

Macedonia

THASOS

SAMOTHRACE

Mysia

TU

Vardar

IMBROS

LEMNOS

AEGEAN SEA

LESBOS

SEA OF MAR

Thessaly

GREECE

1
Thracian foundations

The Thracian lands

The territory generally called Thrace today – Turkey-in-Europe, north-eastern Greece and most of Bulgaria – stems from the Emperor Diocletian's creation of the administrative Diocese of Thracia and is only a fraction of what were once the Thracian lands. More than seven hundred years earlier, Herodotos (V, 3) had described the Thracians as the most numerous of peoples after the Indians, commenting that only their chronic disunity prevented them from being the most powerful of all nations. Archaeological and linguistic evidence is increasingly supporting Herodotos' concept of a multitude of Thracians who, despite a fundamentally common language and heritage, failed ever to achieve a national consciousness.

Like the English, the Thracians were an ethnic amalgam of many different peoples assimilated over a long period, but their homeland was centred on intercontinental crossroads. It ranged from the lands enclosing the north Aegean to the northern foothills of the Carpathians and from the Vardar – (southern) Morava – Tisza valleys and much of Slovakia east into the open Pontic steppe and partly wooded forest-steppe of the Ukraine and into north-west Anatolia. The borders were mostly ill-defined and variable. In South Thrace, the Aegean region enjoyed a Mediterranean climate which also moderated that of the Thracian Plain between the Rhodope-Rila-Pirin and Stara Planina (Balkan) ranges, whilst the Sofia uplands were climatically and geographically closer to Central Europe. Danubian Thrace, between the gentler northern slopes of the Stara Planina and the steeper ones of the southern Carpathians, opened westwards into the central European plain and eastwards into southern Moldavia, the edge of the Pontic steppe. The Carpathian arc presented its most formidable face to the east, dividing North Thracians in Transylvania, east Slovakia and the west Moldavian foothills from the East Thracians of the forest-steppe and Pontic steppe to the Dnieper. Tributaries of the Tisza made communication easy between Transylvania and the central European plain, as did low Carpathian passes only less easily with the plains of northern Europe and the Thracian-inhabited territories of Galicia, Volhynia and Podolia. Notwithstanding many, sometimes drastic changes in the balance of population, this region maintained a fundamental cultural homogeneity lasting some six millennia.

The first farmers

The Carpatho–Balkan region was settled during the late 7th–6th millennia BC by Near Eastern Neolithic farmers, crossing on foot what has since become the Marmara, and possibly by sea to the north and north-west Aegean coast. They were drawn by the rich new opportunities offered by the fertile lowlands of south-east Europe in the Post-Glacial Atlantic climate.

The newcomers, proficient farmers with a mature social structure, spread along the north Aegean coast into eastern Macedonia and Thessaly, into the Thracian Plain, the Sofia uplands and the Vardar–Morava valleys, into the lower Danube valley, Transylvania and north of the Danube delta. Beyond the Prut they gradually merged with a hunting-foodgathering economy centred on the (southern) Bug valley. The various regional cultures – Early Thessalian and Pre-Dimeni, Karanovo I, Kremikovtsi I, Starčevo, Criş-Körös and, on the fringes, the Linear Pottery, developed individual identities but basically remained closely related in their agricultural economies, social organization, arts and anthropomorphic cults which strongly stressed fertility (Raduntscheva n.d.). Their original home has yet to be located, but the new settlers adapted successfully. In especially fertile areas, notably the Thracian Plain, many settlements persisted on the same site, building level upon building level, raising tells that record continuous occupation through the two millennia or more of the Neolithic and Chalcolithic periods and, in some cases, re-use during the Bronze Age and later (Piggott 1965, 44ff).

Tells excavated in the Thracian Plain show that continuity did not necessarily equate with progress (Georgiev 1967). The standard of the fine pottery of the initial stage was not maintained. Indigenous, originally aceramic hunting and foodgathering groups may have inhabited the mountains and forests. The Karanovo III stage here and in adjacent areas, often using stylized zoomorphic handles on cruder, monochrome ware, perhaps represented their descent on the plains and harsher social attitudes. A transitional stage (Karanovo IV) introduced the early Chalcolithic phase (Karanovo V) which, with corresponding developments elsewhere in the Carpatho–Balkans, laid the foundation for the later brilliant Chalcolithic cultures.

The Chalcolithic flowering

The later Carpatho–Balkan Chalcolithic phase, probably beginning late in the 5th millennium and lasting into the middle quarters of the 4th, was an era of unprecedented prosperity and artistic achievement. On the evidence of incised dishes and sherds at Gradeshnitsa and elsewhere tentative steps may even have been taken towards evolving a form of writing (Nikolov and Georgiev, 1970; Todorova, 1978, tables 30, 31). Although on the periphery, especially in the west, neighbouring influences were growing stronger, the various cultures still maintained a basic homogeneity. In the north-east was the Cucuteni–Tripolye; in Transylvania and the Tisza basin, the Petreşti and Bodrogkeresztúr; between the southern Carpathians and the north

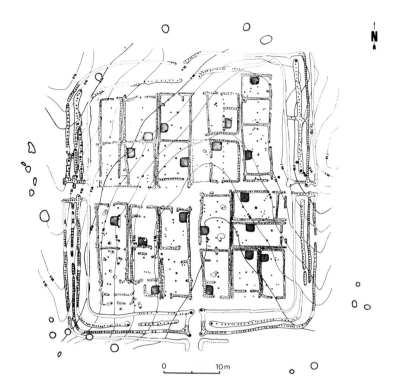

1 Plan of earliest settlement level at Polyanitsa. Early Chalcolithic settlements were usually sited on Neolithic tells which largely influenced their plan, but an expanding population spread to undeveloped north-east Bulgaria where relatively sophisticated planning appeared.

Aegean, and the Black Sea and Olt, Iskur and Maritsa valleys, the Gumelniţa (Karanovo VI in the Thracian Plain); west of this riparian divide to the Morava–Vardar valleys, the Sălcuţa and Vinča-Pločnik; in Macedonia, the Kritsana; in Thessaly, the Dimeni-Rakhmani.

A settlement founded in the early Chalcolithic phase at Polyanitsa in north-east Bulgaria shows a developed capacity for urban planning (Todorova 1976). The first step was fortification. Palisades, generally triple, had entrances at central points in the east, south and west walls. Outer and inner palisades used posts 25–30 cm thick; the intermediate one or, in places, two were less substantial, as were the northern defences bordering a swamp. That only the last of the eight Chalcolithic building levels was destroyed by fire was largely due to the constant attention paid to the defences. The second level saw the inner palisade replaced by a clay wall enclosing lines of tree trunks up to 50 cm thick. Horizontal beams with an earth fill joined inner and outer facings of wattle, thickly plastered with clay. The whole wall may have been 3–4 m high; burning of the outer palisades only served to harden the inner wall's clay surface. Later improvements were buttressing and strengthening the outer wall, with more ramparts at vulnerable points, especially gateways, which were also defended by clay-faced wooden gate-towers and by ditches 2 m deep crossed by removable bridges. Towards the end, crowding ruined the symmetry of the settlement, but its defences received increasing priority.

Polyanitsa is so far exceptional in its regular plan of a new and quite small settlement; most were rebuildings on earlier sites or dependent on the contours of river promontories. But such orderly planning was not confined to the Gumelniţa culture. That of the fortified settlement at Dimeni in Thessaly is well known. In the Ukraine, aerial and geophysical surveys have supplemented excavation to confirm the existence of large Tripolye settlements. At Maidanets in the Cherkassy district one covered some 300 ha of a plateau within a river bend; a population of about 20,000 may have inhabited the 1,500 identified dwellings, many of them two-storeyed (Artemenko 1974). The original circum-radial plan provided for open spaces, communal houses, presumably for family groups, and industrial quarters.

This Chalcolithic phase was boosted by a vigorous mining and metalworking industry in which copper played the major and gold a minor part (Renfrew 1969). Copperworking was centred on the Thracian Plain, northern Bulgaria, eastern and especially north-eastern Yugoslavia, central and western Romania and southern Hungary, but it served an area from the Adriatic to the Dnieper and from Thessaly to the north Carpathians and Tatra valleys (Chernykh 1974). Within the nuclear region, finds of crucibles, slag and artefacts in settlements far from sources of ore testify to extensive trade in untreated ore and to the intensity of production, largely of axeheads, axe-hammers, axe-adzes, awls and chisels, but also of ornaments and cult objects. Copper had already been mined at Rudna Glava in north-east Serbia. Now at Ai-Bunar, near Stara Zagora in the Thracian Plain, surface workings extended over 400 m and pits sunk 15–20 m deep (Chernykh 1978). Other mines worked in this region included Hrishtepe, near the rich Azmak tell, where one shaft ran to a depth of 27 m (Merpert and Chernykh 1972). A hoard found at Karbuna in Moldavia contained over fifty copper tools, pendants and plaques and nearly four hundred copper beads and other trinkets (Sergeev 1963; Klein 1968). Objects were generally forged, but latterly casting in closed moulds was also practised while welding was known to Tripolye smiths. Spectral analysis of Chalcolithic metal finds now in Bulgarian museums shows that at least 5 per cent were bronze, copper being artificially alloyed with, sometimes, more than 10 per cent of tin, an import from outside the Balkan peninsula (Merpert and Chernykh 1974; Chernykh 1974).

Specialist craftsmen produced the fine graphite-painted and encrusted incised ware of the Gumelniţa and Sălcuţa cultures and the Thessalian and Cucuteni–Tripolye painted wares, the almost baroque shapes of the last echoed more simply in the monochrome pottery of the west Carpathian and Bodrogkeresztúr areas. Their development of traditional Carpatho–Balkan Neolithic meander, volute and spiral motifs and, especially in Gumelniţa ware, of new, apparently abstract patterns reached heights of artistic achievement paralleling the elegance of the pot forms.

Decorative motifs chiefly originated in and reflect the basically agricultural Carpatho-Balkan society. The sun, represented by circles and by spiralling lines which rise and fall and rise again, is the most common, especially in the north. Fire, indicated by volutes or so-called 'wave' patterns but which really represent flames, gained additional importance by its use in metallurgy. The symbolic transference of the

2

3, 4

qualities of warmth and fruition to vessels and their contents was a natural act. Snakes also appear. In parts of the Balkans today, house snakes are still cherished; their role of preserving grain stocks from vermin may have preceded their symbolism of immortality. Small shallow 'cult tables', probably used for burning aromatic, perhaps hallucinatory substances, were an early Neolithic legacy preserved in the Gumelniţa, Sălcuţa and Vinča cultures, often with zoomorphic or anthropomorphic ornamentation. Bowls with high, hollow pierced pedestals were Cucuteni–Tripolye and Bodrogkeresztúr counterparts and, as biconical 'egg-cups', are found in the Thracian Plain and Sofia uplands.

Anthropomorphic figurines, and sometimes vessels, were ubiquitous except in the north-west. Most common were simple figurines, female,

2 Clay 'cult table' from Azmak. Ht 11 cm. The horns from the animal's head are missing.

3 *Left*: Painted clay Cucuteni–Tripolye 'incense-burner' from Truşeşti. Ht 37 cm.

4 *Right*: Biconical 'incense-burner' found near Plovdiv. Ht 36 cm. These 'egg-cups', undecorated, also appear at Troy (Schliemann 1880, No. 480).

5 *Opposite above, left*: Anthropomorphic clay vessel from an upper level at Gumelniţa, a forerunner of Early Bronze Age Trojan forms. Ht 22 cm.
Right: Fragment of a large vessel from the same level. Ht 28 cm.

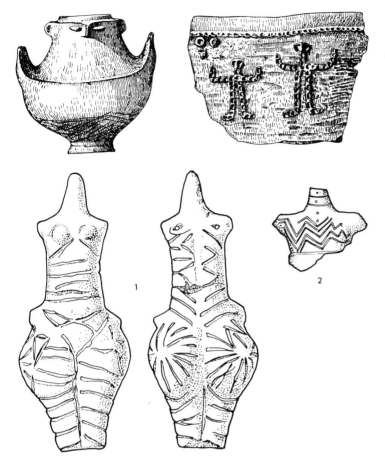

6 *Centre Left (1)*: Clay figurine from Luka Vrubletskaya. Ht 13 cm. *Right (2)*: Fragment of clay figurine from Olynthos. Ht 8 cm. Incised decoration on clay figurines may represent clothing or ornaments or emphasize bodily contours. Flat bone figurines, often highly schematic (*see Ill. 8*) are common in the Gumelniţa and Sǎlcuţa regions, sometimes partly encased in copper.

7 *Below*: Marble figurine from Blagoevo, near Razgrad. Ht 32.3 cm. Marble figurines are comparatively rare, but many in all materials have small holes drilled along each side of the head.

male or asexual, of clay or bone, but sometimes marble or limestone, varying in style from naturalistic to highly schematic. Clay figurines were sometimes seated in separate or integrated high-backed chairs. The more common type rarely reached 20 cm in height, averaging 8–12 cm. Bone figurines were smaller, the most schematic barely recognizable as human, only 6–7 cm high, the flat polished type seldom over 10 cm. S. N. Bibikov (1953, 206ff) believes the female clay figurines from the Tripolye site at Luka Vrubletskaya in west Podolia may represent a young girl at the point of maturity. This observation has a general application throughout the region and argues against the 'Great Mother Goddess' hypothesis. Grave goods in inhumation burials indicate provision for an afterlife but rarely include figurines, which are usually found broken, together with potsherds and animal bones, in what are often called 'rubbish pits' but may have had a ritual purpose. Almost all the intact specimens were single finds or excavated from destroyed houses.

In some cases, symbolism of fertility, whether personal or agricultural, such as sowing and harvesting, may be represented by pregnancy and steatopygy, or by clay phalloi. Figurines could also be talismanic symbols of the spiritual *alter ego*, perhaps conferred at a 'coming of age' ceremony and ritually broken and deposited away from the body in a sacrificial pit when death or other causes had ended their intended role. The lower parts of many bone figurines are often unworked or crudely fashioned, suggesting that they were held in the hand during ceremonies or stuck into a soft surface, such as grain in a jar. A stand for a group of seven, perhaps originally more, was found in a late Cucuteni–Tripolye level at Costişa in Moldavia (Passek 1949, Fig. 50, 1). An unusual group found with what may be symbolic models of houses, stoves and chairs at the bottom of a pit at Ovcharovo in north-east Bulgaria suggests the association of anthropomorphic and hearth-fire cults (Todorova 1973).

The cultural and socio-economic flowering due to agricultural prosperity and copperworking on an industrial scale had brought the late Chalcolithic Carpatho–Balkan region to a point where, given continuing favourable circumstances and political unity, it might have developed into a rival of the early civilizations of the Near East and Egypt. The geographical situation was favourable. Southward it faced the wealthy lands bordering on the east Mediterranean. Northward primitive herdsmen and hunters roved the north European plains and the contiguous forest-steppe where several millennia of 'Atlantic' climate had greatly extended the habitable area and increased its population. From here came amber, furs, skins and also useful immigrants.

8 Religious symbols of the later Chalcolithic period reflect a gradual evolution away from the anthropomorphic and towards solar cults throughout the whole Carpatho-Balkan region.

1 Vinitsa, bone Ht 7.6 cm
2 Karbuna, copper, Ht 10 cm
3 Karbuna, copper, Ht 10 cm
4–8 Salmanovo, bone (no. 6: Ht 8 cm)
9 Traian, Moldavia, gold, Ht 2.5 cm
10 Karbuna, copper, Ht 14 cm
11 Sesklo, clay
12 Sesklo, silver, Ht 3.5 cm
13 Sofronievo, gold, Ht 3 cm
14 Tirgu Mureş, gold, Ht 15 cm

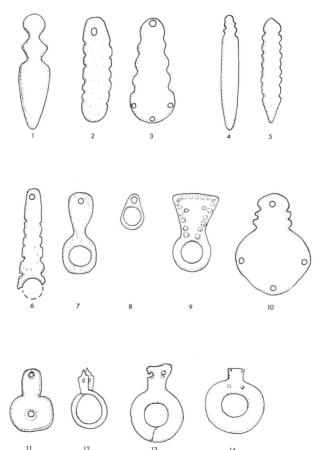

Yet even at its peak the late Chalcolithic era was undergoing fundamental changes. Side by side with the stylization of the anthropomorphic cults, solar cults were increasingly emphasized, tending to assimilate the former. The process foreshadowed in the Neolithic period by a shell pendant from Luka Vrubletskaya can be followed in the Chalcolithic pendants of the Karbuna hoard and in others from the Salmanovo (formerly Denev) tell in north-east Bulgaria (Gaul 1948). Gradually what had represented a human head became a tab. The object was no longer stood up or hand-held but was either a neck-pendant, as on the figurines on the terracotta altar from Truşeşti in north Moldavia, or an appliqué attached to clothing. The lower part became circular, either solid, usually concave, or a ring. The semblance of breasts still lent an anthropomorphic element to the predominantly northern Tîrgu-Mureş, Moigrad, Tisza-Szöllös, Hăbăşeşti, Progar and Hatvan pendants, although the number of bosses in the two last shows the loss of the original meaning. Eventually, in a cultural, not chronological progression, the tab disappeared. Gold was understandably the favoured metal for a solar symbol (H. Dumitrescu 1961); those illustrated are only a few of the many found – after the passage of over five millennia – but clay was also used freely. Unusually, the Karbuna copper hoard contains the full range from a stylized human figure to a cross-decorated circular sun symbol as well as signs of even more revolutionary forces which were also appearing at other eastern sites.

8

15 Moigrad, gold, Ht 22.6 cm
16 Tisza-Szöllös, gold, Ht 15 cm
17 Progar, gold, Ht 12.5 cm
18 Hăbăşeşti, clay, Ht 5.2 cm
19 Truşeşti, clay, Ht 9 cm
20 Hotnitsa, gold, Ht 3.4 cm
21 Varna, gold, Ht 2 cm
22 Gumelniţa, gold
23 Hatvan, gold, Ht 8.5 cm
24 Tibava, gold, Ht 2.8 cm
25 Hotnitsa, gold, diam. 5.4 cm
26 Luka Vrubletskaya, shell, Ht 6.5 cm
27 Dimeni, stone, max. diam. 3.17 cm
28 Varna, gold, diam. 0.6–1 cm
29 Rousse, clay, Ht 3.5 cm
30 Tibava, gold, Ht 2 cm
31 Karbuna, copper, diam. 9 cm

2
Thracian ethnogenesis

Transition to the Early Bronze Age

The transition from the Chalcolithic to the Early Bronze Age (EBA) was long and uneven. The many late Chalcolithic solar symbols, notably more common in the northerly Carpatho–Balkan lands, probably relate to a climatic change affecting vast areas of the northern hemisphere. Towards the mid-4th millennium the Atlantic climate deteriorated into a colder and wetter phase lasting a full quarter-millennium (Frenzel 1967). Resulting environmental changes were naturally especially severe in the north Eurasian land masses; even in the Thracian Plain a survey of the Nova Zagora region has shown severe disruption of Neolithic and Chalcolithic natural drainage systems. Erosion covered previously fertile land with extensive deposits of riverine clay. At the Dipsis tell at Ezero, in an especially vulnerable situation, a sharp difference between the lighter Cinnomonic soil of the Chalcolithic layers and the overlying darker, heavier clay of the EBA drastically changed the ecology of the site (Dennell and Webley 1975). There may be a relation between such changes and the large gap between Chalcolithic and EBA radiocarbon dates.

Reacting to the worsening climate, the Yamnaya (Pit-Grave) culture people from beyond the Volga migrated westward into the less severely affected lands of the Pontic steppe and forest-steppe. On the lower Dnieper these nomadic pastoralists overran the early Chalcolithic Sredny Stog group (Telegin 1973). They brought wooden, two-wheeled, ox-drawn carts and a new burial rite. Their dead, strewn with ochre, lay on their backs, legs contracted with knees upright, in a square or rectangular timber-lined and usually timber-roofed pit up to 1 m deep. A low earth mound, often encircled by stones, covered the grave. Grave goods, when present, were minimal and simple. Secondary burials in older tumuli were common but were dug through the mound into the subsoil (Shmagly and Chernyakov 1970).

Yamnaya people probably infiltrated the north European plain before coming to the Carpatho–Balkans. The absence of natural barriers and a common stock-breeding economy made for easy intermingling, peaceful or otherwise. An early Yamnaya group may have crossed the low north Carpathian passes into the Tisza valley and caused the break between the Chalcolithic Tiszapolgár and Bodrogkeresztúr cultures.

9

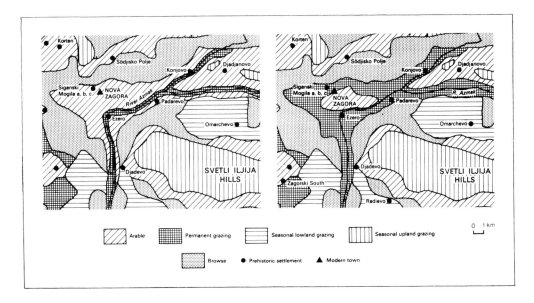

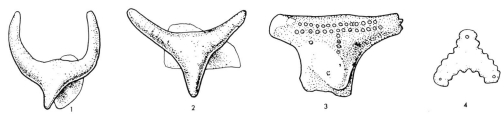

In the Carpatho–Balkans the intrusion was probably slower and intermittent, lasting possibly two or three hundred years. In the climatic circumstances the earliest newcomers' stock-breeding skills must have brought increased wealth. Their traditional livelihood was associated with a cult of horned animals, chiefly cattle but also sheep, usually symbolized by their horns. In the late Chalcolithic period horns and solar symbols appear together. At Hăbășești, in Moldavia, as well as anthropomorphic and solar symbols, semi-naturalistically modelled zoomorphic heads decorate pots and are accompanied by miniature horned animal figurines (V. Dumitrescu *et al.* 1954). At Rousse (Georgiev and Angelov 1957, Fig. 56) and in the Karbuna hoard the horns are schematic, the latter still influenced by accompanying anthropomorphic and solar forms. Other examples appear at Gumelnița, on Cucuteni pottery at Sărata-Monteoru and on part of a ram-head 'cult table' at Gradeshnitsa in north-west Bulgaria.

Both solar and horned animal symbols are present in the newly found cemetery at Varna (I. Ivanov 1974; 1975; G. I. Georgiev *et al.* (ed.) 1978). Gold tabbed pendants, circular appliqués and eye-discs appear with stylized horns symbols of both crescent and 'anchor' types. An especially rich grave also contained a gold sceptre and two gold appliqués of cattle. It is questionable whether the schematic bone figurines are anthropomorphic or zoomorphic.

9 *Above left*: At the end of the Chalcolithic period ecological changes seriously disrupted agriculture. *Above right*: In the Ezero region heavy flooding drastically reduced the area of arable land in the EBA.

10 Immigrant steppe pastoralists popularized the horned-animal cult in Moldavia. Relatively naturalistic forms, as found on pottery at Hăbășești (1, 2) persisted throughout the Bronze Age, appearing in the Thracian Plain in Ezero level V (3). A copper appliqué from the Karbuna hoard (4) probably represents a pair of schematized horns.

11 Ritual objects from the Varna cemetery. 1. Crescent-shaped horns symbol, gold, W. 3.5–3.7 cm. 2. Anchor-shaped horns symbol, gold, Ht 1.2–2.1 cm. 3. Bull profile appliqué, gold, Ht 5.8 cm. 4. Anthropomorphic or horns symbol appliqué, bone, Ht 18 cm. Wealthy burials at Varna show the penetration of the horned animal cult even at the Chalcolithic peak. Besides numerous round gold appliqués (*Ill. 8.21*; *Ill. 8.28*) there were many horns stylized in the form of crescents or anchors, as well as two bulls in profile. With them were schematic bone figurines of a type found elsewhere in the region, as at Gumelniţa, Rousse and Golyamo Delchevo.

In favourable conditions this eastern infiltration might have given new impetus to the flowering Carpatho–Balkan civilization. Instead, the climate continued to deteriorate and the Yamnaya trickle became a torrent, causing a general population surge southwards with increasing conflict for land capable of supporting fewer and fewer people. Complete destruction overtook the wealthy Chalcolithic settlements north and south of the Danube. Few ever recovered. At Hotnitsa, near Turnovo a gold ritual treasure was left undisturbed in the ruins (N. Angelov 1958). An extensive Chalcolithic layer in the Devetaki cave near Lovech ceased abruptly, to be overlaid with no discerned hiatus by a much smaller transitional EBA layer (Mikov 1960).

How much the devastation was due to pressure of refugees and how much to Yamnaya raids is impossible to say. There is no doubt about Yamnaya presence in Moldavia (Zirra 1960). Their stone horsehead sceptres, relics of raids, have been found at Fedeleşeni near Iaşi, at Casimcea in the Dobroudja, Sălcuţa in Oltenia and as far south as Rajevo, near Plovdiv and Suvodol in western Macedonia (V. Dumitrescu 1957; D. Berciu 1962). Their graves have been found in tumuli in Moldavia and the lower Danube valley and at Endje (Popov 1930–31) and Madara in north-east Bulgaria.

In the open steppe between the Bug and the Danube estuaries an early consequence of Yamnaya migration was the emergence of the Usatovo–Folteşti culture. Formed mainly from indigenous Tripolye

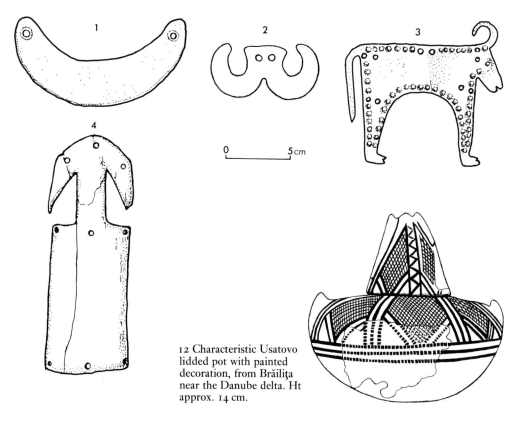

12 Characteristic Usatovo lidded pot with painted decoration, from Brăiliţa near the Danube delta. Ht approx. 14 cm.

people and Yamnaya-influenced Chalcolithic refugees from the lower Dnieper, characteristics of both are reflected in its pottery. Usatovo, now a suburb of Odessa, was a major settlement covering some 500 ha where remains of stone dwellings and pits filled with potsherds, animal bones and ash have been excavated. Its cemeteries included two groups of tumuli and two of flat graves. The tumuli, ringed with stones dug into the ditch made by the removal of earth for the mound, contained one to five crouched inhumations in pits roofed by timber or stone slabs. Ochre staining was rare. Offerings in primary graves included copper weapons and tools and painted pottery. As at Varna, several were symbolic burials or cenotaphs. The flat-grave inhumations followed a similar ritual but with poorer offerings (Passek 1959; Zbenovich 1973).

In the steppe between the Dniester and the Danube a 1964–66 expedition excavated twenty-six tumuli of various periods, containing over three hundred graves (Shmagly and Chernyakov 1970). Six of the earliest, all primary burials, were Usatovo, and these tumuli, like the five with Yamnaya primary burials, two of them double, contained a total of eighty-six secondary Yamnaya graves. A single Usatovo tumulus, at Nerushai, had more than eighty later insertions. Two large Yamnaya secondary graves at Glubokoe had no human remains, although burnt horse, dog and other animal bones were found. Other Yamnaya graves inserted into the tumulus here were roofed by stone slabs which included anthropomorphic stelai like many others found in the Pontic steppe, the Crimea, at Baia-de-Criş in Transylvania, the Dobroudja and north-east Bulgaria. At Ezerovo, near Varna, three were found in a row 2–2.5 m apart; below one were human bones and EBA potsherds (Toncheva 1967). Such discoveries may be evidence for a Yamnaya ancestor cult, whether the stelai stood on the tops of mounds or in a sanctuary associated with a cemetery, as the Ezerovo find suggests.

During the same period in the Dobroudja and lower Danube valley displaced groups from east and north moved into Gumelniţa territory, forming the Cernavodă I culture (Morintz and Roman 1973). At first, settlements were unfortified and the many handmills in wattle and daub surface or, occasionally, semi-dugout dwellings testify to a settled agricultural economy. Absence of mound burials refutes direct Yamnaya influence. The finer pottery still used high quality clay but mixed it with crushed shells. Graphite painting was discarded and the plain, polished surfaces were usually decorated with cord-like or comb-streaked impressions. Stone tools were typically late Chalcolithic; antlers and cattle bones made hammers and hoes. Copper artefacts – awls and knives – seldom appear and the absence of flint weapons and tools points to a breakdown in contact with the Stara Planina area as well as loss of technological skills.

In northern Moldavia the short-lived Gorodsk–Horodiştea culture succeeding the Tripolye–Cucuteni was under ever-increasing pressure by new Yamnaya arrivals and by northern Globular Amphora people. Burials reflect the confusion. Tumuli co-existed with flat graves, pits with timber-lined chambers, and skeletons, with or without ochre, were extended or variously crouched. The stronger and more stable

Folteşti II culture was the outcome, although waves of Yamnaya intruders persisted (Zirra 1960).

About the same time and under perhaps even more confused conditions the alien Cernavodă II culture (Morintz and Roman 1973), strongly Yamnaya-influenced and related not to Cernavodă I but to Folteşti II, penetrated the Dobroudja, east Muntenia and south Moldavia. It is represented at Cernavodă by a layer up to 2 m thick.

Dwellings were flimsy, two levels of the plastered floor of a large surface building being the main structural find. Pottery, quite unlike that of Cernavodă I, was made of clay mixed with sand, crushed potsherds and fine gravel. Characteristic decorations were horizontal bands of cord-impressed, incised or sometimes hatched motifs and finger-impressed cordons applied below rims. Crude channelling was occasionally used in the Danube valley. The intrusion of Cernavodă II people forced Cernavodă I groups southwards into the Dobroudja and west along the Danubian flats of Muntenia and Oltenia. Assimilating local influences, Cernavodă I evolved into the basically pastoral Cernavodă III. In the north Dobroudja and east Muntenian steppe the Cernavodă II group remained to become a formative element of the important EBA Glina III–Schneckenberg culture.

The Central European Baden and related cultures, also under Yamnaya pressure from the north but mainly to fill the void left by the breakdown of the Carpatho–Balkan cultures, expanded east and southeast to gain control of the desolated but strategically desirable lands. Trade routes already linked the Baden lands with the north Aegean, '. . . the most characteristic types of Hungarian EBA pottery', writes I. Bognár-Kutzián (1963, 552), 'the two-handled jugs of the Perjámos culture, the one-handled jugs of the Nagyrév culture or the analogues of the bowls with obliquely flattened broad upper rim, and even their prototypes, recur in the Lower Danube regions, in the Morava valley, Macedonia, Thrace, the Turkish part of Thrace and in Asia Minor.' The Morava–Vardar was probably the main route and its protection would have been a strong incentive, but the direct Niš-Sofia-Plovdiv-Edirne 'Diagonal' road was also important and the fertile Thracian Plain a worthwhile prize.

A substantial Yamnaya intrusion into the Tisza valley is marked by tumulus burials and by potsherds with corded and channelled decoration (Kalicz 1968, 16ff.). Its scale probably explains the hiatus between the end of the Bodrogkeresztúr culture and the arrival of new Baden settlers (Hájek 1961; Bognár-Kutzián 1973). Eventually Baden migrants overcame the Yamnaya opposition and pushed eastwards into Transylvania, west Oltenia and north-west Bulgaria, absorbing or eliminating native Chalcolithic elements to create the Early Bronze Coţofeni culture.

In north-west Bulgaria Chalcolithic settlements had suffered the same fate as those in the east. Only Krushovitsa was resettled in the EBA. Here, as in new settlements, the pottery shows a complete acceptance of Baden influence. In the Sofia uplands an excavation at Peklyuk illuminated the end of one village. It was first attacked by slingstones. By one house four pots inside a fifth were smashed, three stones remaining among the shattered fragments. Others were scattered round a potter's kiln, filled with the vessels and other objects he was firing. No other pots, household goods, tools or skeletons were found, suggesting that after this first attack the inhabitants fled with their possessions, leaving the unfinished contents of the kiln. Three querns were used by the raiders to break it open while still burning, so deforming some pots and smashing others. The village was then burnt down, unintentionally completing and preserving the potter's work inside the kiln to the present day (Petkov 1964).

Preliminary reports of excavations at Dikili Tash and Sitagroi (Photolivos) in the plain of Drama and Paradimi, near Komotini, suggest that here the Rhodope barrier led to a more gradual transition. At Sitagroi a layer (IV) with inferior monochrome pottery separated the Gumelniţa (III) and the EBA (V) layers (Theocharis 1971, 20; Renfrew 1971). Any EBA occupation of Dikili Tash was brief; at Paradimi it is clearer and probably lasted longer (Theocharis 1971, 26), but it is not yet certain if either had a transitional stage or was temporarily abandoned.

In Macedonia and Thessaly the transition was smoother. Mountain ranges protected both areas from the main Yamnaya impact and diverted displaced groups towards south-eastern Thrace. Central European and other influences coming by the Morava–Vardar, Strymon (Struma) and Nestos (Mesta) routes were not disrupted. Yet in Thessaly the new Dimeni culture was closely related to northern Carpatho–Balkan changes, and the subsequent Thessalian III Tsangli and Tsani Magoula pottery, the increasing trend towards the Rakhmani monochrome black ware, the use of parallel incised lines sometimes smoothed to produce a rippled effect, were all reaching into a common EBA.

A site could be destroyed in a day, but the settlement of new peoples and the general adoption of new ideas and customs took centuries. The old population may have been decimated but was not exterminated. Some crossed into north-west Anatolia and the north Aegean islands; others took refuge in the mountains where, adapting to hard and dismal conditions, they retained relics of their Chalcolithic customs, temporarily safe from the essentially plains-dwelling newcomers, to become with them permanent elements in the fusion of races making up the people whom the Greeks were to call Thracians. We do not know if they had a common name for themselves.

Transylvania and the Lower Danube

Early in the Carpatho–Balkan EBA, which occupied much of the 4th and most of the 3rd millennium, emerging earlier in some places, later in others, the Baden-influenced Coţofeni culture established itself in Transylvania. What little is known of the first phase comes mainly from stratified levels in caves, notably at Băile Herculane in west Oltenia. In Transylvania seldom more than collections of potsherds mark its advance across the plateau (Roman 1976; 1977).

In the second phase a few settlements with both surface huts and semi-dugouts suggest a more stable society. Pottery improved in quality. Punched lines, using an almost vertically held instrument, and cord impressions were new decorative techniques, and latterly a form of red slip.

The third phase of this essentially pastoral culture was the longest. Permanent settlements occupied naturally fortified sites. Most tools and weapons continued to be of stone, flint, bone and horn, but primitive copper tools appear – awls, fishhooks, chisels, flat axeheads, cutting blades, spearheads and daggers. The last had short double-edged pointed blades with rivet-holes in the triangular or rounded head.

Pottery improved. Wide-bodied, high-necked amphorae with small handles on the bulge or flat strap-handles on the shoulders and cups with rising handles and slant-cut mouths were new developments and, in the Danube area, small 'dippers' or 'scoops'. Ornament was more careful and restrained. Incised, including 'herring-bone', patterns, punched lines with encrustations and the red slip continued, but cord imprint was rarer. Hatched triangular motifs were common. Part of a clay anchor-type horns symbol pendant was found at Govora in north-east Oltenia (V. Dumitrescu 1974, Fig. 488/12).

Diversity of burial ritual, including tumulus and flat graves, reflects mixed origins and influences, with a strong Yamnaya element. In tumuli at Turnava, in north-west Bulgaria, one mound contained ten single burials, all close in time and all in rectangular pits, carefully roofed lengthwise with poles and neatly covered with earth (B. Nikolov 1976).

The primary grave, 1 m below ground level, was the ochre-stained crouched inhumation of a middle-aged man with a white-encrusted two-handled pot by his skull and ox or other bovine bones strewn outside the pit. Seven secondary burials were also ochred inhumations, one crouched like the primary grave, the rest (one man, two women and three children aged six to twelve) laid Yamnaya-fashion on their backs, knees raised. Two cremations, both carried out elsewhere, lay on specially levelled platforms, partially walled with uncut stones. One platform was shared with a female skeleton. Grave goods were few or non-existent: one or two pots (bowls, askoid jugs or a two-handled vessel identical with that in the primary grave), ox and sheep bones, usually outside the pit except in the platform cremations. One child wore a shell necklace; another had a tiny copper ring on the right shoulder, and the third a similar ring on either side of the skull. A gold lock-ring lay by one woman's neck.

One contemporary mound close by covered a single urn burial. Another hid parallel pits containing the skeletons of two middle-aged men lying on their backs, probably both buried at the same time. Only one had slight traces of ochre, on the skull; he had no grave goods. In the other pit were two open-ended gold rings. No animal bones were found.

During the formative Coţofeni stage, the Glina III–Schneckenberg culture, named from the third layer of the Glina tell, near Bucarest (Nestor 1927–32), and the south-east Transylvanian settlement at Schneckenberg (now Dealul Melcilor) was evolving from Cernavodă II. Covering much of Muntenia and Oltenia, it gradually replaced Cernavodă III, absorbing Gumelniţa and Sălcuţa elements as well as

Cucuteni remnants in the south Carpathian foothills, whence groups pushed through the Olt gap and over the south-eastern passes into Transylvania. At some sites a Glina level appears above a Coţofeni and in others below, and the picture is further confused by Monteoru elements coming from Moldavia, but gradually the Glina–Schneckenberg people gained supremacy. Clay model wheels show that, like the Baden people, they used wagons (Bichir 1964).

Often old Cucuteni sites were resettled, especially those with natural defences, but as elsewhere in the Carpatho–Balkan EBA, there was a drastic break with the past. Pottery retained few Chalcolithic features. Cruder in quality and in decoration, the main new forms were cups, jugs with spherical bodies and high necks, two-handled vessels with high necks, biconical bodies and handles descending from the rim to the top of the bulge, 'tureens' with low everted necks. Usually surfaces were plain, but occasionally with wart-like ornamentation. Human figurines still appeared, but zoomorphic ones, especially horned animals, were more common, also miniature clay axeheads. At Glina the horns symbol appears on pottery (Nestor 1927–32, Fig. 13). Burial ritual was inhumation, the skeletons usually crouched in stone cists, many reopened for subsequent burials.

Like the Coţofeni, Glina–Schneckenberg society was mainly based on a stockbreeding economy suited to the rich Carpathian pastures, with cultivation and hunting as important adjuncts. Stone and flint continued in use even when copper metallurgy had been re-mastered. As well as simpler instruments, Glina–Schneckenberg smiths learned to cast axe-adzes, one blade vertical and the other horizontal. Partly, perhaps, because of superior metallurgical skills, although there is no evidence that either produced bronze, before the end of the EBA the Glina–Schneckenberg culture superseded the Coţofeni in west as well as east Transylvania, and in turn was absorbed by two powerful new cultures, the Wietenberg and Otomani.

During the later EBA, two new groups developed south of the Carpathians from Glina–Schneckenberg, the Tei (Leahu 1966; A. Vulpe 1960) and Verbicioara (D. Berciu 1961). The Tei group lay south-west of Monteoru territory, covering most of Muntenia. A. Vulpe (1964) synchronizes its beginnings with a late stage of Moldavian Monteoru I C 3, but its development was more strongly influenced by the Transylvanian Wietenberg culture. Tei and Verbicioara groups had much in common, but the latter, in Oltenia, developed under western influences and extended south of the Danube to the Stara Planina.

Moldavia and the east

The confused transitional period in north-east Muntenia and the southern Moldavian foothills was resolved by the emergence of the Monteoru culture, to the formation of which Cucuteni, Folteşti, Usatovo, Yamnaya, Glina–Schneckenberg and north European cultures all contributed (M. Florescu 1965). Its people, stockbreeders and primitive farmers, occupied settlements on high terraces within river bends and promontories eroded from parent ridges. One such was the great acropolis-like site of Sărata-Monteoru in north-east Muntenia. Here, lying immediately above a Cucuteni B layer, each Monteoru phase has been excavated and identified consecutively, if confusingly, as IC4, IC3, IC2, Ib, Ia, IIa and IIb.

During the long IC3 period which, with IC4, covered at least the first three-quarters of the 3rd millennium, the Monteoru people settled on the Carpathian slopes and expanded into the Folteşti II area of central and southern Moldavia to near Bacău, strongly influencing the neighbouring north Moldavian Costişa culture. At the latter's eponymous site a Costişa layer contemporary with Monteoru IC3 was overlaid by one of Monteoru IC2 (A. Vulpe 1961).

Bogdăneşti, a typical Moldavian Monteoru settlement, occupied a dominating promontory of the Carpathian foothills south of Bacău (M. Florescu and C. Buzdugan 1972). Here Monteoru IC3 succeeded a Folteşti II settlement, but the early levels suggest new influences rather than a new population. Folteşti features, notably semi-dugout huts and cord-decorated pottery, continued for a while, as did the ditches defending easier slopes throughout the IC3 period, although not all settlements were artificially fortified.

Ashy remains show the usual IC3 dwelling was largely wooden. Metal finds are rare and limited to copper. Characteristic pottery included small bowls or cups with globular bodies and two handles with flattened, often drooping, crest-like projections. Decoration usually consisted of incised concentric circles, bands of incised or punched straight or zigzag lines and pitted pendant triangles.

At Sărata Monteoru (Nestor 1953; 1955) a saddle joined the fortified 'acropolis' to the Poiana Scoruş cemetery, where a demolished IC4 structure of large boulders and stone blocks was overlaid by a big IC3 platform-pyre. Covering approximately 125 m² and probably stepped, this was built of layers of fist-sized pebbles with an earth fill. Corpses had been burnt with offerings of bone artefacts, flint arrowheads, curved stone knives and pottery. Burnt bones from the last cremations, with big vessels broken on the spot, were on top of a thick layer of carbonized bone dust. I. Nestor considered that some previous bones and offerings had been collected and buried in urns, but none have yet been found.

Ezero, the Thracian Plain and the Black Sea coast

Unlike the Danubian and Carpathian regions, the Thracian Plain seems for a time to have been almost depopulated, although current or future excavation may qualify or disprove this. Pending publication of the most important Bronze Age (BA) site here, the Dipsis tell at Ezero, near Nova Zagora, information comes largely from interim reports and articles written since 1961 by the excavators, G. I. Georgiev, R. Katincharov and N. Ya. Merpert and by E. N. Chernykh.[*]

*I am also indebted to them and to Mrs A. Raduncheva for much helpful explanation, whilst assuming personal responsibility for any conclusions drawn. Material on Ezero is listed separately in the bibliographical references.

13 Askos from the Yunatsite tell, near Pazardjik. Ht 11 cm. Others occur in Ezero phase A, more rarely in phase B, and, generally more upright, in the Varna inlet pile village, Ezerovo II.

The Dipsis tell was watered by an immensely powerful, still active spring which surrounded the settlement with protective marshes. A sterile layer followed the fire that destroyed the last Chalcolithic level and when the site was resettled it was by a new people with an already clearly defined EBA culture.

The Gumelniţa graphite-painted pottery and anthropomorphic figurines had completely disappeared. The better quality EBA pottery, although lacking Gumelniţa elegance, used well-purified clay, sometimes mixed with sand to produce a burnished black or dark brown ware. In the first BA levels, the pot shapes – askoi and simple 13 bowls with conical sides and straight rims, jugs and mugs with band or loop handles rising scarcely, if at all, above flat or slanting rims – showed affinities with the northern neighbours, Cernavodă III, Glina III–Schneckenberg and Coţofeni.

Throughout the first phase (A) of BA Ezero, usually equated with levels XIII–VIII, the pottery reflected increasingly strong Baden influence in its single-handled cups and high-necked, wide-bellied globular jugs, twin-handled amphora-type vessels, bowls with inverted 14 rims, urns with concave necks and wide everted mouths with or without two small band or rounded handles or pierced lugs, big cauldron-shaped cooking pots and large grain-storage vessels. The main forms of decoration were finger- or fingernail-impressed cordons at or just below the rim of the larger jars, a rough form of channelling made by short parallel, vertical or oblique cordons or incisions, grooved or vertically ridged handles. Wart-like protuberances were also common; incised or scratched geometric motifs, including pendant hatched or pitted triangles, appeared in increasingly complex patterns. Towards the end of phase A tubular handles (tunnel lugs) were popular. The horns motif, usually a simple arc but sometimes with 14 upturned ends, was a common decorative feature in all EBA levels.

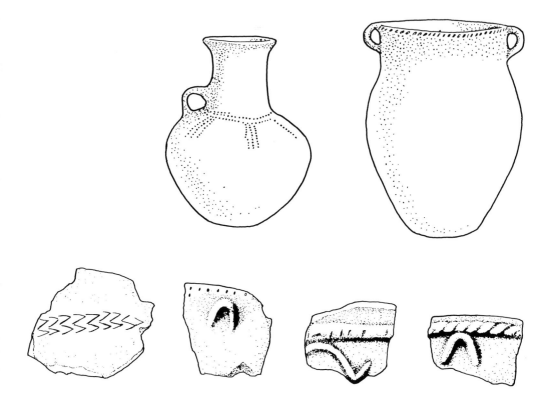

14 Pottery of Ezero phase A. Jug from levels XII–XI. Ht 13 cm. Two-handled urn from level X, Ht 27 cm. Potsherds with horns symbol decoration from levels XIII–X.

Recent excavations in the Magoura cave in north-west Bulgaria are considered to have established a synchronization of the pottery there with that of Ezero A and the Coţofeni cemetery at Turnava (Djambazov and Katincharov 1974).

From the beginning the BA settlement, 60–80 m in diameter, was fortified by a powerful wall 1.5–2 m thick at the base. Set in heavy yellow clay brought from elsewhere, the inner and outer faces were of massive uncut stone, the fill was smaller stones and rubble. Parts of the lower rows were traced, including a western entrance from which a lane led to the settlement's centre. There was another gateway, approached by a ramp, on the north side, its precise nature obscured by reconstruction during level V. The wattle and daub huts inside were regularly oriented but, in contrast to the fortifications, were much flimsier than their Chalcolithic predecessors.

Life in the early levels was precarious. During level X the walls on the excavated west side were moved slightly inwards, although the original gateway remained. Mixed cultivation and stockbreeding formed the basis of the economy. Copper working reverted to a primitive scale and the mines in the neighbourhood were not used in the BA. In Ezero's two earliest levels copper finds were limited to simple four-sided awls. Level X contained leaf-shaped knives and in IX and VIII the range widened with awls and chisels, adzes, axes and hafted knives. Besides slings the main weapons were stone maces and locally cut simple wedge- or boat-shaped stone shaft-hole axes.

Infant burial under house floors or hearths was practised at Ezero throughout the EBA. In addition, five preserved and two destroyed adult intra-mural inhumations were found in early levels. The skeletons were sharply contracted, heads to the south, without grave goods except for one skeleton with a necklace of *spondylus* shells and a white stone oval pendant with a drilled hole. A contemporary necropolis by the Bereketska tell near Stara Zagora contained seventy-eight graves, mostly single but several with two, three or four skeletons (Katincharov 1974). All were crouched, most lying on the left side, head to the south. Often the Chalcolithic practice of placing a piece of ochre by the head was followed. The multiple graves were almost certainly family ones, a child usually in its mother's arms. Clay vessels lay by the head or sometimes by the arms. Copper objects were rare. These burials clearly have close affinities with Baden inhumations.

By the end of phase A migratory pressures from east and west had ceased. Already on the Varna gulf (since silted up to form a lake) such destroyed late Chalcolithic pile villages as Ezerovo IV and Strashi-mirovo A had been succeeded by a similar type of EBA settlement. Ezerovo III, opposite its predecessor, had groups of five or six rectangular pile dwellings standing on a tongue of land about 40 m long and 8 m wide. Pottery, showing the same complete break with the past as at Ezero, corresponds to the latter's levels IX–VII. The stronger steppe influence here led to a greater emphasis on stockbreeding in the economy. Among domesticated animals were cattle, sheep, pigs, horses and dogs, and a number of unidentifiable clay animal models have been found. Fishing, hunting and wild fruits also provided food (Toncheva 1973; Margos and Toncheva 1962; Margos 1961; 1965a, b).

Levels VII–V and perhaps IV are considered Ezero's EBA phase B, although VII followed naturally from VIII, likewise IV from V. In VII and VI the population expanded beyond the walls and during V a new stone outer wall was built. With a diameter of about 160 m, it encircled the lower slopes of the tell. The inner wall was also reconstructed. A new steep ramp enclosed by stone walls approached the north gate at right angles to the circuit walls. Paved with clay-plastered stone, it was 2–2.5 m wide and 8 m long. Heaps of charred wood found on the floor suggest a gate tower from which to assault an enemy force, effectively limited by the width of the ramp to two or three deep.

By this time Ezero and probably other 'metropolitan' tells had acquired small, unfortified, dependent hamlets. When in danger their inhabitants could take refuge at Ezero where, in the middle of the original settlement, a space was ready with densely grouped ovens and large, unfired clay grain-storage jars beside them.

Elsewhere the available space was crammed with dwellings, terraced and detached. Four of the former in level IV were two-roomed, about 10 m long and 4–5 m wide. The long sides were party walls, each slightly curved rear wall projecting a little beyond its neighbour. The best preserved house foundations showed an outer room almost entirely filled by six storage jars, 0.60–1.20 m in diameter. Charred wheat grains lay in and around them. The rear room had a stove and hearth and in the debris was part of a stone mould for casting a metal shaft-hole axehead (Katincharov 1974).

Ezero B pottery was basically a development of earlier forms, although latterly shallow bowls with inverted rims, askoi and slant-mouthed cups and jugs became rarer. An important technical innovation – or reintroduction from the Chalcolithic (Bognár-Kutzián 1972, 84, Pl. LXX, 11) – of *c*. level VIII was a primitive potter's wheel, a round clay platform 20–25 cm in diameter mounted on a low cylindrical base about 8 cm high with opposing holes through which a stick could be thrust to turn the platform. Decoration changed more substantially. There was less incised ornament and pitting was rare; but corded decoration, only found occasionally towards the end of phase A, became common. Whether the imprint was fine or heavy, it was skilfully used to reproduce patterns sometimes more complicated, otherwise identical to those previously incised or pitted.

On the Black Sea coast Ezerovo III was succeeded by Ezerovo II, which returned to the old Chalcolithic site. With the contemporary EB pile village at Strashimirovo, it corresponded to Ezero's phase B, the pottery often similarly distinguished by corded decoration and use of the hand-turned clay platform. Variations of askoi continued to be common. Clay models of bulls(?) have been found.

At Ezero, metalworking was concentrated in a small sector of the inner settlement. Open stone and clay moulds were used for casting shaft-hole, flanged and socketed axes, stone grooves for awls, clay ladles and heavy stone hammers for forging. A socketed axe cast in a stone mould, found in a level IV house, has analogies primarily in Transcaucasia and in the neighbouring Anatolian Karaz type. During phase B metallurgy developed to include bronze-casting; copper began to be artificially alloyed with arsenic, usually as little as 1 per cent but sometimes 3–5 per cent. Tin was not used. Arsenic concentrate is not found in Carpatho–Balkan Chalcolithic copper and the sources of EBA ore have not been located.

The use of arsenical bronze – with its harder cutting edge – brought the Thracian Plain into what Chernykh has termed the Circumpontic metallurgical province. Probably originating in the Caucasus and its spread a Yamnaya legacy, this 'province' extended across the Pontic steppe, the forest-steppe as far as the middle Volga, and reached the Thracian Plain during Ezero EBA phase B. The earliest types of socketed bronze axeheads cast in open moulds, found in the Kura–Araxes and early Maikop culture, preceded Carpatho–Balkan entry into the province, but the later axeheads with a smooth arched curve of the blade and other contemporary weapons and tools are common to the whole Circumpontic zone.

Yet metallurgical production remained small. The decline from the Chalcolithic era is illustrated by an examination of copper and bronze artefacts in Bulgarian museums. About 370 belonged to the late Chalcolithic period (Gumelniţa–Karanovo VI) and only some 150 to the Early and Middle Bronze Ages combined, a period three to four times longer (Chernykh 1974).

The final levels of Ezero C are co-terminous with an open Middle Bronze Age (MBA) settlement at near-by Nova Zagora, suggesting a peaceful transition from the Early to the Later Bronze Age in the Thracian Plain.

Carpatho–Balkan relations with Anatolia

Baden influences on north-west Anatolia, as Bognár–Kutzián suggests, probably came first via Macedonia, but pottery analogies relating Troy I to the later levels of Ezero EBA phase A and most of phase B, when contact was probably eased by the waning of the Yamnaya pressure, illustrate another link. Troy I especially, as well as offshore Poliochni (Bernabò-Brea 1964) in phases II–V (Blue to Yellow) and Thermi (Lamb 1936), additionally show the strength of the late Chalcolithic Carpatho–Balkan presence in north-west Anatolia. Here many of its traditions continued into the local EBA to become important factors in the foundation and development of Troy and in the surrounding area, including Kum Tepe Ic (Sperling 1976).

Carved in relief on a limestone slab, a starkly stylized, heart-shaped face with drilled holes lining each side of the head greeted or menaced all comers at the corner of the east tower flanking the south gate of Middle Troy I. The schematic design which, as C. W. Blegen comments (1963, 56), 'implies a long preceding period of experiment and development', is clearly Chalcolithic, arguably in the Tripolye rather than Gumelniţa tradition; a closely comparable head of a figurine was found at the Dnieper site of Zolotechna (Makarenko 1926, Pl. 6ii), but many marble, clay and bone Gumelniţa and Cucuteni analogies also exist. Near the Troy slab are two others which 'seem to be tables of offering that probably once had their place in a shrine'. (Blegen 1963, 56; Blegen *et al.* 1950–58, I(1)157, I(2) Pls 193f). Analogous 'offering tables' were excavated in an exceptionally large three-roomed building, clearly neither dwelling nor workshop, in the late Chalcolithic level IV at Azmak in the Thracian Plain (Georgiev 1963). The fortified ramps of Poliochni and Troy may be related to that of Ezero but we must await publication of the last.

The occasional faces on the rims of bowls in Troy I again have Tripolye analogies (Kozlovska 1926, Figs 17, 19, 20, 22, 23). The many

15

15 Described by Blegen (1963, 56) as 'the oldest sculptured monument yet found in Western Anatolia', this Troy I relief of a human head has analogies with Cucuteni-Tripolye and Gumelniţa figurines (*see Ill. 7*).

16 Carpatho-Balkan elements in Troy I and II. *Left*: Troy II face-pot with horns symbol, clay, Ht 28 cm. *Right*: Troy I pedestalled bowl, clay, Ht 23 cm. *Below*: Troy II marble figurine, Ht 6.5 cm. The face-pot reflects Gumelniţa influence (*see Ill. 5*); often, instead of handles, stylized arms reach upwards from the bulge. Schliemann (1880, 224) perceptively called the pedestalled bowl, a Trojan version of the Cucuteni vessel (*see Ill. 3*), a 'Curious Vessel, use unknown, perhaps a censer.' Facial indications on the figurine show Chalcolithic anthropomorphism continuing in the Trojan Early Bronze Age.

17 *Opposite above*: Bone figurines (*see Ill. 8*), like those of the solar cult, were carried to Troy, Poliochni and Thermi by Carpatho-Balkan immigrants. 1. Troy I. Hts 16 and 15 cm. 2. Poliochni II. Hts 8.5 and 8.2 cm. 3. Poliochni V. Ht 12.3 cm.

18 *Opposite centre*: For a time in the Early Bronze Age clay anchor-shaped horns symbol pendants were adopted over a wide area, being found in Ezero level VII, in the south Carpathians at Govora, in Macedonia, Thessaly and south to the Peloponnese. Hts 5–10 cm. 1. Mihalich. 2, 3. Poliochni II. 4. Servia. 5. Gremnos-Magoula, near Larissa. 6. Eutresis, Boeotia. 7. Lerna, EH III.

Trojan face pots, characteristic of Troy II–V, derive from Gumelniţa and its Neolithic antecedents. Schliemann's shallow bowl on a high pierced pedestal (1880, No. 50) has Cucuteni origins.

Stylized bone figurines of the simplified Carpatho–Balkan type occur in Troy I and Poliochni II onwards and in Thermi IV (Lamb 1936, Pl. XXVII, 36). Clay and marble symbols of the Carpatho–Balkan transition from anthropomorphic to solar cults also appear in Troy I–VI, Poliochni and Thermi. At Troy they include Schliemann's 'hideous and barbaric idols' (1880, 232f) the upper parts of which bear facial indications.

'Anchor-type' pendant horns symbols, like those from Varna and Gumelniţa but invariably of clay, are found in the Macedonian, Thessalian and Boeotian EBA and as far south as Lerna in EH III, as well as at Mihalich, near Svilengrad on the Bulgarian–Turkish frontier. Usually shaped like a clumsy anchor, finer, less schematic examples from Poliochni emphasize their bovine character. The anchor-type symbol was ephemeral but, as at Ezero, Govora, Glina III and elsewhere in regions affected by the Yamnaya migration, the horns symbol became a common 'decorative' motif on pottery, appearing so in Kum Tepe Ic 2, Troy II–V, Poliochni V, Thermi and Thessaly.

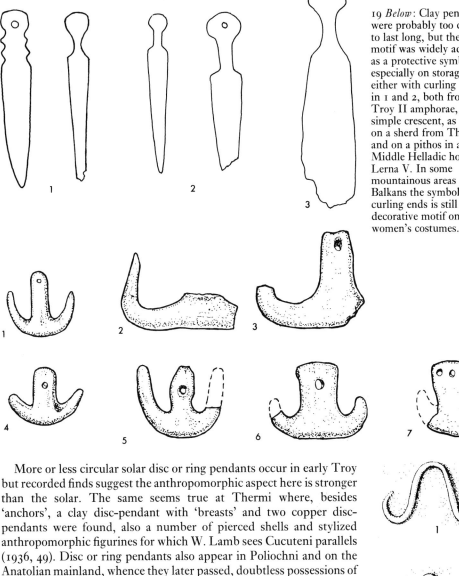

19 *Below*: Clay pendants
were probably too clumsy
to last long, but the horns
motif was widely adopted
as a protective symbol,
especially on storage jars,
either with curling ends as
in 1 and 2, both from
Troy II amphorae, or as a
simple crescent, as in 3,
on a sherd from Thessaly
and on a pithos in a
Middle Helladic house in
Lerna V. In some
mountainous areas of the
Balkans the symbol with
curling ends is still a
decorative motif on
women's costumes.

More or less circular solar disc or ring pendants occur in early Troy
but recorded finds suggest the anthropomorphic aspect here is stronger
than the solar. The same seems true at Thermi where, besides
'anchors', a clay disc-pendant with 'breasts' and two copper disc-
pendants were found, also a number of pierced shells and stylized
anthropomorphic figurines for which W. Lamb sees Cucuteni parallels
(1936, 49). Disc or ring pendants also appear in Poliochni and on the
Anatolian mainland, whence they later passed, doubtless possessions of
descendants of Balkan Chalcolithic migrants and once again made of
gold, silver and clay, to Cretan EM II sites such as Mochlos, Krasi and
Myrtos.

On the Carpatho–Balkan mainland, pottery analogies suggest a date
roughly contemporary with the end of Ezero A for the strategically
situated fortified settlement at Mihalich (Mikov 1948). Near-by finds
of corded ware and four examples of the Trojan *depas amphikypellon*
show that the site was inhabited well into Ezero B – and Troy II.
Although stratification was not observed, Mihalich is of particular
significance both as a south-eastern outpost of corded ware and because
north-west of it Anatolian and Aegean BA pottery appears as an import
or foreign influence.

The absence of cord decoration in north-west Anatolia or the Aegean islands and its limited appearance in Macedonia and Thessaly mark the rise of an independent north Aegean zone of the Carpatho–Balkan region ready to assert its own individuality. A reversal of the flow of dominant influences is stratigraphically illustrated at Hisar in the Kosovo–Metohija district by two levels corresponding to Ezero A and B, both with characteristic Baden ware but the later also containing Kritsana-type pottery, reflecting a northern expansion of the Macedonian EBA (Todorović 1973). In Ezero B two fragments of *depata* were found (Merpert 1969, 251); a single-handled tripod vessel from Ezerovo II is probably a local copy of an Anatolian original (Toncheva 1973, Fig. 7/2). The capped amphorae which came to north-west Anatolia from the Usatovo culture may even have been another example of a re-export to the Thracian Plain, as the example from Ezero suggests. On the other hand, the characteristic Aegean beak-shaped or 'cut-away' mouths of jugs and 'sauceboats' remained essentially southern forms which the more northern Carpatho–Balkan lands did not accept.

The Vulchi Trun gold treasure

Like the end of the Chalcolithic era, the latter centuries of the EBA were a time for rulers to amass great wealth. The Maikop royal burials in the north Caucasus, those of Alaca Hüyük in central Anatolia, the Schliemann treasure from Troy IIg, the gold bowls from Euboea in the Benaki Museum, Athens, illustrate an established tradition of goldworking and access to rich sources of ore.

The isolated gold treasure-hoard found by chance at Vulchi Trun in the Pleven district of north Bulgaria was first dated (Mikov 1958) to the 8th century BC, then considered as the end of the Bronze Age. More recently it has been attributed, using a longer chronology, to the

20 Clay *depas amphikypellon* from Mihalich. Ht 20 cm.

21 *Below left*: Lidded pot from Ezero. Overall Ht 14.5 cm.

22 *Below right*: Lidded pot from Thermi. Ht 24 cm.

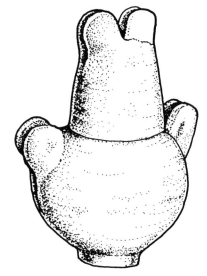

13th–12th centuries. In both cases a Carpatho–Balkan provenance is assumed (Bonev 1977, summarizing opinions of various scholars).

The treasure, which is incomplete, consists of thirteen gold objects weighing a total of 12.5 kg. A bowl with two handles rising from the rim and riveted to the bulge is the largest item, weighing nearly 4.4 kg. One large and three smaller cups are similar in workmanship. There were also seven covers, the two largest inlaid with silver, and a triple vessel with trident-shaped communicating tubes of electrum, inlaid with niello, possibly made as a censer but later altered by adding two larger tubes linking the vessels from below. A comparable bowl, as yet unpublished, was recently found near Odessa.

Although on a much smaller scale, Transylvanian analogies exist for the covers, in the discs, tutuli and phalerae of the Later Bronze Age (LBA), the gold dishes from Bihar, near Oradea, are the only known vessels possible to date to *c.* mid-2nd millennium (Mozsolics 1965–66). These are very different from the Vulchi Trun vessels. Technique and the thickness of the gold also exclude a Mycenaean provenance.

A toreutic tradition using thick sheet gold for vessels existed towards and about the end of the 3rd millennium. The Trojan gold sauceboat weighed 600 g. The thickness of the Alaca Hüyük 'champagne cup' and jugs varies between 2 and 3 mm and the Euboea bowls are about the same. The channelling on the triple vessel and the silver inlay of the two large covers again recalls Alaca Hüyük.

If this earlier period is accepted for the Vulchi Trun treasure, instead of regarding it as a later Thracian toreutic masterpiece, it may have been a royal gift. Were there in the Carpatho–Balkans at this time rulers sufficiently wealthy and powerful to receive such a magnificent present? So far, the Vulchi Trun collection is unique, but the Varna cemetery is only one recent reminder that there is still a great deal to discover about Carpatho–Balkan prehistory.

23

23 The large gold bowl from the Vulchi Trun treasure. Wt 4.395 kg; Ht 17.1 cm; including handles 22.4 cm.

3

The Bronze Age Flowering

Transition to the Later Bronze Age

The later centuries of the 3rd millennium brought changes affecting variously the general prosperity achieved by the end of the EBA. Troy II ended abruptly and successive 'cities' followed quickly until stability was regained with Troy VI about 1800. Elsewhere in Anatolia the old order was changed by a series of invasions, the Hittites finally emerging as the dominant force. In Greece the fortified city of Lerna was sacked and rebuilt as an open settlement, grey Minyan ware appeared at Orchomenos and elsewhere. There is a possibility that the changes inaugurating the Middle Helladic period were partly due to intrusive peoples or influences from the north or perhaps Anatolia.

Migratory movements brought incursions of north Caucasian pastoralists of the Catacomb culture into the Pontic steppe while others of the Middle Dnieper culture moved into the forest-steppe west of the Dnieper. Their impact on Yamnaya and Globular Amphorae people as well as on indigenous survivors set up a series of pressures across the north European plain that spilled over the north Carpathian passes down the Tisza valley with reverberations felt as far as Macedonia and Thessaly.

Fast-moving raiders from the steppe, bent on the riches of the Troad, may explain the final destruction at about this time of the EBA settlements on the Varna inlet. The appearance in the late levels of globular amphorae, not found earlier here nor in Thracian Plain settlements, suggests the arrival of northern refugees who may have been precursors of more savage raiders. Future excavation, especially in Turkish Thrace – for the Bronze Age (BA) an archaeological void – may show whether this route was used in the destruction of Troy II and Poliochni V (Yellow). Work in progress at Ikiz-tepe near Samsun in north Anatolia may disclose whether seaborne invasion played a part in the Anatolian upheaval.

In Moldavia, during Monteoru IC2 the population of Bogdăneşti declined sharply. A deeper, wider ditch replaced the Folteşti construction and hitherto open settlements were fortified. Monteoru elements appeared in Costişa and Tei areas. The natural defences of Sărata–Monteoru were strong, but late in phase Ia or early in IIa the citadel was for the first time protected by a ditch on its eastern access. At the end of IC2 many early Monteoru settlements ceased to exist, probably owing to a population expansion across the Pontic steppe to the Dnieper and in places beyond it, which in turn shifted large numbers of people westward. Thus, at Cîndeşti in south Moldavia, during late IC3 and IC2 a biritual (cremation and inhumation) but chiefly inhumation cemetery came into being, its many cist graves recalling those of the Usatovo culture (V. Dumitrescu 1971, 108). During Ia at Sărata–Monteoru inhumation suddenly replaced cremation in a new cemetery with some four hundred graves. No Monteoru ritual 'offering vessels' were found among the grave goods here or at a similar cemetery at Poiana.

With the north Caucasus remaining their source of metal, the Catacomb people spread over the steppe between the Volga and Dnieper, with only sporadic settlements farther west but, despite the evidence of the Varna lake villages, not unduly disturbing the earlier inhabitants. Near Nikopol on the right bank of the lower Dnieper, the old Tripolye and Yamnaya site at Mikhailovka, with multi-roomed stone-built houses and stone wall defences, became an important trading centre between the Caucasus and – via Usatovo traders – south Moldavia and the lower Danube.

The rise of the Otomani–Wietenberg cultures

The impact of the new steppe migrations was short-lived and, on present evidence, had little direct effect on much of Transylvania, the lower Danube valley or the Thracian Plain. Having borne the initial brunt, the upper Tisza region began to recover while the chain reaction of displaced peoples was still bringing disruption farther south. The emergence of the Otomani culture was an important factor in this recovery. Its apparently brief initial phase probably dates to about the third quarter of the 3rd millennium. Related to the Únětice culture and influenced by the east Hungarian Nagyrév, the possible role of new elements in the population is unclear. A militant local reaction against adversity is an alternative explanation. It was and remained closely linked to the contemporary and adjacent Wietenberg culture of Transylvania (Horedt 1960; Horedt and Seraphin 1971).

Settlements usually had natural defences and were also fortified by strong ramparts and ditches. At Barca in east Slovakia, where an Otomani layer, predominantly belonging to the third phase, followed a

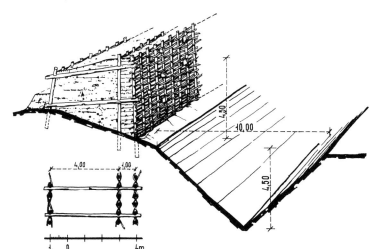

24 Section of fortifications, Nitriansky Hrádok. Otomani mountain settlements, like Spišský-Štvrtok, were usually fortified by powerful drystone walls, W. 6–7.5 m with inner and outer faces of roughly cut blocks. Where stone was scarcer, as at Barca and Nitriansky Hrádok, palisades replaced stone faces, linked by horizontal beams passing through the earth fill. Another palisade usually surmounted the wall, which was encircled by a formidable ditch.

Baden-*cum*-Corded Ware one (Hájek 1961; Vladár 1973), an earth rampart was enclosed by posts interlaced with branches and 24 strengthened by struts laid horizontally from front to back. The same technique was used at Nitriansky Hrádok in west Slovakia (Vladár 1973). At Otomani, north-east of Oradea (Ordentlich 1963), the first settlement was on the triangular head of a ridge above marshland and within a river bend. A ditch 20 m wide and up to 4.30 m deep, backed by an earth rampart, protected this 'citadel' settlement from attack along the ridge and continued round it, narrowing to about 16 m wide on the other two sides and apex of the triangle. On a lower terrace, a second ditch 14 m wide and 3.75 m deep reinforced the first on the more gradual north slope.

Early Otomani pottery was simple. Flat-based pots with or without small handles had moderately convex bodies, the rims sometimes everted. Common forms of decoration were patches of textile impressions, streaked lines or brushed hatching, with, occasionally, notched bands or cordons at the rim and wart-like protuberances. In the Otomani I layer at Barca conical *Buckeln* or bosses (Hájek 1961) revived an early Chalcolithic Tiszapolgár motif (Bognár-Kutzián 1972).

The average depth of the Otomani II layer at the 'citadel' was 1 m, about four times as deep as that of Otomani I. There was abundance of pottery with much greater variety of form and decoration. Cups were common, their single strap handles rising slightly above the rim and descending to the widest part of the slightly bulging body. Larger pots were usually more spherical and had high necks with emphatically everted rims. These were of well purified clay, but many coarse fragments of large storage jars were also found. Some vessels still had impressed cordons at the rim, but the usual ornamentation was by careful incision of horizontal lines with pendant hatched triangles combined with arcs or spirals, parallel oblique incisions and bands of short hatching or pitting.

Dwellings were surface huts of wattle and daub, the clay mixed with chaff, earthen floors and roofed by reeds from the marshes. Before the end of phase I and in part of phase II, a space in the centre of the settlement was devoted to hearths with storage jars beside them, suggesting a refuge for unprotected neighbours such as existed at Ezero.

No copper or bronze was found in phases I or II, only some bone artefacts and a horn hoe. The many sheep and cattle bones are evidence of stockbreeding, but deer, boar and other wild animal bones show that hunting was also a major occupation.

Towards the end of phase II, the 'citadel' became so overcrowded that the ditch was filled in to provide more housing space. Although the site was long occupied, the main settlement gradually moved to an island, the *Cetatea de Pămînt* (earth fortress), of 6–7 ha surrounded by the river marshes. The island lay barely 1 m above water level, so, in a remarkable feat of planning and construction, a layer of yellow clay subsoil was brought in and spread over the naturally porous light grey earth to form an insulating 'damp-course'. This was raised to form a rampart along the shore, not against attack, for which the marsh was adequate, but against flooding. Especially here, but also in the interior, the clay course was reinforced by rows of posts, also serving as the framework for wattle and daub huts. The concentration of successive levels of housing in the centre of the island gradually formed an artificial hill, for which the crannog of the second Glastonbury lake village phase provides an interesting analogy. The reinforced periphery similarly rose.

Evidence about Otomani burials is still confusing, possibly because of varying Wietenberg influence. Inhumation was practised initially as in east Slovakia and at Pir, near Otomani, (Székely 1955) where it continued into Otomani II, but in a late Otomani I cemetery at Ciumeşti, also near Otomani, all twenty-six burials were cremations, with the remains in ordinary domestic pots, sometimes turned upside down and often accompanied by another, presumably containing food for the afterlife. I. Ordentlich and C. Kacsó (1970) note the difference from the ritual common in neighbouring cultures of scattering the ashes on the earth beside the offering vessels. At the fortified site of Sălacea, just north of Otomani, excavations have uncovered remains of what at present appears to be a unique Otomani II ritual building. Only 8.8 by 5.2 m, its contents included three altars, two of them hearths and one on wooden legs, also many clay figurines and clay models of wheels, wagons and a boat (Coles and Harding 1979, 86ff.).

Co-terminous with the near-by eponymous site of Otomani, an important Wietenberg settlement has been partially excavated at Derşida, a naturally fortified hill north-west of Oradea (Chidioşan 1968). Semi-dugout and surface dwellings were found in the first phase, the former roughly oval and some 4–9 m long, the latter of wattle and daub with exterior hearths. The little pottery recovered showed the influence of both Glina–Schneckenberg and late Coţofeni. Ornament, in general more sophisticated than at Otomani, beside notched bands or cordons at or just below the rim, with fingertip or fingernail impressions, achieved more complex patterns of bands of incised crosses or groups of incised lines slanted to give a zigzag effect.

No dugouts but two types of surface hut were found here in the Wietenberg II phase. The larger, more substantial huts had thick stamped clay floors, hearths and storage pits; the rest had a flimsy superstructure, a thinner floor of ash and sherds mixed with stamped clay and no hearths. In the second half of the phase, bigger post-holes in the large huts were probably for gabled roof supports. The pottery had developed in elegance of form and decorative techniques, with channelling as well as incision. New motifs – or rather Chalcolithic Cucuteni revivals – were running spirals and variations on the horizontal linked 'S' pattern.

Although most Wietenberg metal artefacts are dated to its third phase, copper and bronze metallurgy developed gradually in phases I and II.

The third Otomani–Wietenberg phase

The second phase of Otomani and Wietenberg coincided approximately with the growth of the Únětice culture, which spread from Moravia into Bohemia, west Slovakia, southern Poland, Silesia and north Hungary, to reach a peak in the following Mad'arovce culture. Mad'arovce–Otomani III contacts were probably responsible for the powerful stone walls protecting northern settlements, such as Spišský Štvrtok in east Slovakia. Up to 7.50 m thick, inner and outer drystone facings each 1.70 m thick had an earth and stone fill. The extent to which Únětice tin reached Otomani and Wietenberg smiths earlier is not known, but in the third phases of both these cultures, beginning in the first or early second quarter of the 2nd millennium, the trade was the basis of a flourishing bronze industry.

The stratified excavations at Otomani and Barca have proved the relative longevity of Otomani III. On the Otomani island the dwellings had floors of smoothed clay. An exceptionally large house in the centre measuring 24.5 m by 12.5 m, had two building levels, both with stamped clay floors, the earlier 40–50 cm thick and regularly shaped. Destroyed by a violent fire, much of the clay floor was reddened; the remains of molten bronze objects lay in the centre and elsewhere the debris contained much white ash, charred wood and circular lumps of clay probably used to shut ventilation 'windows' in the walls. After an interval, a new floor was laid. The remains of eight hearths were found in the corners, around each four to six conical clay supports. Three rows of three holes up to 50–60 cm deep were dug along the two long sides and the middle of the floor, the last being the largest and able to take two posts at an oblique angle as well as one upright, clearly to support a gabled roof. The surviving household goods after its final destruction suggest the building was the home of the ruler. Most of the pottery was of very fine quality, thin-walled and richly decorated with conical bosses and curved channelling, common forms being dishes or bowls and cups with low pedestals bases and single handles sometimes rising and often with a small knob at the rims or highest points. There were two rows of hearths near the house with storage jars containing charred grain beside them.

25
26

Most of the bronze artefacts were unidentifiable, but included two spearheads, fragments of bronze pins and most of a razor with spiral ornament. Among other objects were three-sided bone arrowheads and horn cheekpieces of a snaffle; bones of sheep and cattle, and many from deer and wild boar were found, also horses' hooves. Outside a corner of the house were two crouched inhumations with no grave goods but a single dog skull.

34

In Otomani III, the concealment in time of danger of often immense hoards of valuable metal objects was a common practice. Much of our knowledge of the Otomani–Wietenberg flowering comes from their discovery and the practice probably explains the few bronze remains found in the island ruler's dwelling. A hoard, perhaps a bronzesmith's stock, of ninety-nine bronze objects including seventeen phalerae and seven tutuli, buttons and pins, found elsewhere on the site show that the Otomani culture persisted here until the end of the Bronze Age. Also found in the dig or in ploughing were Cypriot-style pins, open-ended incised bracelets, sickles, a flat-headed pin displaying a sun symbol and the mould for a disc-shaped axehead. At Derşida erosion has destroyed most of the contemporary levels, but the equal prosperity of Wietenberg III is confirmed at other sites such as Wietenberg itself (now Sighişoara).

Inhumation and urn burial were common to both cultures and cemeteries were often biritual, although, on present evidence, cremation was more common. A cemetery 400–500 m from a Wietenberg III settlement at Bistriţa in north-east Transylvania contained thirty-eight incinerations in urns. Analysis of twenty-three identified eleven adults, five adolescents and seven infants (Crişan 1961). Of sixty-seven Otomani graves at Streda nad Bodrogom in east Slovakia, thirty-four were urn cremations, nine symbolic and the rest inhumations (Polla 1958). In general, grave goods were minimal.

Pot forms common to the third phase of both Otomani and Wietenberg included cups with rounded bodies, high necks, everted rims and handles rising sometimes slightly, sometimes quite high above the rim. Often, especially in the Otomani ware, there were small pedestal bases and little knobs on the top of the handles. Less frequent on Wietenberg pots, the knob became an *ansa cornuta* – a Baden legacy – or a lobe on the rim opposite the handle. Shallow vessels richly ornamented on the under side were common to both, with Wietenberg rims only slightly everted, whilst the Otomani dishes or 'soup plates' had widely everted, decorated rims.

Pointed conical bosses, enclosed by concentric circles or semicircles, protruding from the walls of vessels are a distinctive Otomani motif, although earlier they had been a feature of Precucuteni III pottery. Decoration of Wietenberg ware is more varied and complex, using spirals, meanders and other geometric patterns on graceful, simpler shapes.

First found on Wietenberg II pottery, the return of Chalcolithic motifs to a region where they had been dormant, apparently dead, for over a millennium is one of the surprising features of the Otomani–Wietenberg flowering. Similar sun and fire symbols characterize many cultures but their lively revival here, compared with neighbouring lands, and the intensity of concentration in areas inhabited by or greatly influenced by the Otomani–Wietenberg peoples argue a native origin. As before, these symbols were not merely

25 *Above left*: Otomani III channelled clay cup from Derşida.

26 *Above right*: Otomani III high-necked clay jar from Barca. Ht 28 cm. Conical bosses, whether on shallow bowls or on the bodies of high-necked pots, were characteristic decorative motifs, reviving a local Chalcolithic tradition.

25

26

27

27 Urn from Deva, with characteristic Wietenberg III running spiral decoration.

28 *Below*: Clay ritual hearth found in a Wietenberg III settlement layer at Sighişoara (previously Wietenberg). Diam. approx. 1.5 m.

Opposite above.
29 *Left*: Bronze axehead and detail of head with incised flame motifs, from Păuliş. *Centre*: Bronze spearhead with incised running flame motif, from an unknown Hungarian findspot.
Right: Bronze axehead with a flame motif in horns symbol form, from Szirmabesenyö.

30 *Opposite far right*: Bronze sword from the Apa hoard. L. 62 cm. Hoards of the Hajdúsámson–Apa and Koszider horizons, probably dating to around the second quarter of the second millennium, contain many of the most magnificent Otomani-Wietenberg weapons.

31 *Opposite below.* Otomani III horns symbol pendants. *Left*: Barca, bronze. Max. W. 1.32 cm. *Centre*: Spišský Štvrtok, gold. Max. W. 6 cm. *Right*: Plain bronze pendants, Max. W. usually between 1.5 cm and 12.5 cm, found in large numbers in some Otomani graves and hoards. The in-curving ends of the first and second may indicate a tendency by some groups to adopt rams' rather than bulls' horns to symbolize strength and apotropaic power, *inter alia* accounting for the use of rams' heads on Late Bronze and Early Iron Age firedogs (*see Ill. 64*).

ornamental. The running spiral incised on the clay ritual hearth at Sighişoara (Wietenberg) in eastern Transylvania often appears on fine Wietenberg pottery, sometimes abbreviated to a horizontal linked S. The sun-fire symbol is as clear in its meaning as it had been in the Chalcolithic era. A new but related motif consists of delicately incised parallel lines representing individual curling flames, either arranged symmetrically, as on one sword in the Apa hoard and an axehead in the Ashmolean Museum (Mozsolics 1967, Fig. 12), asymmetrically, as on

the Apa and Păuliş axeheads, or in a linked line, as on a spearhead from Hungary. The round disc-butts project the image of the burning sun, sometimes as simplified versions of the running spiral. A second Apa sword has a variant of the burning sun motif on the pommel; this and others appear later on phalerae and other circular ornaments.

The running spiral of the Sighişoara hearth is unquestionably a Wietenberg form. A parallel, perhaps distantly related development had also brought it to Mycenaean art. The curling flame motif appears chiefly on costly bronze weapons, which although made for use in battle were clearly owned by warrior chiefs, nobles, princes or kings whose status and prowess were enhanced by the symbolic decoration. Usually found in hoards, they may have been made to order, been gifts between rulers or trophies of war. No special workshops have been located, but finds of moulds are widespread and extend west to the Danube.

The curling flame motif may have been common to both cultures. The plain spiral is rare in either, whether on pottery or armour, except in the form of armband terminals, the solar symbolism here a practical protection against sword slashes.

A motif peculiar to Otomani was one that had appeared in the late Chalcolithic and persisted through the EBA – the horns symbol. Incised on weapons, often repeating the pattern of a double flame, or

31, 32

dictating the shape of bronze ornaments, especially pendants but also bracelets and armlets, representations are rare in Transylvania but are found in large numbers in the Otomani lands of Slovakia, the Tisza valley and the central European plain. A common Otomani pottery motif like a torc but with inturned ends may be a development of this symbol.

Portable altar-vessels consisting of a bowl and stand appear in Otomani–Wietenberg and neighbouring related cultures (Kacsó 1975), perhaps a new version of the Cucuteni–Tiszapolgar 'incense-burning' bowls. Clay model wagons or wagon wheels, both solid and spoked, are testimony of both a symbolic aspect of this vehicle and its wide use. At

33 Lechinţa de Mureş model wagon fragments included a bovine head – suggesting comparisons with the bird-drawn model from Dupljaja in the Banat, but here signifying a syncretism of the horned animal and

63, 64, 137 sun-fire-hearth cults from which zoomorphic firedogs derive.

The emphasis on the development of weapons leaves no doubt that this was an 'heroic' age. Society was stratified. We do not know how

32 In shape and decoration this massive gold bracelet from Bilje, near Osijek in northern Yugoslavia, syncretizes the horns symbol with that of the fiery sun. L. 11.8 cm.

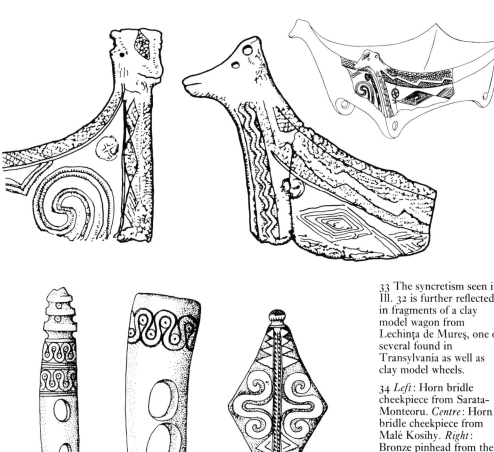

33 The syncretism seen in Ill. 32 is further reflected in fragments of a clay model wagon from Lechinţa de Mureş, one of several found in Transylvania as well as clay model wheels.

34 *Left*: Horn bridle cheekpiece from Sarata-Monteoru. *Centre*: Horn bridle cheekpiece from Malé Kosihy. *Right*: Bronze pinhead from the Borodino hoard. While wagons were probably ox-drawn, horn cheekpieces are probable evidence of riding horses. The incised undulating band decoration, especially common on horn objects but related to that on the Borodino bronze pinhead, is often ascribed to Mycenaean influence. The pin more likely represents the native horns symbol, from which the undulating band on circular artefacts may derive to produce a continuous effect.

35, 36

rulers arose or if a dynastic principle existed. The many hoards buried (Rusu 1963; Mozsolics 1965–66; 1967; 1973; Hänsel 1968; Petrescu-Dîmboviţa 1977) in periods chiefly of Otomani and Wietenberg expansion suggest considerable internecine warfare.

Transylvanian hoards such as those of Ţufălău, which included five gold axeheads, and of Şmig with many gold rings, phalerae and other objects, show that gold was used lavishly and no less skilfully than bronze. The treasure of Perşinari, in Muntenia, with part of a gold sword and eleven daggers, ten still showing casting flashes, may be of Transylvanian origin, as may that of Ostrovul Mare, in Oltenia, with three bracelets, ten lock rings, three phalerae and thirty appliqués, all of gold. Ornaments were probably worn as much by men as by women.

35 *Above*: Fragment of ceremonial gold sword from Perşinari. L. 29 cm.

36 *Below*: Gold phalerae and buttons, from Ostrovul Mare. Diams 6.8 and 3.5 cm.

In an heroic society, smiths, users of fire to fashion weapons, objects of beauty and religious meaning, must have held that special place in society which has been transmitted in the mythologies of other peoples. Bronzesmiths' skill was directed primarily towards efficiency. Swords were designed for slashing and thrusting. The battle-axe had to be heavy enough to be effective, but sufficiently light and handy for use by mounted warriors, whose horses had horn cheekpieces and, perhaps, leather bits as none of metal have been found. The first bronze axes copied the stone shaft-hole axe, but gradually it was found that a narrower blade could take the same cutting edge, and that a lighter blade could be effective and the axe easier to wield, although no less strong, with an elongated butt or when a tube replaced the shaft hole. Later, a shorter tube or ordinary shaft hole and a pointed disc-butt became popular.

Although bronzeworking was primarily concerned with weapons and ornaments, notably toggle-pins, armlets, bracelets and necklaces, many hoards, increasingly in the later centuries of the BA, contain industrial and agricultural tools, especially celts and sickles, showing the role of bronze in developing the economy. Limited to casting from moulds until the last century or two of the BA, the Carpathian bronzesmiths manufactured vessels only from then on. For these clay had been the appropriate medium, although gold was sufficiently malleable for cups such as those from Bihar (Mozsolics 1965–66) and possibly even birch-bark for Otomani cult purposes, as at Gánovce in Slovakia (Vladár 1973, Fig. 76). Sheet bronze does not appear to have been so used until the 13th century, if we interpret Reinecke Ha A1 to fit the higher chronology. To this period belong fragments of vessels at Guşteriţa in south Transylvania and two bronze buckets of G. von Merhardt's (1952) 'Kurd' type at Brîncoveneşti in central Transylvania.

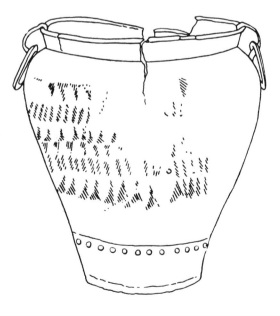

Otomani–Wietenberg expansion

The Carpathian arc – the Carpathian basin extending into east Slovakia and the Tisza valley – was agriculturally self-sufficient and had rich deposits of copper, gold and salt. That the nearest known source of tin was Bohemia would explain links established between Otomani II and the metallurgically more advanced Únětice. At an early stage in Otomani III the Únětice evolved into the Mad'arovce culture of west Slovakia and the Věteřov of Moravia and Bohemia, possibly influenced by an Otomani conquest or alliance. In any case it was a profitable association which was shared with their Wietenberg neighbours. A. Mozsolics (1967, Figs 35, 36) has shown that the rich early Hajdúsámson group of Otomani III hoards are mostly in Transylvania. A century or two later a considerably larger wealthy horizon of hoards, the Koszider group, still occurs in Transylvania, but most of the findspots lie in the central European plain, many clustering along the Danube and farther west. At a late stage in the BA, between about 1400 and 1200, the Otomani-type hoards designated by Mozsolics as the Ópályi group, no longer appear in the central European plain but are concentrated in north Transylvania, east Slovakia and the Carpatho–Ukraine (Mozsolics 1973, Fig. 17). These hoards demonstrate the existence for perhaps some 300–400 years of a powerful Otomani influence spread over the whole plain, where its legacy was to affect its peoples and their neighbours for many centuries.

Increasing archaeological evidence shows that Otomani and Wietenberg groups extended a contemporary and parallel influence north and east of the Carpathians. Otomani elements crossed the north Carpathian passes to mingle with the early mound grave culture centred on the upper Dniester and evolved the Komarów culture (Sulimirski 1968; 1970, 158ff). In the large cemetery at Komarów, tumulus burial was retained; there were some cremations but many more inhumations, with grave offerings of food, personal ornaments and, rarely, weapons. On the other hand, as T. Sulimirski, its excavator, observes, 'all the metal (bronze and a few gold) ornaments excavated in the Komarów barrow graves were of 'Hungarian' origin; so were most of the stray bronze objects and hoards found within the Komarów territory and in the area farther to the east in west Podolia. Thanks to these, the sub-Carpathian area and west Podolia acquired the character of a 'Hungarian Bronze Age province,' (1970, 159).

North-west, north-east and east of the Komarów area, the west and east Tshinetsky (Polish Trzciniec) cultural groups emerge about the second quarter of the 2nd millennium, contemporary with and closely related to the Komarów. All three in some degree possessed a Tripolye substratum. I. K. Sveshnikov (1965) and S. S. Berezanskaya (1972, 144f) consider the three cultures are so close that they make up a single cultural and, probably, ethno-cultural region. Metal artefacts are basically similar in type since the main mass of bronze objects came ready-made from Carpathian centres. The Komarów people had most metal objects, the east Tshinetsky least. Conical bosses like those on Otomani pottery appeared on Komarów and west Tshinetsky but not on east Tshinetsky ware. Even if Komarów is considered a separate

38

37 *Opposite*:
Bronze bucket from
Brîncoveneşti. Ht approx.
45 cm. Introduction of
forging about the 13th
century enabled the North
Thracians to use sheet
bronze for buckets,
although wood or antlers,
it seems, remained in use
for plough coulters.

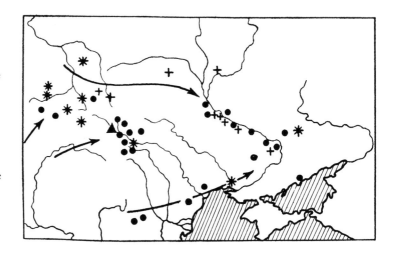

38 Evidence (1970) of the extension of Koszider horizon Otomani-Wietenberg influence north and east of the Carpathians.

✱ bronze hoards of Koszider type
● chance Koszider-type finds
+ bronze objects connected with the Tshinetsky culture
▲ Komarów cemetery

culture, this Thracian penetration, aided by a chiefly Wietenberg expansion into south Moldavia and the Pontic steppe, established a Carpathian sphere of influence that extended to and beyond the Dnieper, where the east Tshinetsky group assimilated Middle Dnieper cultural elements (Artemenko 1967, 131ff), contemporary with and as powerfully based as the westward Otomani expansion.

The EBA 'metallurgical province', based on metalwork of the Caucasus that had penetrated the Carpatho–Balkans, was now replaced
39 by a Carpathian 'province'; its exports reached east to the Caucasus and as far north as Strelitsa, over 400 km north of Kiev, where chemical analysis of bronze objects from a flat cemetery showed them to be of Transylvanian origin (Artemenko 1965).

Thus it appears that a vast Otomani–Wietenberg 'empire' – an hypothesis needing rigorous examination before acceptance – was a North Thracian equivalent of the Mycenaean and Hittite empires. Approximately their contemporary, it almost certainly began before either.

The Tei and Verbicioara cultures of Danubian Thrace and the Mokrin of the Voivodina probably developed as dependent provinces. About the middle of the 2nd millennium the Vatin group, succeeding the Mokrin (Tasić 1974), seems to have acted as an intermediary, via the Morava–Vardar route, in trade with Mycenae. J. Vladár (1973) in a valuable survey identifies various analogous motifs, but the assumption that inspiration always came from Mycenae must be questioned, likewise Mycenaean influence on objects in the hoard buried at
34 Borodino in south Moldavia (Gimbutas 1957; Safronov 1968).

The Gîrla Mare intrusion

Early in the third quarter of the 2nd millennium a middle Danubian people known from their distinctive pottery as the Pannonian Encrusted Ware culture migrated eastward into the lower Tisza valley, inhabited by people of the Pecica culture who were closely related to their Otomani northern neighbours. With displaced Pecica groups they

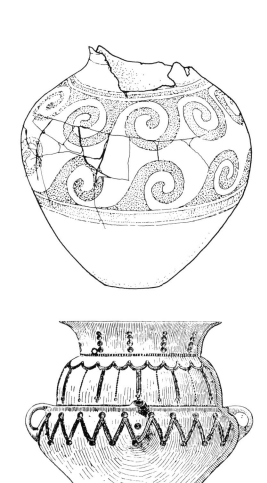

then spread into the Voivodina, Banat, west Oltenian Verbicioara lands and north-west Bulgaria to form the Gîrla Mare–Dubovac culture distinguished by cremation burial in flat 'urnfield' cemeteries and the ritual importance of clay female figurines (V. Dumitrescu 1961; D. Berciu and Comşa 1956; Mikov 1970; Tasić 1974). Whilst a mainly western, non-Thracian culture, many of its basic pottery decorative motifs – including the boss, incised sun-flame and in-curling open-ended rings – illustrate the legacy, treated in a foreign, baroque manner, of the Otomani expansion into central Europe. It was a strong and lasting intrusion, but its cult of female figurines failed to make headway against Thracian aniconism.

The Suciu de Sus culture

Another consequence of Otomani–Wietenberg expansion was the Suciu de Sus culture (known as Felchesevch–Stanovo in the Ukraine). It developed in a limited area around the upper reaches of the Tisza and

39 *Left and above right*: Caucasian finds with characteristic North Thracian decoration. Fragments of gold plaques from the Kelermes tumulus and a Middle Bronze Age painted pot bearing Carpatho-Balkan flame symbols, from Tumulus XVII, Trialeti. Ht 72 cm.

40 *Below right*: 'Villanovan-type' urn from the Gîrla Mare cemetery at Balta Verde. Ht 32.6 cm.

53

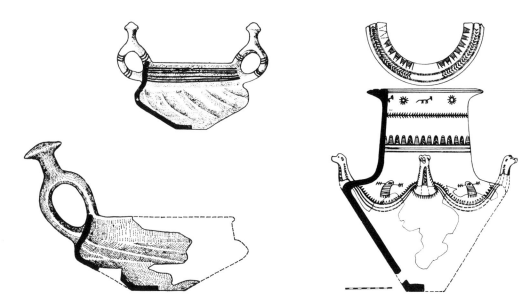

41 Pottery from Lăpuş. Single-handled clay bowl. Ht 23 cm. Two-handled clay bowl. Ht 16 cm. A development of the Otomani high-necked urn (*see Ill. 26*) with painted decoration and four bosses terminating in horned animal heads, the horns now mostly broken. Ht 46 cm.

Somes, occupying parts of the Carpathian Ukraine, north-west Romania and north-east Hungary in the second half of the Later Bronze Age (Kacsó 1975; A. Vulpe 1975; Balaguri 1969; Bader 1972). This was an inter-Thracian development, mainly a peaceful infiltration of Komarów influences into adjoining Otomani–Wietenberg territory. Although some settlements were protected by marshes and other natural defences, no artificial fortifications have been found and other settlements occupied extensive areas of open country. Dwellings were usually surface huts of wattle and daub, occasionally semi-dugouts; inside, many hearths and firedogs.

The burial rite was cremation, the calcined bones being placed in a pit or sometimes in an urn. Normal grave goods were one to three cups, bowls, spindlewhorls, beads and, less often, bronze artefacts. Graves were usually flat, but there were exceptions, as at Lăpuş, where, near a flat-grave cemetery, there was another with groups of four tumuli or single isolated mounds. Certain ritual differences among the groups suggest the cemetery was used over a long period by communities from various parts of the surrounding country. A comparison of grave goods shows that tumuli were heaped over graves of persons of special importance, the normal Otomani–Wietenberg flat graves belonging to ordinary people.

Metal finds in the tumuli included gold rings and beads, bronze disc-butted axes, one a miniature only 10 cm long, dagger-blades, a spearhead, even an iron celt. Only fragments of ritually broken pottery were placed with the cremated remains, the great variation of pot forms between tumuli providing a chronological sequence. Thus cups varied

41

from plain to biconical shapes, sometimes with button knobs on rising handles. Some dishes were decorated with exquisitely incised and relief spiral motifs, baroque versions of Otomani–Wietenberg sun symbols. The customary urn had a truncated biconical body, horned bosses on the shoulders and a high, slightly tapering neck, the rim often everted.

Both here and in the Gîrla Mare culture the high-necked Otomani jar was evolving into an early version of the 'Villanovan' urn. On some early vessels shoulder bosses terminated in ram heads. Several mounds had the remains of portable 'altar-vessels'. Lăpuş was in a particularly wealthy area and Komarów practices evidently attracted the local leaders.

Late Monteoru developments

Practice of inhumation and, at the western end of Sărata–Monteoru, a new cult building are dated to phase IIa (Nestor 1953). A terrace 2 m high was carefully faced with stones and stepped on the north and south sides. On the platform two large, pointed-base offering-vessels placed side by side, one containing charred grain, were supported by stones. Around them were fragments of cups, a larger vessel and a deep, wide-based pot, thought to be a 'cult table' – 'incense–burner', and animal bones. Close by a second group comprised a single pointed-base offering-vessel, empty but similarly propped up, with stag's antlers on one side and a carbonized beam on the other. There were also fragments of a 'cult table', a large pot, four cups, a clay disc, animal bones, some of them burnt, a copper needle and a great deal of ash from a fire that had fiercely scorched the surrounding stones. Large amounts of ash about the ritual platform suggested frequent use.

42 Clay offering-vessel from Sărata-Monteoru.

Use of stone in the construction of dwellings was developed in Monteoru IIa, but a more significant change was the preference for open settlements in lowland sites, as at Pufeşti on the Siret (M. Florescu et al. 1971). Here some half-dozen low mounds, 35–45 m in diameter, each 25–30 m apart and spread over an area of 10 ha, were identified as remains of dwelling complexes. Two were partially excavated. The first covered the burnt ruins of four huts, the second three; phases IIa and IIb were both represented, the two layers clearly separated by deposits of ash mixed with earth and debris. Floors and hearths had sometimes been remade, in one case a new floor overlaid one of the same phase.

The huts were large and substantial. One was at least 7 m long with post-holes 15–25 cm wide sunk to 50 cm in the soil. Some wattle and daub walls were 45 cm thick and one fragment showed that the interior had been polished and decorated with channelling or relief lines. Another had an outhouse annex, unfloored but with a hearth. In the debris above the floors were potsherds and stone tools, including curved gritstone knives and axes, and various bone implements, among them skates.

Between the huts, which stood 5–7 m apart, rubbish deposits heaped on a slightly hollowed base formed low mounds of charcoal, ash, bones, shells, broken pots and tools and hearth fragments. Similar deposits begun in pits some 3 m deep on the peripheries of the housing complexes formed other mounds.

On the north edge of the settlement was a small ritual pit, only 1 m in diameter, its walls carefully and repeatedly plastered and enclosed by three raised concentric clay rings. A jar at the bottom held ashes, bones, wheat grains, chaff and charcoal. Outside, lining the outer circle, were more bones, wheat and fragments of a pot. The pit wall and vessels had been much burnt and the excavators attribute this to continued offerings to fuel a sacred fire; they draw attention to a similar pit altar in a cult building of phase IC 2 at Cîndeşti.

South Thrace and relations with Anatolia and Mycenae

For the first half of the 2nd millennium the Stara Planina seems to have been the southern boundary of Otomani–Wietenberg III influence. Metallurgical progress in the Thracian Plain came only towards the middle of the millennium with access to central European tin. Gradually open moulds for casting axeheads and other objects were replaced by two-leaved closed moulds, allowing improved and more varied shapes (Chernykh 1974). In contrast to the north and to the Chalcolithic past, metallurgy remained a small-scale industry although from early in the millennium there is evidence of population growth and increasing prosperity. Ancient tells resettled early in the EBA, as Ezero, or by its end, as Karanovo, were deserted for larger open sites,

43 Cherven, south of Rousse, where later ruins overlie Thracian remains, is a typical promontory site, with steep sides dropping to the almost encircling river offering both natural protection and access to water supplies. Only a narrow neck of land needed ramparts and ditches.

44 Postholes outline a two-roomed apsidal-ended dwelling in level VI at Nova Zagora, whose max. L. is 12.7 m and W. 5.15 m.

although the Yunatsite tell in the west was inhabited longer (Mikov 1937–39). The final levels of Ezero were contemporary with the first ones of a new settlement 3 km away at Nova Zagora, where six building levels have already been identified (Katincharov 1972). There was identical pottery in both and also in the last Karanovo (VII) layer. The latest levels of Nova Zagora apparently overlap the earliest of a settlement at Razkopanitsa, east of Plovdiv (Detev 1968) and, with new excavations at Pshenichevo, near Stara Zagora (Chichikova 1972), supply stratigraphic continuity for the Late Bronze and Early Iron Ages in the Thracian Plain.

Both Pshenichevo and Razkopanitsa lay on promontories within river bends, the latter needing a ditch and vallum to protect its more accessible sides. There was progress in urban planning, and houses were more substantially built than in the EBA. As well as rectangular single-roomed huts, the two-roomed dwellings with curved ends already noted in level IV at Ezero, have become fully apsidal in early Nova Zagora levels and at Razkopanitsa. South of the Thracian Plain another was excavated in the contemporary layer at Sitagroi (Renfrew 1970).

Pottery, like metallurgy, was almost untouched by the northern exuberance. Except in the later stages, decoration was simple or entirely absent. Among typical forms were brown or burnished black single-handled 'milk jugs', shallow bowls with inverted rims and often with spouts, and small high-handled cups or dippers, the handles, like those on the jugs, usually knobbed at the top. These last were especially characteristic of the north part of the Thracian Plain and of the Devetaki (Mikov and Djambazov 1960, 106ff.) and Magoura (Djambazov and Katincharov 1974) caves of the Stara Planina. Their southern counterparts at Razkopanitsa and Yunatsite – also found at Devetaki – were probably small single- or two-handled pots, usually

45 *Above left*: Clay dipper from Ezero. Ht 9.5 cm. These small slant-mouth cups with high knobbed handles found in Ezero's final levels, Nova Zagora levels VI and V, Karanovo VII and other north Thracian Plain sites, as well as in the Devetaki and Magoura caves, were probably scoops and measures for grain or liquids.

46 *Above right*: Clay dipper from Yunatsite. Ht 13 cm. At Razkopanitsa and Yunatsite, but also at Devetaki, dippers often had pointed bases, sometimes two handles and incised decoration.

45

46

47 *Opposite above*:
Indications of Otomani-
Wietenberg contact with
South Thrace. Two
schematic horn figurines
from Ezero. Hts 9 and
6.9 cm. A sherd from
Pokrovnik. Two horn
figurines, one definitely
and the other questionably
anthropomorphic, in level
II of the north-east
sounding at Ezero,
immediately above the
level containing the
Thermi-type lidded
vessel, form a link with
Otomani I and II. Close
analogies appear in early
Otomani levels at Barca.
Others occur at Gánovce
and Mad'arovce, at the
Ljubljana marshes site
and at several in Hungary,
also at Braşov in
Romania (L. Hájek, *Slov.
Arch.* VII/2, 1959, 285
ff.). Decoration on the
Pokrovnik sherd, as on the
Tsepina jug (*Ill. 48*)
suggests a strengthening
of Otomani-Wietenberg
links with South Thrace
towards the end of the
Bronze Age.

8–14 cm high with concave sides and conical bases. At Yunatsite most were near hearths and often held carbonized grain. With the same form in layer II levels at Bubanj Hum, near Niš, relations within this area were obviously close.

After *c.* 1500 this quiet backwater – its peace perhaps an archaeological illusion due to the absence of the many hoards which illuminate the Otomani–Wietenberg culture – assumed a new strategic importance through its situation between the North Thracians and two southern great powers, Hittite Anatolia and Mycenaean Greece. Nearer still, since *c.* 1800 a strong north-west Anatolian state had controlled the Dardanelles. Its bounds are unknown and probably varied. J. G. Macqueen (1968) has argued that here was Ahhiwaya, an independent kingdom friendly with the Hittite empire. Troy VI, nearer the coast than now, guarded the entrance to the straits and was probably the capital. It is unlikely that the rulers and main occupants of Troy VI were Thracian. Indeed from the end of Troy V to the final levels of Troy VI a Thracian presence seems to have been minimal. Then the appearance of knobbed or crested high handles (Blegen *et al.* 1950–58, III/2, 318; 296/12, 14; 396/20), horizontal rows of small flat bosses (*ibid.* 372/17; 396/20) and larger single bosses, here usually termed lugs (*ibid.* 371/17; 372/18; 438/18), suggest the revival of the Thracian element for whom the 'flattened ovoid or piriform clay objects' (*ibid.* III/1, 31f; III/2, pl. 305) were sun symbols rather than loom weights.

Outside Troy and on both sides of the Propontis the population probably remained basically Thracian. D. H. French (1965) notes surface sherds on a mound some 50 km east of Istanbul with parallels 'from the Bursa region . . ., from Troy (*late* Troy I) and especially from S.E. Bulgaria . . . The best parallels in S.E. Bulgaria are to be found at Karanovo (VII) and Dipsiska-Mogila-Ezero.'

The legendary voyage of the Argonauts reflects perils facing Mycenaean seafarers braving the passage to the Black Sea. A few must have succeeded for the myth of the Colchidian gold fleece to evolve, but, perhaps significantly, the Argonauts were helped by Thracian Orpheus. Their adventures – passing through the Dardanelles at night to avoid the watch maintained by Troy, then along the Asiatic shore of the Marmara to a welcome by Cyzicus, king of the Thracian tribe of Doliones, who afterwards mistook them for pirates and lost his life attacking them, then to Mysia where Hylas was abducted, and to the land of the Thracian Bebrykes with their savage king Amykos, then across to the kingdom of the blind Thracian prophet-king Phineus, without whose support passage through the Bosporos was impossible – all indicate strong Thracian as well as Trojan obstacles to shipping passing from the Aegean to the Black Sea (Mihailov 1972, 185ff). Homer's list of Trojan allies also suggests a united Thraco-Trojan interest in confining the Mycenaean Greeks to the Aegean.

The existence of trade along the west Black Sea coast in the LBA, suggested by the underwater archaeological discovery of pottery and stone anchors off the Sozopol area, has been further supported by the find of an 'oxhide ingot' off Cape Kaliakra, north of Varna. The ingot, weighing 1.46 kg and a mixture of 32 per cent gold, 18 per cent silver

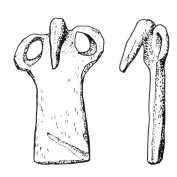

and 43 per cent copper, plus traces of nickel and sulphur, has been dated by East Mediterranean analogies to *c*. 1200 (Lazarov 1974; 1975). Recently a similarly shaped copper ingot, weighing 26 kg and dated to *c*. 1500 has been reported near the inland village of Chernovo, west of Bourgas (Karaiotov 1978). Troy, it seems, may also have been an entrepôt for Mediterranean–Black Sea trade.

There seems no reason for the Otomani–Wietenberg people, who had expanded over vast areas to east, west and north, to have contemplated a southward move which could lead to conflict with sea-based Mycenae. South Thrace was a useful buffer region. The Morava–Vardar trade route may even have been in abeyance at this time. Had links been closer, surely Carpathian bronzesmiths would have adopted southern forging techniques. Instead, as N.K. Sandars (1971) states, 'the northern sword was cast with no subsequent forging, whereas the Greek swords had been subjected to heating and forging.' A.D. Alexandrescu (1966) lists only seven Mycenaean swords in Transylvania and two in Muntenia, a small number when contrasted with the Carpatho–Hungarian types, of which nearly three hundred are known, besides those which Thracian mercenaries probably introduced widely into east Mediterranean lands.

On the other hand, Mycenae's attention turned to the north as knowledge of its wealth became more definite and Mediterranean piracy increased. During the 14th–13th centuries settlements were established in Thracian territories in south Macedonia, Khalkidiki and at Axiochorion, north of Thessalonica, and possibly elsewhere (Casson 1926, 134f), a development which may have instigated the Phrygian emigration to Anatolia. Perhaps further penetration was partly blocked by defence measures taken in South Thrace with, or without, Otomani–Wietenberg support. Northern presence or influence is suggested by potsherds found in the middle Strymon valley, at 47 Pokrovnik near Blagoevgrad (Stoyanova–Serafimova 1970) and by vessels, sherds and firedogs at the Tsepina fortress, near Velingrad in 48 the west Rhodopes (Gizdova 1974) although continuity of Chalcolithic tradition may have existed here as in the Carpathians. At the magnificently naturally defended fortress site of Gela, near Smolyan,

48 Clay jug from the Tsepina fortress in the west Rhodopes. Ht 8 cm (*see Ill. 47*).

LBA pottery, as yet unpublished, has been found (Naidenova 1977). Not far away V. Mikov (1928–29) found BA sherds at G'oz-tepe, the peak reputed later to be a sanctuary of Dionysos. The strongly walled refuge fortress at Ostur Kamuk near Kurdjali is dated by pottery to the LBA (Balkanski 1976). Many other unexcavated Rhodope fortresses used in later periods may also have been fortified at this time, as was the Krakra fortress at Pernik on the upper Strymon (Raduncheva 1970).

Whether the Mycenaeans seriously contemplated an invasion of all South and possibly North Thrace must remain doubtful, but, although slow to move, they certainly made a bid to seize control of the Dardanelles after an earthquake had destroyed Troy VI, leaving its successor VIIa more vulnerable. Were Troy the capital of Ahhiwaya, not only would possession of it eliminate a dangerous rival, linked by sea – as Hittite records show – with Amurru (the Syro–Lebanese coast), Alasiya (Cyprus) and, in the 13th century, the overlord of Millawanda (Miletos), but domination of the Dardanelles would have been a major step towards control of trade between Anatolia and Europe, possibly a main source of Anatolian tin (Mellaart 1968), as well as potential access to the Black Sea, two dreams of fabulous wealth. In the event, the siege and destruction of Troy VIIa was a hollow victory, exhausting the Greek kingdoms beyond recovery. Troy VIIb 1 was occupied briefly by Trojan survivors. With Troy VIIb 2 the whole north Aegean, the Propontis and Macedonia reverted to Thracian control.

49 A massive seven-angled drystone wall, L. 262 m and W. 2.20 m, using roughly cut but carefully laid blocks sometimes more than 1 m long protects the accessible sides of the Late Bronze Age Ostur Kamuk fortress, near Kurdjali, and distinguishes it from Iron Age neighbours, roughly built of smaller stones. Like Tsepina, it was sited to defend the Thracian Plain from the south, perhaps a precaution against Mycenaean expansion.

4
Late Bronze to Early Iron Age:
_c_. 14th–11th centuries BC

Disintegration of the empires

The middle of the 2nd millennium was a time of prosperity, not only for the Thracian lands but for central Europe, Anatolia and the eastern Mediterranean, and the outlook for the future seemed full of promise. Yet the 13th and 12th centuries saw the destruction of Troy VI and its short-lived successor VIIa, the fall of the mighty Hittite empire, the collapse of Mycenae and the invasion of the 'Sea Peoples' in the east Mediterranean. The Otomani–Wietenberg 'empire' had retracted in the west, urnfield cultures succeeding it in the central European plain and a tumulus culture from the north appearing in Slovakia. For a time metallurgical production in Transylvania continued unabated, but its technological leadership was declining.

Although these major events may be used to mark the transition from the Later Bronze to the Early Iron Age, the chronology of social change is more complicated. From the mid-2nd millennium the climate again deteriorated, growing gradually colder and wetter, but the change was minor compared with that which had introduced the EBA (Frenzel 1967). Again, too, there was a westward migration into the Pontic steppe, a branch of the Srubnaya (Timber-grave) people advancing from beyond the Volga, but on this front the Otomani–Wietenberg expansion across the Dnieper had established a settled and powerful East Thracian community in the west Pontic and forest-steppe area capable of halting the migration at the Dnieper and of assimilating any smaller groups successful in penetrating farther west.

50 LBA ornaments. _Above_: Bronze phalera or shield boss from Bădeni. Diam. 14.4 cm. _Below_: One of two bronze stylized figurines from the Ulmi-Liteni hoard. Ht 11.4 cm.

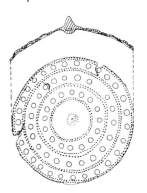

Transylvania and the Gáva–Holihrady culture

The Otomani–Wietenberg culture probably began its gradual disintegration about the second half of the 14th century. Evidence for its course is based largely and very strikingly on hoards of bronze and – to a lesser extent – gold objects, dated approximately to the later 14th, 13th and 12th centuries. The earlier hoards are mainly concentrated in the Someş and upper Tisza valleys, with a few in Slovakia, north-east Hungary and the upper Mureş. A contemporary group round the upper Olt are perhaps due to Noua expansion from Moldavia. Whilst still numerous, although declining, in the Someş and upper Tisza basins, by about the 13th–12th centuries some of the largest and wealthiest appear in the valleys of the Mureş and its tributaries, many also for the first time in the Banat (Rusu 1963; Mozsolics 1973; Petrescu-Dîmboviţa 1977).

Weapons are prominent in the later hoards, especially disc-butted battle-axes, now rarely decorated but often with an unpleasant spike at the centre of the disc, flange-hilted slashing IIa swords, daggers and spearheads. Celts and sickles were common among tools, bracelets and armlets among ornaments, the latter varying from simple, open-ended rings to elaborate spiralling guards; there were also phalerae, a form which spread widely across central and northern Europe (Merhart 1956). Ornaments were of gold as well as bronze. The hoards are impressive evidence of the scale of Transylvanian metallurgy in the final disturbed phase of Otomani-Wietenberg. Five great *c.* 13th–12th century upper Mureş hoards (Uioara, Şpălnaca, Guşteriţa, Dipşa and Band) together yielded a total of 4000 kg of bronze; from Uioara alone, some 5,800 items weighed 1300 kg. Tin was lavishly used in fine work, its ratio to copper sometimes 17–25 per cent (Rusu 1963).

Not surprisingly, many fortified settlements increased in size during this period (Horedt 1974). Although the Otomani 'island' of 6–7 ha, one of the largest at the beginning of the Later Bronze Age, continued in use, about the 13th–12th centuries two immense fortified enclosures were founded near the lower Mureş-Sîntana, 78 ha and Corneştii–Jădani, 67.5 ha. In north-east Transylvania the *c.* 12th century upper Someş site of Ciceu–Corabia occupied 30 ha.

The two Mureş sites, exceptionally strongly fortified, marked a significant change in the fortunes of Transylvania. No longer was the Mureş an open gateway to the west, the gate was shut and barred. The *c.* 13th–12th century fragmentary bronze corselets of Čierna and Tisou in eastern and Čaka and Ducové in western Slovakia (Snodgrass 1971) suggest the presence on the western marches of a people with superior arms and technology, including forging. The Brîncoveneşti buckets are the nearest contemporary parallels yet found in Transylvania. After the destruction of Sîntana's first wall, 10 m thick and 4 m high with a ditch 3.5 m wide and 3 m deep, it was replaced by a massive construction some 25 m thick and 7 m high with a ditch 13 m wide and 4 m deep. Corneştii–Jădani, south of the Mureş, was encircled by two additional outer walls, the inner enclosing over 200 ha and the outer 586 ha. Such vast fortified areas could accommodate an urban industrial population and give refuge to the thickly populated countryside. At the other end of the scale were forts so small as to be simply strongholds of local chiefs.

The opposing phenomena of an intensive metallurgical industry and a constant desperate concealment of the finished product could not long coexist. Transylvania increased the export of ingots or semi-finished goods to new manufacturing centres east and south of the Carpathians. M. Rusu's explanation (1963) is a state of acute inter-tribal warfare, from which during the 13th century the Gáva culture (László 1973) evolved in the north-west sector of the Carpathian arc. Closely related to the preceding Suciu de Sus culture, the Gáva group spread into Transylvania and across the north Carpathians into Komarów territory, where it has been identified as the Holihrady culture (Smirnova 1974).

Whether fortified or not, Gáva sites were usually chosen for

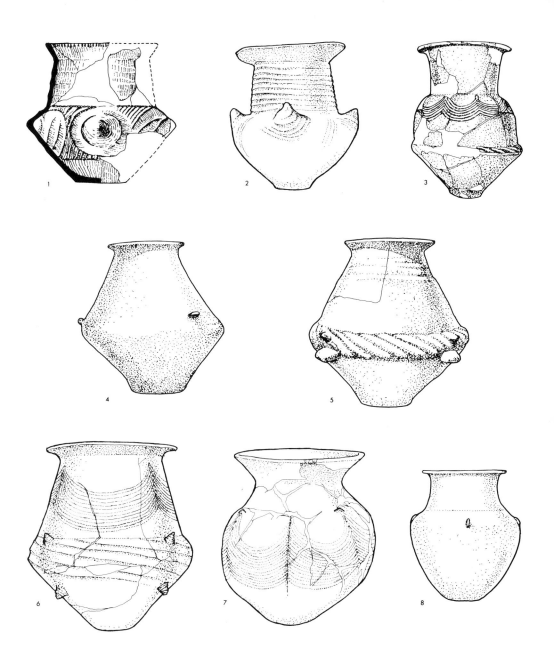

defensive potentiality. Surface huts and semi-dugouts had hearths both inside and outside, also domed ovens. In some settlements a system of 'pit-ovens' seems to have provided a kind of under-floor heating. Unmarked flat graves held urns containing the ashes of the dead and accompanying pots. Pottery was generally of high standard, although lacking the élan of Otomani III or Suciu de Sus, from both of which Gáva inherited and disseminated widely two features: bossed decor- 51 ation (*Buckelkeramik*) and the truncated biconical 'Villanovan' urn.

Gáva elements moving southwards into Transylvania had been forestalled in the south-east by the Noua infiltration from Moldavia but the check was temporary. The basically Wietenberg character of the first phase at Reci shows strong Noua influence, later replaced by Gáva. At Mediaş, north of the Olt gap, Noua *zolniki*, or ashy mounds, are found together with Gáva bossed ware (Zaharia 1965). Conversely, Gáva or Holihrady infiltration may account for the cremation burials at Piatra Neamţ and elsewhere in west Moldavia during the Noua period. At Mahala, in north Moldavia, Holihrady levels succeeded Noua (Smirnova 1969; 1974).

52

The Noua culture

In Moldavia about the end of the 14th century and closely connected with Sabatinovka developments east of the Dniester, the late Monteoru, Costişa and Belopotok–Komarów cultures gave way to the Noua culture with a marked drop in living standards (A. C. Florescu 1964). Strongly concentrated at first in the basin of the middle Prut, in the 13th century the new culture spread into Transylvania and southwards to east Muntenia and the Dobroudja.

The Noua people lived in open settlements, using surface huts, sometimes later semi-dugouts. Among their characteristic pots were simple sack-like jars, with a plain or notched cordon and often a ring of small holes below the rim. Cups or bowls had one or two handles that, rising slightly from the rim and returning to the shoulder of the rounded body, were frequently knobbed at the peak. In the essentially pastoral economy, animal bones, preponderantly cattle, account for as much as 60–65 per cent of recovered archaeological material. The many bone implements had metal prototypes, Transylvanian imports having fallen, seemingly for lack of purchasing power. They included needles, piercers, sickles, buttons, arrow- and spearheads, with only the working part carefully executed. Stone and flint were once again used for axe-hammers, curved knives, bill-hooks and sickles. Bronze pins, most commonly the knot- and ring-headed types, are occasionally found in graves. Thirteenth-century Moldavian bronze hoards further illustrate the scarcity of metal. Ulmi–Liteni yielded a sickle, a celt, a chisel, an engraver and a few ornaments, including two highly stylized anthropomorphic pendants of a type then popular in Moldavia and Podolia (M. Florescu 1961); Duda two celts, four sickles and one dagger (Petrescu-Dîmboviţa 1966); and Bozia Nouă one celt, three sickles and some lumps of crude bronze (Petrescu-Dîmboviţa 1964). Even the larger hoards – at Ruginoasa fourteen sickles, two celts, a chisel and a lump of crude bronze (Ursachi 1968) and at Ilişeni three celts, twenty-seven sickles, two swords and a spearhead (Foit 1964) – in no way compare with the hoards in Transylvania, whence most of the objects derived.

The Noua lands straddled a trade route carrying bronze ingots and partly worked artefacts from Transylvania to the more prosperous Sabatinovka country and some of the goods were retained and copied. A small local industry grew up to make tools, especially celts and sickles, but swords and daggers, needing more skill, still came from Transylvania (Dergachev 1975).

53

50

52 *Opposite above*: Table comparing artefacts from settlement layers at Mahala. I Noua, II Early Holihrady (also called 'Thracian Hallstatt'), III Evolved Holihrady.

53 *Opposite below*: Noua clay bowl from Teiuş, west Transylvania.

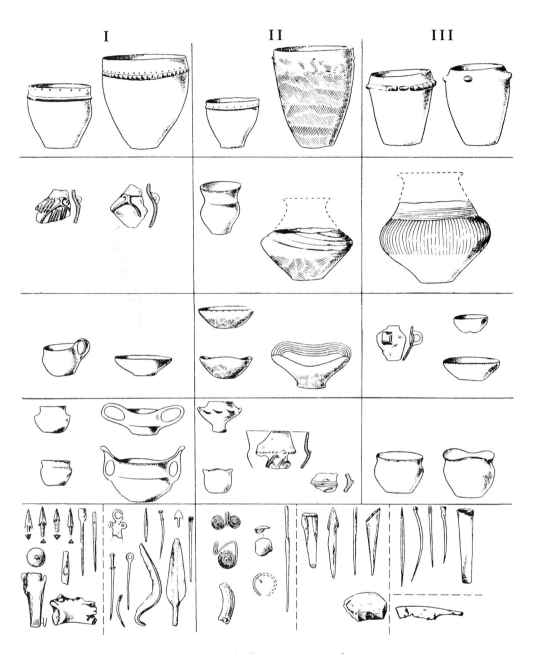

The normal burial rite was inhumation in flat graves; cremation was rare. Skeletons, moderately or sharply crouched, were laid in earth pits. In the Noua cemetery at Truşeşti thirty-four out of forty-nine graves contained offerings, but twenty-three of them only a single pot, usually placed near the head. A small gold ring was the sole valuable offering.

The Noua culture is especially associated with *zolniki*. These had already appeared in late Monteoru sites, as at Pufeşti (M. Florescu *et al.* 1971), but were not a Komarów feature. In the Truşeşti settlement (Movila Şesul Jijiei), three successive levels of *zolniki*, all pre-

ponderantly ashy, were recorded, their diameters approximately 17, 25 and 30 m respectively. Finds characteristic of late Monteoru–Belopotok appeared in the two lower levels, the third being clearly Noua (Petrescu–Dîmboviţa *et al.* 1954).

Some *zolniki* seem to embrace the remains of whole houses, others to be deposits of ashes and other hearth and stove remains, together with broken pots, animal bones and whole or fragmented hearths. At Gindeshty, near Floreshty in north-east Moldavia, a drystone wall had enclosed a scattered group of nine (Melyukova 1961). Normally associated with settlements, they rarely contain a burial. *Zolniki* have also been noted in the related Coslogeni culture in east Muntenia and the Dobroudja, in adjacent Sabatinovka sites such as Belgorod, and in Bilohrudivka settlements. They were later widespread in the Chernoles culture and have been found as far east as the Donets and the north Caucasus (Melyukova 1961; Shramko 1957; Krupnov 1949).

As the domestic or kin hearth represented continuity of existence in primitive society, so *zolniki* combined ancestral and solar cults, the frequency of hearth fragments and broken tools linking the hearth with forefathers who had earlier dwelt on the spot (Grakov 1971, 153ff.). The ash assumed the sacred nature of the hearth. Ethnographic study of the Caucasian Udmurti tribe showed that ash was taken when moving from their old homes and that a new generation took ash from the family hearth to start their own (Shramko 1957). The *zolniki* may have served a like function and thus become a form of shrine. There is an analogy in the bearing by Greek colonists of brands from the *prytaneion* of the mother city for rekindling in their new one overseas (Jeffery 1976, 56).

The Sabatinovka and Bilohrudivka cultures

In south-east Moldavia, between the Prut and the Dniester, the last Monteoru phase merged with the Sabatinovka culture (Sharafutdinova 1968; Novikova 1976) which evolved during the 14th century as an eastern outlier of the Otomani-Wietenberg 'empire' in the Pontic steppe between the Dniester and Dnieper.* Beyond the Dnieper, Srubnaya tribes from east of the Volga continued for a time to depend on the Urals for bronze, but increasingly turned to Caucasian sources. Some Srubnaya sites were fortified; the open Sabatinovka settlements suggest a peaceful life and co-existence, and trans-Dnieper trade may be responsible for their greater prosperity compared with the Noua.

Stone, used earlier in the area, became common in house-building, usually the lower parts of walls, sometimes the whole of them; rubble mixed with clay was also used. Stone dwellings have been found in an

---

*The Sabatinovka culture is a matter of controversy. *Inter alia*, contrary to the views of T. Sulimirski and I. N. Sharafutdinova here adopted, A. I. Terenozhkin (1961; 1976), following O. Krivtsova-Grakova (1955) considered it in essence Srubnaya and covering the whole Pontic steppe from the 16th–7th centuries, with a proposed chronology as follows: Pokrov (early Srubny) 1600–1400; Sabatinovka 1400–1150; Belozero 1150–900; Chernogorovka 900–750 and Novocherkassy 750–650 (the historical Cimmerians). A. C. Florescu (1964) equates the Noua and Sabatinovka cultures.

area stretching from Bolgrad, near the confluence of the Prut and Danube, Cherevichnoe and Anatolevka, between the lower Dniester and Bug, the eponymous Sabatinovka site on the middle Bug to Zmievka on the lower Dnieper and even farther east. At Anatolevka cut stone blocks enclosed a rubble fill. There were hearths indoors and outdoors; large rooms had two or three, as well as domed ovens. At Zmievka a *zolnik*, the result of piling hearth ash, broken pottery and other domestic debris, was found beside a three-roomed house, an oven showing one room to be a kitchen (Chernyakov 1964; Pogrebova 1960).

The dead were inhumed and buried, Yamnaya fashion, in existing tumuli or in flat cemeteries where earth pits, sometimes stone-covered, or stone cists were used. The crouched skeleton normally had a vessel by the head, and besides other pots grave goods included bronze knives, lock rings, what seem to be buttons, bone spindlewhorls and food remains. Sharafutdinova (1968) notes evidence of a fire-hearth cult linked with zoomorphic figurines and little clay 'loaves'.

Pottery was usually grey or black, often highly polished. Handles were rare except on cups or dippers where they were sometimes knobbed. Cordons or patterned incised bands below the rim were frequent at first on larger vessels but decoration tended to greater simplicity in the later or Belozero phase (Leskov 1971). The conventional horns symbol appears on a clay cauldron from the Sabatinovka I settlement (Sulimirski 1970, 176, Fig. 41).

A flourishing pastoral economy provided ample bone for arrowheads, needles, piercers, polishers, skates, harpoons and bridle cheekpieces and this was only gradually superseded by bronze. Sickles, then knives and celts, were the most common of the many bronze implements found in settlements and hoards, with spears and daggers as the preferred weapons. It was a local industry, as the many stone moulds show, but raw material – ingots, scrap or unfinished work – had to be imported.

Initially some sickles and axeheads came from the Kuban and north Caucasus, but chemical analysis of Sabatinovka bronzework showed it to be generally identical with Transylvanian and Komarów. Yet, although ore continued to come from the west, the Belozero phase marks a gradual strengthening of relations with the Srubnaya on the middle Dnieper. Finished goods began again to come from the Caucasus, which was superseding Transylvania not only in bronze metallurgy but in the use of iron for swords, daggers and axes.

North of the Sabatinovka-inhabited Pontic steppe the Bilohrudivka culture followed somewhat later in the forest-steppe. 'The various elements contributing to its formation', writes T. Sulimirski (1970, 38) 'are well reflected in its remains: tulip-shaped pots evidently inherited from the Trzciniec (Tshinetsky) culture; bowls from the Komarów culture; ashy mounds adopted under the influence of the Noua culture; Tripolyan clay figurines and some pottery; in moulds for casting socketed axes and some other elements from the Sabatynivka culture in the south and the Srubnaya culture east of the Dnieper; and stone battle-axes, flanged bronze axes (Sandraki on the Boh (Bug)) and a bronze spearhead from the Catacomb culture of the preceding period.' They were a settled population, with new dwellings built on the debris

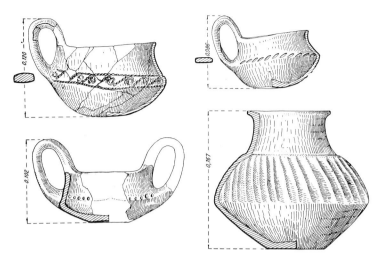

54 *Left*: Clay bowl of the Plovdiv-Zimnicea group, from Gradeshnitsa. Ht 9.5 cm.

55 *Right*: Pottery from Babadag I.

of the old, concentrated especially strongly in the Uman region (Terenozhkin 1961, 6ff.).

Danubian and South Thrace

These events were not without their impact on the complex and still confusing situation in Thracian lands along and south of the lower Danube. Besides the changes in the north and north-east, Urnfield cultures were relaying new ideas from the west, while in the south the Mycenaean expansion included Thessaly and the north Aegean region.

For a while a group known from two important pottery finds as the Plovdiv-Zimnicea or, in B. Hänsel's terminology (1976) the Cherkovna, continued to maintain earlier traditions. The find-spots are mainly in the Thracian Plain and between the lower Danube and the Stara Planina, with a few on the north bank of the Danube. At Zimnicea sixty-four inhumations, moderately crouched and lying on either side, were found in a flat-grave cemetery (A. D. Alexandrescu 1973; 1974). Grave goods were minimal; two graves contained two pots each and forty only one. Almost all were either black mugs, wide-bodied jugs or globular bowls with concave-profiled necks and two rounded handles rising from the bulge and rim, and of poor quality clay. The only other offerings were two bronze finger-rings, a curved bronze fragment, an amber bead and four snail shells. In the whole cemetery one Gîrla Mare jug was found. The limited contact between these two groups is reciprocally shown by the find of only one Zimnicea-type bowl in the 116 BA graves at Cîrna (V. Dumitrescu 1961, no. 121, Pl. LXVIII) and one, with the handle rising from the join of neck and shoulder, at Balta Verde (D. Berciu and Comşa 1956).

In north-west Bulgaria twenty graves in a cemetery at Krushovitsa (B. Nikolov 1964) yielded almost the whole Zimnicea-Plovdiv repertoire. A closely related Oltenian group (Hänsel's Govora) also used similar pot forms although retaining Verbicioara traditions in decoration.

54

The Plovdiv find was unusual: fifty-eight whole and many fragmented vessels had been carefully stored in rows, many pots showing signs of long use (Detev 1964). No burial was found, but a near-by well or spring may be relevant; the eight vessels found at Cherkovna near Razgrad were also near a well. The Plovdiv pots were identical with those at Zimnicea and Krushovitsa, but added globular jars with two or more handles on the bulge and a deep bowl with a pail-like handle. The same jugs and bowls were also found at Razkopanitsa, the bowls sometimes with incised decoration (Detev 1968).

The Plovdiv–Zimnicea group could not have lasted far into the 13th century. Gáva influences from the north and Noua from the north-east were stimulating new expressions of traditional concepts in hitherto conservative South Thrace.

At Babadag in the north Dobroudja, excavations of a hill fortress (Morintz 1964) uncovered three stages of a long-lived culture identified at other sites, fortified and open, in the Dobroudja, at Rousse on the Danube (Georgiev and Angelov 1957) and extending to a cemetery at Stoicani in south Moldavia (Petrescu–Dîmboviţa 1963). The pottery contains elements of Noua, but Gáva influence, introducing its horned boss, is stronger, as is that of the Pshenichevo culture of the Thracian Plain, characterized by its stamped decoration and incised tangented circles. Another feature, deep parallel excisions, is foreign. The earliest phase of Babadag, in which were two small pieces of impure iron and a much oxidized iron bar, has been dated from the early 12th century to *c*. 1000, although the appearance of the same pottery in a mature form in Troy VIIb 2, dated by C. W. Blegen (1963, 174) to *c*. 1190, argues an earlier beginning. By putting the Babadag I phase, whether at Babadag or elsewhere, back to the 13th century and assuming cultural unity along the west Black Sea coast, for which Hänsel (1976, 213ff.) has adduced evidence, extension of this culture to the Thracian Bosporos and as far as Troy in phase VIIb 2 is logical. Turkish Thrace is a gap in our knowledge but settlements in the hinterland of Varna (Todorova 1972 a, b) and on the Meden Rid, near Sozopol (Venedikov *et al.* 1976)

56 *Above*: Clay bowl from Troy VIIb 2, Ht (with handles) 20.5 cm. The identical shape, with a small central boss, is found at Babadag and Rousse.

57 *Below left*: Fragment of a clay bowl from Troy VIIb 2 with Pshenichevo-type, stamped tangented circle decoration. Ht (to rim) 8.2 cm.

58 *Below centre*: Clay cup from Troy VIIb 2, with three small bosses. Ht (to rim) 7.5 cm. The peaked handle, like that of Ill. 56, is also found at Malko Kale (*Ill. 68*).

59 *Right*: Clay bowl with three horn bosses, from Troy VIIb 2. Ht (to rim) 24–25.8 cm. A similar vessel with more pronounced bosses is illustrated by Schliemann (1880, No. 1369) and parallels exist in the west Pontic coastal belt at Golyamo Delchevo and nearby Dulgopol.

67, 68 provide increasing support for such cultural unity, to which, besides
Babadag, Gáva and Pshenichevo contributed substantially.

Westwards, in the region of the Danubian Iron Gates, the Insula
Banului culture (Morintz and Roman 1969) supplanted the remnants
of Gîrla Mare. It differed considerably from its predecessor in that
decoration on the pottery, so far almost all fragmentary, largely
consisted either of lines of cord-like impressions made by a comb-like
clay tool used also on Gáva, Babadag and Moldavian pots, or
impressed motifs, notably patterns resembling S, M and the

conventional horns symbol, an Otomani legacy received either via the central European plain or direct. At Devetaki, farther east, potters were also making bossed ware and using applied horns symbols, incised 'comb' and channelling decoration. Curved pointed bosses were also common on Insula Banului ware and parallel incised garlands were another Transylvanian link. Finds in the later dwellings show more use of channelling, a link with pottery at Pecica, west of Arad and the Belegiš culture of the Voivodina.

In the Thracian Plain a contemporary development was taking place at sites such as Pshenichevo, near Stara Zagora, (Chichikova 1972) and Razkopanitsa (Detev 1968). Here Gáva-influenced bossed ware came with Wietenberg rather than Otomani accompaniments, Pshenichevo potters transforming them into tangented circles, linked S patterns and incised running spirals. 'Comb' decoration and channelling were common here, too, but an original contribution was the use of many and varied stamped motifs in both traditional and new designs. The Pshenichevo culture, barely apparent north of the Stara Planina, contributed greatly to the growing homogeneity of South Thrace, including the new south-east Thracian Megalithic culture. The Pshenichevo culture may also, as Hänsel (1969) has inferred, have introduced an early South Thracian group of stone firedogs, with incised decoration difficult to date to any other period. In this ritual context the horse appears as well as the more usual ram. Perhaps legendary 'horse-breeding' Thrace and its hero-king Rhesus, a mighty warrior and Trojan ally famed for his white horses, is not entirely without archaeological support.

East Muntenia and neighbouring areas south of the Danube were a meeting place of the final Tei phase, the Gáva, Sabatinovka, Noua and Babadag. The heterogeneous consequence of this intermingling has been termed the Coslogeni culture (Morintz and Anghelescu 1970). It is doubtful whether the various elements were ever sufficiently

Opposite.
60 *Above left*: Bossed urn from Gabarevo, near Kazanluk. Ht 23 cm. Bossed ware, revived by Otomani III, Gáva and Suciu de Sus cultures, had appeared as early as the Tiszapolgár and Precucuteni, the latter exhibiting developed horn bosses at Traian in central Moldavia.

61 *Above right*: Late Bronze Age sherds from Pshenichevo showing punched, incised, pricked and channelled decoration.

62 *Below*: Continuity of the tangented circle motif is shown by this 5th to 6th-century AD altar screen from Osenovo, near Varna. Ht 24.5 cm.

63, 64

63 *Above*: Stone firedog representing a horse, with Pshenichevo-type decoration, from Markovo, north of Chirpan. Ht 23 cm.

64 Clay firedog from Brno Obřany, Moravia. Max. Ht 23 cm, L. 47 cm. This firedog with a stylized representation of a ram was one of several found near hearths in the settlement.

65 *Opposite above*: A single-chamber megalithic tomb close to a small hill-fort near Harmanli, Haskovo district. Ht 1.45 m, L. 2.80 m.

66 *Opposite below*: A complex megalithic chamber tomb near Lalapaşa. A passage with sides 1.20 and 1.60 m long leads to an antechamber and main tomb chamber, together 2.70 m long, with rounded holes approx. 30 cm wide in the dividing slabs. At entrance W. is 2.20 m and at rear 2.80 m. Ht 1.50 m.

integrated to form a distinctive culture, but it is valuable to locate the crossroads of all these influences.

A south-east Thracian Late Bronze – Early Iron Age culture was characterized by megalithic chamber tombs, the so-called dolmens, almost all concentrated in a narrow band of country stretching southwest from the Black Sea coast between Sozopol and Ahtopol to the eastern Rhodopes of Bulgaria and Greece and including the western Strandja (Istranca) hills of Bulgaria and Turkey, where groups have been located round Lalapaşa and Hacidanişment, north-east of Edirne (Kansu 1963; 1969; Köylüoğlu 1976). Of some 650 recorded since 1900 in Bulgaria P. Delev (1975) estimated about 85 per cent were in the Sakar hills. Originally there may have been twice this number; some reported earlier in the Sredna Gora and Stara Planina no longer exist.

The simplest structure was a rectangular chamber of five skilfully fitted monoliths forming front, sides, back and roof, the sides sometimes sloping slightly inward to fit grooves carved in the capstone. The front usually had a rectangular or arched hole 40–70 cm high, perhaps to give spirits access to food in the entrance. More complex graves possessed an antechamber with similar openings both to the end chamber and to a passage walled by rather smaller slabs leading to a stone ring that encircled the mound of earth or small stones originally heaped over the whole structure. Local slate used in the Evros prefecture had gaps instead of holes between the outer or dividing slabs and one of the walls (Triandaphyllos 1973). Very exceptionally a mound covered more than one tomb, but continued use seems to have been common, perhaps for a family or kin-group. Inhumation, the earliest rite noted, was succeeded by cremation.

Generally standing on hills or low ridges, some are isolated; others, grouped, form the cemetery of a settlement near a fortified refuge. Greater size or complexity probably reflected status, as at Büyünlü north-east of Edirne where one large and two much smaller ones stood together. None have been found on the coast, where intensive settlement from the Greek colonization onwards could easily account for their removal for one purpose or another. Inland, erosion and later re-use of stones from cairns and rings have left the megaliths standing alone. Very few have not been completely ransacked. Three skeletons

67 Potsherds from
megalithic chamber tombs
at Studena and Sakartsi,
Haskovo district, showing
analogies with the
Pshenichevo and Babadag
– Troy VIIb 2 cultures.
Ht of broken conical boss,
from Studena, 4.5 cm.

67, 68

were found in one in the Svilengrad region and a few Pshenichevo-type
sherds near by (Mikov 1955). Recent research has produced more
pottery (Venedikov and Aladjov 1976), some of it definitely linking the
megalithic chambers in the Sakar and east Rhodopes with the
suggested coastal culture.

Looting, re-use and perhaps ritual removal of earlier burials make
the appearance of the first Thracian megalithic chambers hard to date.
In the Strandja V. Karaiotov (1976) has reported one with an
(unpublished) pottery sequence from the 11th to the 3rd century, but
such structures may have existed much earlier. Close analogies with the
monuments of a megalithic culture in the north-west Caucasus and
Taman peninsula (Tallgren 1934; Markovin 1973) are helpful. V. I.
Markovin dated the earliest and simplest here to c. 2400–2200; free-
standing, they contained single inhumations with rich grave goods.
Later they became more complex, were re-used and covered by
mounds. I. I. Akhanov (1961) dated fragmentary finds in some near
Gelendzhik on the Caucasian coast from the end Bronze – Early Iron
transition down to c. 4th century. There seems little doubt that the
Thracian megalithic chambers result from a migration from across the
Black Sea, probably towards the end of the Bronze Age. Ş. A. Kansu
also reports (1964) an irregularly shaped passage grave under a mound
at Arpaçay, near Kars in north-east Anatolia. The copper ore of the
near-by Meden Rid (Copper Range) and the north Strandja may have
attracted the newcomers, but the chance find of a stone mould for
sickles (Aladjov 1969) and the Chernovo ingot are no proof of copper
mining here before the 1st millennium b c, the earliest period so far
established.

The importance of Sozopol and nearby inlets as prehistoric ports,
now becoming clearer through underwater archaeology (Lazarov 1974;

68 Jug with channelled decoration from the earliest level at Malko Kale, dated to the 11th–9th century. Ht 20.5 cm.

1975), is reflected in the fortified settlements on the low Meden Rid dominating the gulf. Small soundings in one, Malko Kale, show two distinct layers before the Greek arrival (Venedikov *et al.* 1976). In the earlier phase it seems to have been an open settlement, with defence walls only in the second phase. Enough pottery was found to relate the first phase to the Late Bronze coastal culture and to the earliest Pshenichevo-type ware found in the megalithic chambers. The peaked-handled and channelled jug is almost identical with a vessel in a passage grave at Sakartsi in the Sakar hills. Bossed, incised, stamped and stab-and-drag decoration are other common features. Another link with Troy VIIb 2 as well as elsewhere in the Carpatho–Balkans is a collection of crude anthropomorphic figurines (Blegen 1963, Pl. 66), at Malko Kale a ritual deposit and accompanied by zoomorphic models, miniature vessels and clay rings.

67

Menhirs, seemingly indiscriminately grouped, have been noted by D. Triandaphyllos near the Evros dolmens and by Kansu and N. Köylüoğlu at Lalapaşa and Hacidanişment. Anthropomorphic, including ithyphallic, zoomorphic and solar rock engravings were also found by Triandaphyllos, who tentatively dates them by Italian and Austrian analogies to the 13th–12th centuries, but does not exclude the possibility of a much earlier time.

Inside the defences of the Paleokastro fortress on a peak above Hlyabovo in the Sakar hills is a crest of tooth-like rocks facing east (Venedikov and Fol 1976, 25, 159). Here over 140 discs, 25–90 cm in diameter, have been carved, some excised 3–5 cm, others raised. The granite and gneiss rock contains a great deal of mica, and the discs are placed to catch and reflect the sun's first rays. This 'solar temple' of sun discs is at present unique in Thracian lands and undated, although it is generally associated with the surrounding megalithic culture.

5

The Thracian Early Iron Age:
c. 11th–7th centuries BC

Early ironworking in Carpatho–Balkan Thrace

The break-up of the Otomani–Wietenberg 'empire' must seriously have disrupted Transylvanian imports of tin, but the bronze industry's decline was not offset by a change to ironworking. The small iron finds at Babadag probably came from north-west Anatolia, but a foundry at Cernatu in south-east Transylvania, where, besides a bronze socketed spearhead and two bronze fibulae, an iron knife and chisel, a double-bladed iron axehead, four iron bars and seven or eight fragments of others were found (Székely 1966), may represent an import of technology from the same region. Both discoveries are dated to before the end of the 2nd millennium BC, when iron was being vigorously exploited in Mediterranean lands, yet the few Transylvanian iron finds datable to the first quarter of the 1st millennium, for instance those at Hida, Somartin and Tuşnad-Băi, indicate slowness to adapt to new circumstances, probably due to economic disruption and decline. As elsewhere, the new material seems to have been most commonly used for axeheads and knife blades where the sharper edge it could be given was appreciated. Because of its rarity value, iron was also used for ornaments, but bronze still served for swords and general purposes.

By contrast, evidence for considerable South Thracian iron-working in the 10th century is found in the cemetery at Vergina in Macedonia (Andronikos 1969) and S. Casson (1926, 143f.) has cited other Macedonian iron-using centres at Pateli, Chauchitsa, Vardino and Vardaroftsa which may have existed as early as the 12th century (Desborough 1972, 220). Vergina was the homeland of the Thracian tribe of Pieres before their expulsion to the Pangaean region in 479 by Alexander I of Macedonia (Thuc. ii, 99) and, with the other centres, appears to have maintained the Vardar–Morava trade links with east central Europe. Those buried at Vergina, Pieres or others, may have included northern migrants after the Mycenaean collapse. A warlike people, as seen by the weapons in their graves, their pottery has button-knobbed handles, bossed and other northern forms mingling with Aegean cut-away necked jugs. Although Greek ironworking may have been a stimulus, A. M. Snodgrass (1971, 253ff.) points out Vergina lack of connection with Greek iron-using centres farther south. On the basis of the similarity of its bronze products to those of the lower Danube area and its ready access to raw materials, he concludes that the population may then have been Thracian rather than Macedonian in character.

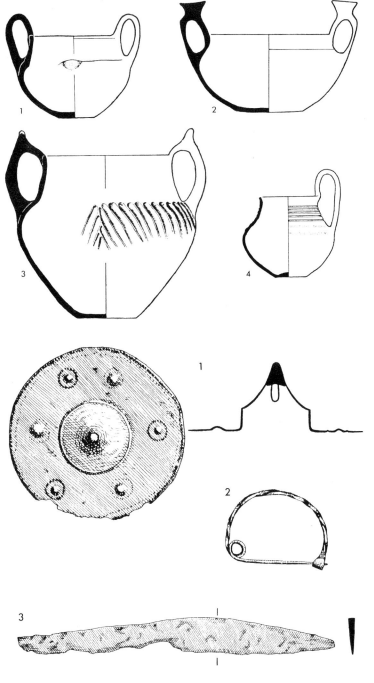

69 Northern influences in pottery at Vergina. *Above left*: Kantharos with rising handles and bossed decoration, 10th century. *Above right*: Bowl with rising button-knobbed handles, 11th–early 10th century. Similar handles were found at Olynthos. *Below left*: Bowl with channelled decoration and rising peak-knobbed handles, early 10th century (*cf. Ill 78, left*). *Below right*: High-handled jug or cup, early 10th century. A shape popular throughout Thracian lands in the first half of the first millennium BC.

70 Metalwork from the Early Iron Age cemetery at Vergina. 1. Bronze shield-boss, early 10th century. Diam. 4.7 cm. 2. Bronze arc fibula, 11th–early 10th century. L. approx. 4 cm. 3. Iron makhaira, early 10th century. L. 24 cm. 4. Iron flange-hilted sword, 11th–early 10th century. L. 69 cm.

71 Rock tomb in a low massive outcrop near Ovchevo with a bier in an arched recess opposite the entrance.

70

During Vergina's three centuries of prosperity iron was used almost exclusively for the many weapons and knives in male graves. In female graves especially, a wealth of jewellery and ornaments, both arc and spectacle fibulae, show the continued importance of bronze. Iron knives and weapons like those at Vergina made their way to other Thracian areas; but, Macedonian centres apart, Carpatho–Balkan Thrace still relied on bronze, the Vergina group, like Glasinac in Bosnia, probably influencing the dissemination of new models.

This is reflected in tumulus cemeteries such as Pavelsko in the central Rhodopes (Mikov 1940–41) where an intact burial with two skeletons containing five bronze fibulae – one spectacle, two single-coil arc and two boat-shaped – together with an unidentifiable iron object can be related to an early Vergina group. Another from a cemetery at nearby Progled is dated to 11th–8th centuries (Gergova 1977). The earliest burial in the tumulus cemetery at Bailovo in the western Sredna Gora, dated by D. Gergova to the end 8th–6th centuries, included an iron fibula and two plaques which were probably shield bosses (Popov 1921). As at Vergina, bronze fibulae were the general rule but, unlike Vergina, evidence is lacking that iron was used for weapons by the South Thracian population east of Macedonia at this early period.

South-east Thracian rock tombs, shrines and niches

A group of what appear to be tombs, carved into rock faces in parts of the megalithic chamber country and thus seemingly related, probably developed later, although no contents have been found to date them. Found in cliffs or large rock outcrops, sometimes at ground level, more often above, some are simple vaulted holes, others have complex interiors. One of the latter , 'Pope Martin's tomb' in the north face of a cliff in the Arda valley (Kolev 1965) has a trapezoidal entrance, which

could be closed by a stone slab, opening into a rectangular chamber; at the rear two narrow steps precede an arcosolium-like niche, and a vaulted trough occupies the west end. Another, near Ovchevo, south of Kurdjali, is hollowed out near the apex of a high, steep outcrop. An eroded arched portal opens into a vaulted antechamber in which a semicircular hole gives access to a cell less than 1 m high. Some 50 m below stands a shallow rectangular monolithic trough with a drainage outlet, probably serving some ritual, sacrificial purpose. The *sharapani* also found in the eastern Rhodopes are usually considered primitive wine-presses, although their hilltop sites, unlike the wine-presses of the Roman period, leave an element of doubt (Tsonchev 1963, 121ff.). A second tomb near Ovchevo in a low, much eroded outcrop, has a dome-shaped chamber with an arcosolium in the rear wall.

In a pyramidal outcrop at Tatoul, also south of Kurdjali, roughly cut steps ascend above a square-cut niche, 1 m high, 78 cm wide and 45 cm deep, to a platform with a central coffin-shaped trough 33 cm deep with ledges on which a slab cover could have rested. To the excavators, I. Venedikov and N. Bihodtsevski (1972), its size suggested a youth's sacrificial grave. More steps climb from the platform round the rock to its peak, where an arcosolium was carved, its situation, open to the sky, appropriate to a shrine. An analogous open sanctuary, possibly also Thracian, is the shrine of Pan by the path to the acropolis of Thasos.

At Gluhite Kameni, south of Haskovo, at the base of a great rock crowning a dominant hill, an arched entrance leads to a domed chamber about 2 m high; an adjacent entrance must have been intended for a similar, never completed chamber. Close by, a staircase ascends, making a left-hand turn to reach the summit, where a deep rectangular trough lies immediately above the tomb. Carefully cut ledges recall those of the Tatoul 'grave', and fragments of Roman masonry suggest that a ritual trough may have been enlarged to store rainwater by a strategically placed garrison.

72 *Sharapani* or troughs for pressing grapes, carved in living rock on hilltops in the east Rhodopes may have had a ritual purpose.

72

71

73

73 Gluhite Kameni, a peak in the low, densely forested east Rhodopes, with a rock-cut tomb; steps lead to the summit.

74 A huge outcrop at Ardino is pitted with niches, most, like those at Gluhite Kameni and elsewhere, trapezoidal in shape, usually between 50 and 100 cm high. From the top, which is flush with the cliff faces, the niches gradually widen and deepen to bases 25–50 cm wide and 25–30 cm deep.

Neither the Tatoul nor the Gluhite Kameni complex were isolated monuments. Some 50–60 cm from the former is a strange rock cavity in the form of an upright pithos, 3.1 m deep and with a maximum diameter of 1.1 m, its only opening – 75 by 65 cm – at the mouth easily closed by a slab. A gold ring in the carefully plastered interior is the only recorded find.

Gluhite Kameni's precipitous rock faces were pitted with niches. At least two or three of the highest were roughly semicircular in shape and larger than the rest. Impossible to approach without climbing equipment, they look very like a niche in the rocky hill above Vize in the east Strandja foothills, where there are also rock chambers, undatable except for one carved into the form of a Byzantine cross-in-square chapel. At Gluhite Kameni some two hundred more niches pit the cliff faces from top to bottom, irrespective of orientation, in the same way as at Ardino, south-west of Kurdjali (I. Velkov 1952) and elsewhere along the Arda and its tributaries, all remarkably uniform in their

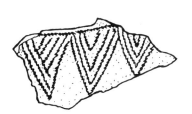

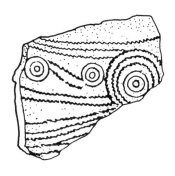

trapezoidal shape and dimensions (Kolev 1965). All within a small area of the east Rhodopes, these massed niches are almost without exception near a rock tomb. One such, at Shiroko Pole on the Arda, contained both inhumation and cremation burials, with iron weapons and a *c*. 8th century single-coil arc fibula (Mikov 1955). But this isolated find only gives a date when this tomb was in use and the purpose of the niches and how they were carved remain unknown. Unpublished Early Iron Age (EIA) sherds, possibly from them, have been found on the ground below. They may have held ritual offerings or ashes of the dead.

75 Sherds from the Mezek fortress area. These have close analogies with finds from the Lake Mandren fortress.

Early Greek coastal settlements

During the 8th–7th centuries the relative peace enjoyed in South Thracian lands was broken by invasions of its Aegean coast and offshore islands. First the Phoenicians, Herodotos (VI, 46, 47) tells us, conquered Thasos and exploited its gold mines. In the 8th century Greeks from Euboea had begun to plant colonies in the Khalkidiki. Parians occupied Thasos *c*. 700 and soon after founded Neapolis (Kavalla) on the mainland, exceptionally, on the evidence of coins, appearing to attain good relations with the local tribes. Ionian Greek cities established colonies further east at Abdera, Maroneia and Ainos. The main object was to acquire land on which to settle surplus population that would in turn supply produce to the mother cities (Boardman 1964, 236). Thracian resistance seems to have been generally fierce, the Greeks being forced to retreat from Abdera.

The establishment of Greek colonies in the Propontis was slower, more dangerous. No Troy controlled the Dardanelles, but warlike Thracian tribes on both shores could easily ambush landings and ships. Clearance of the Dardanelles was largely achieved by Miletos in the first half of the 7th century. Cyzicus, first temporarily settled *c*. 756, became a permanent colony in 675 (Hasluck 1910, 156ff.). The first Black Sea colonies, Histria on the Dobroudja coast, Berezan and Olbia on the west Ukrainian, were probably founded shortly before the mid-7th century, Panticapaeum on the Cimmerian Bosporos (or Kerch Strait) and Apollonia Pontica (Sozopol) by the end of it, the latter probably intended mainly as a staging post.

The fortification of Malko Kale and no doubt the other Meden Rid settlements about the 8th century suggests the Thracian inhabitants – documented here and elsewhere, as on Thasos (Bernard 1964) by pots or sherds – actively resisted the Greeks. Thracian forts around Apollonia were not confined to the hills but, as at Lake Mandren, encircled it to sea-level. Only tiny sherds were found in the second layer of the Malko Kale sounding (Venedikov *et al.* 1976), but the same decoration continued. The layer ended *c.* 500 with upper levels of jumbled Greek and local ware.

76 Basarabi artefacts.
1 Jug from Ferigile. Ht 24 cm.
2 Fragment of bowl from Ferigile. W. 30 cm.
3 Two-handled bowl from Frögg.
4 Jar from Frögg.
5 Curved dagger from Frögg.
6 Curved sword from Balta Verde. L. 51 cm.

Interaction of Early Iron Age cultures

As well as the gradual introduction of ironworking, an important aspect of the EIA was an enormous increase in mobility. Whether, apart from the Phrygians, there were other major migrations during the transition from Bronze to Iron is more questionable. Diffusions of ideas are reflected, especially, in pottery. The spread of bossed ware from the north-west Carpathians to the Dnieper, Anatolia and Macedonia is one example; another is the interrelationship of South Thracian cultures during and immediately after the transition to the EIA. Gradually,

77 *Below*: Thracian artefacts from Sholdaneshty. *Left*: Sherd with running spiral decoration. *Centre*: Piriform vessel. Ht 37 cm. *Right*: Bronze arc fibula, perhaps an import from South Thrace. The Carpatho-Balkan running spiral, rising button-knobbed and peaked handles, bossed 'Villanovan-type' urns and cups like those from Troy VII b (*Ill. 58*), but with horizontal rims and rising handles, are all present at settlements such as Sholdaneshty in the Middle Dniester forest-steppe. New forms include piriform vessels with small bosses and a high neck carrying horizontal channelling and knobbed high-handled dippers, often with incised white-encrusted decoration.

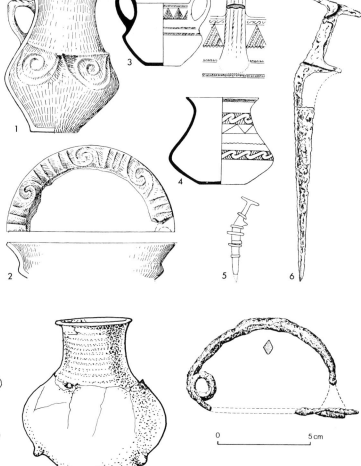

greater cultural homogeneity was achieved and a series of wide-ranging horizons can be traced.

One, recognized by A. Vulpe (1965; 1970), as the Basarabi culture or complex, is characterized by a revival of Wietenberg motifs and has two stages, the mid-8th to end 7th century and end 7th to mid-6th when it was influenced by the Agathyrsi migrations. It is spread over a wide area, notably on the north bank of the lower Danube and central Transylvania with isolated outposts as far south as Plovdiv, east to Sholdaneshty on the middle Dniester and west to Sopron in north-west Hungary and Frögg in Carinthia. N. Tasić (1974, 257ff.) extends it to the Voivodina and E. Pateck (1974) to east Hungary. A. I. Melyukova, analysing east Moldavian and Podolian sites (1958; 1961; 1972 (revising earlier dating)) relates both the middle Dniester 8th to mid-7th century Sakharna–Soloncheny group of settlements and cemeteries and the 7th–6th century Sholdaneshty group to Basarabi Danubian counterparts. Another contemporary horizon may link the last with south Moldavia and part of the north Pontic coast, using the evidence of 8th–6th century pottery at Orlovka, north of the Danube estuary (Golobko *et al.* 1965) and at Berezan and Olbia (Kaposhina 1956; Dzis-Raiko 1959, Pls I–IV).

At present these horizons must be treated with caution. Such appears to have been the influence of the Otomani–Wietenberg culture that we rarely know enough to tell whether common features are due mainly to diffusion of ideas or to continuous autochthonous evolution. Usually both are factors with Thracian conservatism sometimes producing long-lasting pottery shapes and decoration, little influenced by external developments.

H. Hencken (1968a, 440ff.; b, 91ff.) discussing possible Balkan origins of the Villanova culture, cites in particular the so-called 'Villanovan' urn and the horned animal-bird pots. The former, with minor variations is still current, besides in Villanovan Italy, in the 7th–6th centuries at Sholdaneshty, the Kiev (Mantsevich 1959) and Kanev (Khanenko 1899; 1900; Kovpanenko 1971) areas of the middle Dnieper, as well as at Smolenice–Molpír in west Slovakia (Dušek 1974) and the Bosut group in the Voivodina (Tasić 1974, 258ff.).

The bird-shaped vessel, sometimes the head is horned, is more common in the Gîrla Mare area than farther north, although the Suciu de Sus urn with projecting animal heads is a variant. Not generally

78 Pottery from the Middle Dnieper, Kanev district. *Left*: Bowl with rising peak-knobbed handles (cf. *Ill. 69*). *Centre*: High knobbed-handled cup. *Right*: Vessel with faintly bossed decoration.

76

77

79

51
78

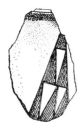

79 *c*. 7th-century
decoration on north-west
Pontic potsherds.
1 Berezan
2 Orlovka

80 *Above right*: Late
Bronze – Early Iron Age
zoomorphic clay vessel,
from Ostrovul Mare. Ht
to rim 14.5 cm.

81 *Below right*: Late
Bronze – Early Iron Age
zoomorphic clay vessel,
from Chotín. Ht 15.5 cm.

popular in Thracian lands, it was a feature of the Slovakian Podoli culture and travelled to west Hungary (Thomas 1956, 130), Vienna and Brandenburg. These zoomorphic vessels, Hencken remarks (1968a, 519), begin in Italy in the Villanovan Iron Age, contemporary with Ha B, but are in central Europe by Ha A and in eastern Europe in the Middle Bronze Age (MBA). The long Otomani supremacy in central Europe – accounting for the 'Basarabi' aspects of Sopron and Frögg – must be reckoned a factor in this dissemination by providing a cultural *koine* in which, as Hencken says, there may have been a slow and gradual movement of small groups of families able to maintain their traditional ways as they moved. We cannot be certain that this happened; nor, if it did, where in the Carpatho–Balkans it began. The same may be said for Villanovan pottery with horn bosses (Hencken 1968b, Pl. 19).

80
81

Cimmerians and Chernoles

About the turn of the 1st millennium, life in the Pontic steppe was transformed by the arrival east of the Dnieper of the warlike Cimmerian nomads. The Caucasian metallurgical industry had regained the leadership lost in the LBA and was able and ready to supply the newcomers with their favourite bronze and iron cross-hilted swords and daggers, snaffles for riding horses, arrows and spearheads. Well armed and mobile, the Cimmerians soon overran the Pontic steppe, which they dominated until the late 7th century. Some of the Thracian and Srubnaya population moved north to the forest-steppe and others west to the Carpatho–Balkans, but the mass undoubtedly remained, initially at least in subjection to a small Cimmerian warrior caste. Distinctive Cimmerian horse equipment and weapons of Caucasian origin are found with pottery retaining characteristic Thracian incised ornament, but impressed motifs are rare (Sulimirski 1959; Terenozhkin 1976).

Caucasian metallurgy also had a revolutionary impact on the Bilohrudivka people in the forest-steppe, who now entered a new phase, known from its eponymous site as the Chernoles, and who imported arms and tools from the Caucasus through Srubnaya intermediaries. The first settlements were open, but after Cimmerian destruction of a group in the Uman area a series of forts were built along a western tributary of the Dnieper, the Tyasmin, with three as far south as the upper reaches of the Ingulets. Some were small hill forts, others large and strongly fortified. The fortress of Subbotovo, in the Tyasmin valley, had a circular inner 'citadel' protected by an earth rampart, probably palisaded; a wide ditch was on its only accessible side, on which was its narrow entrance. Outside was a much larger fortified area of about 2,700 m². No Chernoles remains were found in the 'citadel', but in the outer area a layer with Bilohrudivka-type dugouts and refuse pits was covered by another with Chernoles pottery and surface or slightly dugout huts (Terenozhkin 1961, 34ff.).

Chernoles, on a plateau above the deep gorges of the Ingulets, also had a roughly round, apparently uninhabited citadel on the high end of a promontory, the only accessible side barred by a similar rampart 2 m high, 12–15 m wide, probably palisaded, and by an equally wide ditch, 2 m deep. Some 600 m away on the east side of the plateau was a second line of defence. Two parallel ramparts, still 1 m high with ditches and 45–60 m apart, connected the two enclosing ravines. Yet another rampart, 1.5 m high, and ditch was built 800 m further south. Such well defended sites successfully withstood Cimmerian attacks. The only signs of habitation found at Chernoles were several large mounds, up to 15 m high, covering about a third of the area between the citadel and the second line of defence. One, when excavated, was found to contain a *zolnik* with many Chernoles sherds and burnt animal bones.

Grave ritual varied considerably. Mounds covered inhumations and cremations, the latter apparently preponderating. Cremated remains, in urns, were also found in flat graves, especially in the west. Until the 7th–6th centuries inhumations, sometimes collective, were usually crouched; later they were supine, probably due to Scythian influence. Grave goods included bronze ornaments, more rarely bits, arrow- and spearheads, and iron swords.

Early Chernoles pottery, like that of the neighbouring west Podolian Wysocko culture, evolved from the Bilohrudivka and that culture's nascent bronze industry was likewise strongly developed. Although influenced by new Caucasian styles they continued to obtain ore and perhaps scrap from Transylvania, probably lacking direct access to the Caucasus. The Bondarykha and Srubnaya people in the forest-steppe east of the Dnieper, apparently less affected by the Cimmerian barrier, progressed further in ironworking.

The term 'Thraco–Cimmerian', often used for the eastern raiders – not migrants – responsible for many 10th–8th century hoards in Transylvania and the central European plain, is also often mistakenly taken to imply a genetic relationship. The Cimmerians' superior Caucasian weapons were copied by the Chernoles people and also obtained from their neighbours beyond the middle Dnieper, and where there were opportunities for plunder, Thracians seldom stayed behind. The fortresses built during these centuries to guard the east Transylvanian passes – Sărăţel between the upper Mureş and Someş, Voivodeni on the upper Mureş, Satu Mare, Tuşnad-Băi, Cernatu de Sus, Bodoc and Braşov, all poised round the vulnerable south-eastern passes (Horedt 1974) – were perhaps erected against both East Thracian and Cimmerian intruders, although the latter were undoubtedly more dangerous. Yet the common Cimmerian danger gave new strength to the basic Thracian unity at a time when the old Otomani–Wietenberg links were wearing thin and the Thracians in the Pontic steppe in particular were being increasingly subjected to eastern influences.

Two burials in north-east Bulgaria, at Endje (Popov 1930–31) and Belogradets (Toncheva 1975) are secondary interments in Yamnaya tumuli. At Endje a warrior lay supine, a bronze snaffle by his left hand, at his waist fragments of an iron dagger and scabbard, and beside him an iron spearhead; a gold diadem had apparently been broken in two and tossed on the body. Among the grave goods were a bronze hook, fifty-two bronze arrowheads and two piriform Chernoles vessels. One, black burnished, had horizontal channelling round a relatively narrow neck and wider vertical channelling from the shoulders to the bulge; on the shoulder and below the bulge were rows of small bud-like bosses. It was identical to vessels at Sholdaneshty. The socketed, vertically ribbed spearhead and diadem could be either Cimmerian or Chernoles; there is no characteristic Cimmerian crosspiece on the dagger. The Belogradets grave, not fully published, contains an undecorated pot of similar shape, bronze arrowheads and a Cimmerian iron dagger and amber-encrusted gold sheath. Endje may be Chernoles, Belogradets probably Cimmerian. North of the Danube, the *passementerie* fibulae in the Bîrlad and Rafaila and other central Moldavian and Transylvanian hoards may reflect a Chernoles influence (Terenozhkin 1961, Fig. 110) extending even farther west, being found in the Blatnica hoard in north-east Slovakia (Gallus and Horvath 1939, Pl. 25) and at Érsekvadkert, due north of Budapest (Thomas 1956, 120).

77

One result of Thraco–Cimmerian raids was the introduction of Caucasian animal art to central and south-east Europe. Five miniature bronze axeheads, three from the Iskur and Vit valleys just north of the Stara Planina and the other two of unknown (Bulgarian) provenance, are Caucasian or derive directly from Caucasian prototypes. Their tin content of about 6–10 per cent suggests the latter and perhaps forest-steppe manufacture. Dated between the 10th and the 7th century (Milchev 1955, 361f.; Venedikov and Gerasimov 1975), most of the animals are clearly recognizable as cattle, sheep and goats. A bronze stag amulet hung by a ring, from Oryahovo on the Danube, has an almost exact Koban counterpart (Milchev 1955, Figs 7, 8).

Thus the Thracian Chernoles and also late Sabatinovka–Belozero refugees from the Pontic steppe probably contributed more substantially than the Cimmerians to the introduction of Caucasian bronze and iron metallurgy to the Carpatho–Balkans and central Europe. This contribution was greatly increased by migrations due to the Scythian appearance in the late 7th century. Other eastern influences were coming via Anatolia. The general orientalization so clearly seen in Greece is demonstrated by bronze horse models, such as the *c.* 7th century example from near Philippi (Venedikov and Gerasimov 1975, Pl. 5) and is even more evident in the *c.* 8th century bronze (tin content 15.8 per cent) stag from Sevlievo. The latter's origin is unknown but, despite its affinity with Greek geometric art, analogies with examples such as the animals on the Tli belt suggest Caucasian workmanship (Milchev 1955, Fig. 9).

89

6

Greeks, Celts, Scyths and Persians:
c. 7th–early 4th centuries BC

Greek Black Sea foundations

A Lydian squeeze on the hinterland of Miletos, the city's main source of food and raw materials, was largely responsible for almost all the 7th and 6th century Black Sea colonies. That trade, not territory, was the Miletan objective helped to establish good relations with the native population and archaeological evidence suggests that usually this and even a degree of integration were quickly achieved.

The early northern colonies had the advantage of dealing with local Thracian tribes while the Cimmerians were increasingly involved elsewhere. At Berezan and Olbia the finer local potsherds discovered among the Greek foundations bear incised and white-encrusted motifs analogous to those on Chernoles ware as well as to pottery in 6th century late-Sabatinovka settlements on the lower Dniester and Bug valleys and further east along the north Pontic coast to the Don and north-west Caucasus (Dzis-Raiko 1959). Cimmerian domination of the steppe and the Crimea, although moderating Carpatho–Balkan influences – stamped decoration appears in the forest-steppe but not here – did not prevent a substantial and prosperous Thracian infiltration east of the lower Dnieper, reflected not only in pottery but in the Thracian names of Spartokos, the 5th century founder of the Bosporan dynasty, possibly the son of a Greco–Thracian marriage (Blavatskaya 1959, 38) or a Thracian mercenary (Sulimirski 1970a, 92), and some of his successors, who continued until 303.

Exceptionally close relations between the Greeks of Bosporan Panticapaeum and the Maeotian Sindi of the Taman peninsula and lower Kuban valley brought Greek influence to Kuban metallurgical centres by the early 6th century (Blavatskaya 1959, 92ff.). The first flowering of what is commonly called Scythian art was actually a Greco–Maeotian symbiosis, drawing freely on Assyrian, Iranian and Greek models as well as on Scythian and other Asiatic steppe art. Although they served as Scythian prototypes, the early 6th century tumuli of the Kerch and Taman peninsulas and the Kuban valleys, including the Kelermes and the first Kostromskaya were, as M. I. Artamonov (1969, 22) stresses, Sindi–Maeotian and not Scythian burials.

Scyths in the Pontic steppe

From the last quarter of the 8th century, Cimmerian attention became diverted from the Pontic steppe and east Europe to the more lucrative possibilities offered by Assyrian and Urartian rivalry south of the Caucasus. After routing a Urartian expedition they were themselves defeated by other invaders, the Scyths, who forced them to retreat, destroying as they went, across central Anatolia to the Ionian coast. The Scyths remained in north-west Iran until evicted by the Medes early in the 6th century, when they re-crossed the Caucasus and moved into the Pontic steppe, probably joining other Scyths who had arrived direct from their eastern homeland some decades earlier.

Herodotos (IV, 81) admits he was unable to learn whether the Scythian population was small or large. The conflicting opinions of his sources may have derived from a confusion between the Scythian race and their subjects. Even the independent forest-steppe tribes come within the bounds of Scythia (Hdt. IV, 99–101). The Scyths proper were probably very few in relation to their power and the area they controlled. Herodotos (IV, 46) says they had neither cities nor fortifications but lived a nomadic life in wagons; all mounted archers, they lived from their herds, not by agriculture. As they told Darius, they had no settlements or cultivated lands, but only their ancestors' graves to battle for (Hdt. IV, 127). In such conditions sophisticated metallurgy was impossible and the treasures from Scythian tombs were created for – not by – a Scythian warrior aristocracy, whose patronage none the less impressed its individuality on such objects as weapons and bridles and motifs in the wild animal style.

The Agathyrsi migrations

A degree of Thraco–Scyth integration in the Tyasmin basin and in Moldavia early in the 6th century suggests the possibility of Thracian co-operation in eliminating any remaining Cimmerians in the forest-steppe. But the Scyths soon showed their determination to rule the steppe ruthlessly and alone. There is a reflection of the consequent Thracian migration in Herodotos' legend (IV, 9, 10) of the three sons of Herakles and the snake-woman. Skythes, the youngest (or the latest arrival), able to draw Herakles' bow and thus proved the strongest, inherited the land whilst Agathyrsis and Gelonos were expelled.

The western migration of Thracians from the Pontic steppe, often termed Scythian but here, following Herodotos, Agathyrsi, un-doubtedly contained Scythian elements. The Vettersfelde hoard, the horse and wagon burial at Szentes Vekerzug, east of the Tisza and Körös (Criş) confluence, the gold or electrum stag appliqués from Tápiószentmárton and Zöldhalompuszta in the middle Tisza valley and the bronze pedestalled cauldron from Szöny (Ózöny) on the Danube west of Budapest (Parducz 1974) unquestionably reflect Scythian ownership; but most of the other artefacts attributed to them originate from the Caucasus, the north Pontic Greek cities or the forest-steppe. Some were common to Thracians and Scyths; others were essentially Thracian.

The Agathyrsi migration took place in a series of large and probably many smaller waves as different Thracian areas were conquered or laid waste. The earliest migrants settled mainly in Transylvania about the first quarter of the 6th century. At first they preserved their own

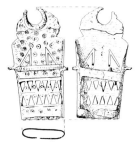

82 7th–early 6th-century bronze metalwork. *Above*: Openwork belt clasp from Ferigile. *Below*: Agathyrsi quiver ornament from Chotín. The impetus derived from migrating East Thracians is reflected in the distinctive forest-steppe quiver ornament found in Agathyrsi cemeteries at Chotín and the Bîrseşti group. The openwork belt clasps in the Sava valley, north-west Bulgaria and Oltenia are Illyrian-influenced.

89

83 Bronze bridle frontlet from Sofronievo. L. 8.5 cm; Ht 3.5 cm. Besides the horned animal, sun symbols include a triskele, circles round central dots and a Gîrla Mare derivation of the Otomani flame motif.

customs. Burial was by inhumation in flat graves with three to four pots, weapons, bronze hand-mirrors, personal and harness ornaments, often a horse or part of one. Of over one hundred graves in Transylvanian Agathyrsi cemeteries, less than ten were cremations (Crişan 1965).

During the century other migrants settled between the south-east bend of the Carpathians and the Siret, and others in the Muntenian and east Oltenian foothills, named respectively after large cemeteries as the Bîrseşti (Morintz 1957) and Ferigile (A. Vulpe 1967; 1977 (with revised chronology)) groups. Both were biritual tumulus cemeteries. S. Morintz comments on the Thraco-Scyth synthesis achieved at Bîrseşti, stressing the dominance of the former. Ferigile graves contained finely made Chernoles-type cups or dippers with high knobbed handles. In this western sector of the lower Danube metalwork had already received a stimulus from emergent Illyrian – and perhaps Cimmerian – influences entering the old Insula Banului area. Its individuality is evident in 7th–6th century openwork metal belt-clasps (Vasić 1971), fibulae and other ornaments, including an early bridle frontlet from Sofronievo in the Vratsa district. Further north and west, other Agathyrsi settlers helped to develop the Thracian Kuštanovice group in the Carpatho–Ukraine, the Vekerzug group in Slovakia and east Hungary (Dušek 1978) and, even touched Slovenia (Jovanović 1976). This migration gained momentum after the failure of Darius' Scythian expedition brought the Scyths to the Danube at the end of the 6th century.

In a large local Thracian and Agathyrsi cemetery of over four hundred graves at Chotín in south-west Slovakia, the proportion of inhumations to cremations was about 2:1 (Dušek 1966). In thirty-four cases, following incineration, usually on special pyres, the ashes were placed in urns; otherwise cremation took place *in situ*, and the ashes and grave goods were piled on the pit floor or strewn in the fill. One double grave was biritual. There were usually a few pots in the simple grave goods. Male graves had spears, trilobate arrowheads, iron knives, but not swords; five had bridle bits. Two female graves had handmirrors and most had ornaments and spindlewhorls. One warrior was buried with his horse. There were ten isolated horse burials, all without harness or wagons.

Thracians and Celts in central Europe

The lingering influences left by Otomani–Wietenberg domination over much of central Europe were weakened as Illyrian and Celtic or proto-Celtic groups asserted themselves. This process was temporarily halted by the Agathyrsi reinforcement of the Thracian element in west Slovakia and the Hungarian Plain. There followed two centuries of fruitful Thraco–Celtic co-existence, the Celts as strongly influenced by Villanovan–Etruscan connections as the Thracians by theirs from the east, and both affected by Greek material culture reaching them through trade. But, although it contributed to the formation of Celtic art, the Thracian strain was the weaker and by the 4th century central Europe was Celtic (Piggott 1965, 215ff.).

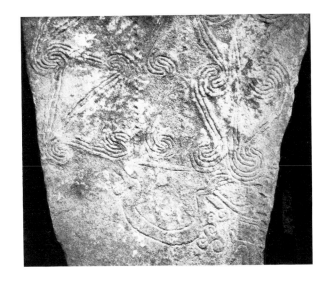

84 The larger of the two Razlog slabs, 1.60 m high, is carved with a field of intricately linked spirals above an ithyphallic figure, a triskele, volutes and a 'sun-boat'. On the smaller slab, in the shape of a right-angled triangle and 1.2 m high, a whirling sun-disc is carved above a spiral pattern repeated on the left of the larger.

The great carved stone slabs near Razlog in the upper Nestos valley are isolated phenomena in Thracian lands. B. Hänsel (1969), rejecting T. Gerasimov's second half of the 3rd century dating (1962), suggests the late Urnfield or the EIA, with the 7th century as just possible. Given the Celto–Villanovan aspects, the early mingling of Celts and Thracians in the Pannonian plain and the situation on an important trade route, the 8th–6th centuries are probable. 84

As the origins of Celtic culture lay in parts of Europe little affected by Asiatic steppe migrations, horns symbols such as appear at Hallstatt, a Celtic linch-pin at Niederweis in the Rhineland and a Celtic scabbard from Jenišův Újezd in north-west Bohemia (Neustupný 1961, Fig. 45) are unlikely to have retained more of their ancient symbolism than some superstitious association with power and magic. But superstition is strong, so the motif was not discarded but transformed, the form but not the meaning being retained in the Celto–Villanovan sunboat with bird- or animal-head terminals, a rare example in Thracian lands seen on a Razlog slab. Finally it developed into the highly stylized 'lyre' motif, appearing transitionally as a bronze ornament from Faardal in Jutland. 85 86 84

From *c.* the 8th–7th centuries to early La Tène, Celtic art used the Otomani flame symbol, identical on the Băiceni and Amfreville helmets. The Wietenberg 'running flame' was rarer, but ornamental bronzes, weapons, razors and 'belt-boxes' from Denmark and Sweden (Sprockhoff 1954; Jacobsthal 1944, Pl. 266/125–133) display both in traditional and evolved forms and with zoomorphic embellishments such as those below the rims of the Agighiol and 'Iron Gates' beakers. 95 116

The Celts preferred the triskele to the tetraskele, but the strong impact of Thracian art is seen in the Celtic copy of a horsehead tetraskele from Magdalenska Gora in Slovenia. It lacks the characteristic Thracian hatching and, with its central hole, is more like a garment appliqué than a bridle ornament. H. Schmidt (1927, Fig. 24) and B. Jovanović (1976) illustrate others. Even more stylized bronze horsehead tetraskeles appear as fibulae at Cristeşti, near Tîrgu Mureş, and Szöny (Parvan 1926, Figs 255, 394). 92

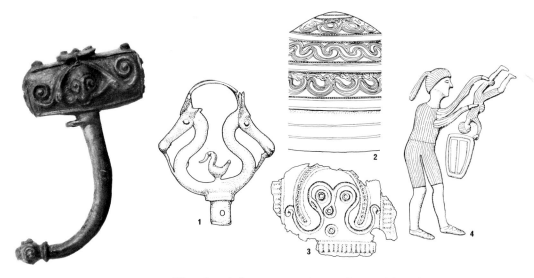

Thracian influence on the craftsmanship of the Gundestrup cauldron, unquestionably Celtic in spirit and symbolism, has been studied, *inter alia*, by O. Klindt-Jensen (1950; 1953), N. K. Sandars (1968) and T. G. E. Powell (1971). Parallels include the use of hatching for clothing, as on the Oguz plaque; as Sandars points out, this technique for smooth-coated animals stems from Hasanlu and earlier in the East. The human profile has a malformation identical to that on the Băiceni and Coţofeneşti helmets, the Lovets belt and the Oguz and Letnitsa plaques, all *c*. end 5th to mid-4th century.

The gods with arms raised in the 'orant' position are like the figure on the 4th century Chertomlyk (near Nikopol) silver dish and probably reflect Greek influence, although the ritual pose long antedates the Greeks; but not so the Gundestrup goddess with one arm raised and the other across her chest and the similarly positioned central figure of the Oguz plaque. Powell perceptively concludes the Gundestrup bowl was made 'in a place where Thracian versions of ancient Orientalizing art were still executed by craftsmen who were not perhaps exclusively Thracian or Celtic, and so their home can be narrowed down to those parts of Carpatho–Danubian Europe where archaeology must continue to explore the interrelations of these peoples.' This identification, however, must also reconcile Gundestrup's turn of the 2nd–1st or 1st century BC dating with 4th century Thracian skills.

Forest-steppe Thracians and the Scythian impact

The Cimmerian southern involvement allowed the Chernoles tribes to expand east of the Dnieper along the Vorskla, thus coming appreciably nearer the Caucasus and in closer contact with the metallurgically more advanced people of the eastern forest-steppe. Towards the mid-7th century the Tyasmin fortresses were gradually replaced by open settlements, as at Zhabotin (Pokrovskaya 1962; 1973), where two bronze buckets of Wietenberg ancestry were found, reputedly in a tumulus (Makarenko 1930). The early dwellings here, mainly dugouts, were replaced by surface huts in the later 7th century. Western associations, an extension of the Basarabi horizon, appear in the finer

87

pottery, Villanovan urns, bowls and cups or dippers with high handles carrying prominent flat-topped projections at the turn. Decoration, incised and often white-encrusted, was commonly composed of slanting lines, intricate hatching, especially of triangular and zigzag patterns, and, occasionally, stamped motifs.

An unusually large building, some 9 m square, preserved much of a carefully smoothed and burnished clay floor with an incised central circle of obvious ritual significance, its decoration including the Wietenberg linked S flame motif, found also on a potsherd, relating it to the Sighişoara hearth. It is almost identical to a contemporary hearth excavated at Bosut Gradina in north Serbia (Medović 1978, pl. V, 1), a striking demonstration of the strength of the Wietenberg tradition. E. F. Pokrovskaya (1962), dating the Zhabotin hearth to about the turn of the 7th century, mentions the find of at least two similar altars in earlier excavations. At Pastyr was one with six concentric circles (Grakov 1971, 124).

Another cult structure was a semi-dugout with two rooms. Both were filled to ground level with lumps of baked clay and plaster, probably from the walls, some small fragments painted in red and brown geometric designs on a white or blue background and others incised with the same decoration as the altar. On the floor of the larger, north room, the debris contained fifty-six astragal bones by the upper part of a human skull. Ashy remains, a horse's skull, horns, jaws and shoulder-blades of a bull, and the fragments of some one hundred and fifty finely made and decorated vessels, including about fifty jars, sixty high-handled cups or dippers and thirty bowls were scattered around.

Living between the two early 1st millennium metallurgical centres of central Europe and the Caucasus, the Chernoles' natural allegiance to the west was modified first by the Srubnaya and forest-steppe tribes east of the Dnieper, and then, more violently, by the Cimmerians. By the 8th–7th centuries they appear as the link, through trade and also, no doubt, through raids, between far-distant areas. A genuine Villanovan bronze helmet was found near Kamenets-Podolsky on the middle Dniester (Szlankówna 1936–37; Sulimirski 1970, 355, Pl. XLIII). The animals of the upper Dniester Mikhalkov hoard are basically

Opposite:
85 and 86 Thracian influence on Celtic art. *Above left*: Bronze linchpin from Niederweis, Rhineland, *Above right*: 1 Bronze ornament from Faardal, Jutland. 2 Detail of bronze belt-box decoration from Mecklenburg. 3 Fragment of bronze plaque from Hallstatt. 4 Detail from Gundestrup cauldron. The Otomani-Wietenberg legacy in central and western Europe included horned animal and flame motifs transformed into a Celtic idiom. Thracian influence, perhaps even workmanship, appears in the Gundestrup cauldron.

87 *Below*: Chernoles bronze and clay vessels. 1 Bronze buckets from Zhabotin. Ht 36 cm. 2 High-handled dipper from Kanev district. Plain or with white-encrusted decoration, these are common in East Thracian settlements and cemeteries. Diam. of rim usually 7–12 cm.

88 Clay hearth altars in the Wietenberg tradition. *Left*: Zhabotin. Diam. approx. 1.30 m. *Right*: Bosut Gradina, detail.

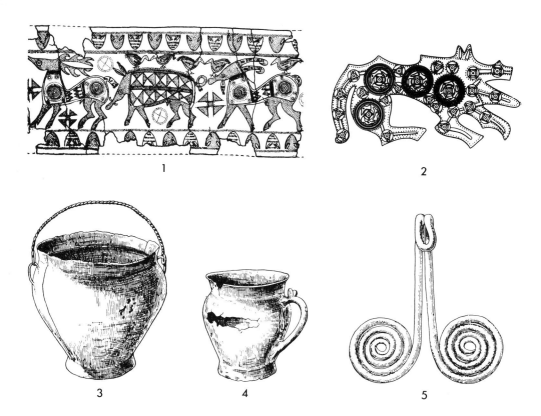

1

2

3

4

5

89 Carpatho-Balkan connections with the Caucasus. 1 Detail of bronze belt, Tli. W. 10.5 cm. 2 Gold zoomorphic fibula, Mikhalkov hoard. L. 16.5 cm. 3–5 Bronze bucket, jug and pendant from Tli, Hts 17 cm, 12.7 cm and 14 cm. Zoomorphic fibulae in the Mikhalkov hoard have close analogies on a belt at Tli in the south Caucasus. A similar 'Kuban beast' ornaments a gold fibula from Dalj in the Voivodina (Vasić 1971). The type reappears on a *c*. 4th-century clay urn at Bolyarovo in the Thracian Plain. Bronze vessels also reflect contact, and there are antecedents in the Middle Dnieper culture for the Carpatho-Balkan spectacle fibula and Tli pendant forms.

Caucasian, with Transcaucasian analogies at Tli (Tekhov 1963), but bear solar medallions with three 'Urnfield' bird heads, a motif found in west Podolia and Volhynia (Sveshnikov 1968, Fig. 3), whilst at Tli similar medallions enclose concentric circles with rays. Yet while its Transylvanian phalerae, twin spiral-terminalled bracelets and elaborate fibulae give the Mikhalkov hoard a western bias, the Tli cemetery also has a single spiral-terminalled bracelet, a form of spectacle-fibula hook or pendant as well as single-coil arc fibulae. The bronze buckets and jugs here are especially interesting, the former, as at Brîncovenesti and Zhabotin, being Merhart's Kurd-type in shape but with the modern pail-handle, the latter having handles on the bulge carrying 'butterfly wing' projections almost identically repeated on the two Zhabotin buckets. More research is needed to interpret this complex relationship.

If the forest-steppe Thracians initially welcomed the Scythian arrival in the Pontic steppe as relief from the Cimmerian nuisance, they were soon disillusioned. The prosperity of Zhabotin was brief. In the first half of the 6th century the pottery declined in quality and lost its rich decoration. About 500 the inhabitants moved to the new fortress of Matronin 2 km away, many retreating farther north to safer homes along the river Ros. Matronin, occupying about 220 ha, with powerful ramparts 4–5 m high and a ditch, had a similarly defended, permanently inhabited citadel in the centre, surrounded by an almost empty refuge area for people and livestock from the countryside. Here and at a smaller Tyasmin fort, Sharpov, fired clay was used to give slippery, fireproof sides to ditches and ramparts. Sharpov and Pastyr, small forts of only 10–20 ha, were quadrangular, a transverse rampart dividing the citadel from the refuge area.

The Scyths, although better armed and organized, were essentially steppe nomads and, in the more rugged but fertile forest-steppe, fortresses naturally and artificially well protected proved effective defences. A similar Chernoles settlement pattern was followed in the Dnieper basin around Kanev and Cherkassy (Kovpanenko 1971; Terenozhkin 1965). Open settlements dated to the second half of the 7th and early 6th centuries were gradually replaced by hillforts. The Bolshie Valki fort covers about 500 ha and is protected on its accessible side by a 6 m high earth rampart and a 3.5 m deep ditch. Inside its citadel among traces of some thirty-five dugout and surface huts, all with stone hearths, was a floor with a plastered clay circle, in its centre a small pit. On this 'altar' lay a bowl and fragments of a 6th-century Rhodian kylix and near by a broken zoomorphic pot and a heap of animal bones.

In 150 tumuli in the same area were 86 graves of the 7th–6th centuries. Most 7th-century burials were insertions in BA tumuli; new mounds were more common in the 6th century. Fourteen flat graves in timber-lined and -roofed pits were also found. The normal ritual was inhumation, the corpse supine, but cremation, usually at the grave, was practised. The most important graves had timber walls and roofs.

To the west, the open settlement of Nemirov, south of Vinnitsa, was converted in the late 7th or 6th century into a fort commanding the Bug valley; it was smaller than Matronin but similarly planned and as formidable (Grakov 1971, 122ff.; Mongait 1961, 159). Still farther west were Bolshaya Sakharna on the Dniester, with bastions and 4 m high ramparts (Smirnov 1949) and Stînceşti–Botoşani on the edge of the Carpathians commanding the Siret and Prut valleys (A. C. Florescu 1971), its south and east sides protected by an earth rampart *c*. 7 m high and 900 m long.

In the 5th century a second fort was added at Stînceşti and almost the whole perimeter of 1900 m enclosed by a reinforced earth rampart. Gradually a north-south line of defence extended to new forts at Cotnari, Moşna (A. C. Florescu 1971) and Arsura (Teodor 1973), perhaps as far as Poiana, above the Siret south of its confluence with the Trotuş. At Cotnari, dated to the early 4th century, palisaded earth ramparts had a complex inner reinforcement varied according to the terrain but including longitudinal and transversal stone walls as well as a 'scaffolding' of oak beams. These forts may have resulted from Scythian reprisals for the Agathyrsi refusal of help during Darius' invasion of Scythia in 512 (Hdt IV, 119) and for the murder of the Scythian king Ariapithes by their king Spargapithes (Hdt IV, 78).

East of the Dnieper, the great double fort and industrial centre of Belsk, occupying some 4,400 ha on a promontory between the Vorskla and a tributary, was enclosed by a rampart over 30 km long and even now 3–4 m high. At Lyubotin, outside Kharkov, another 6th-century fortress-city lasted into the 4th century, but no comprehensive survey of its earthworks exists.

B. A. Shramko (1973; 1974) notes that, like other forest-steppe forts, Belsk was fired near the end of the 6th century and suggests that this

90

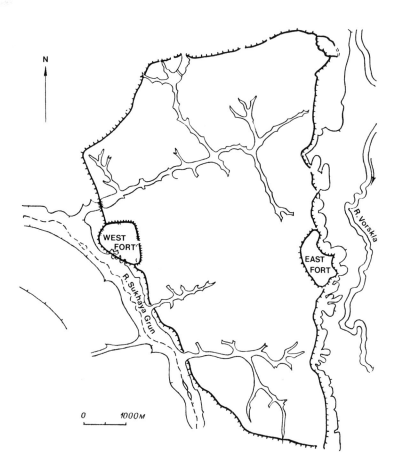

90 Belsk, plan of fortified
settlement.

may have happened during the Scythian retreat into the territory of the
non-Scythian tribes who had refused to join them against Darius.
Herodotos (IV, 123) mentions the Persian burning of a Budini 'wooden
town', possibly the partly Hellenized one named Gelonos (IV, 108),
after their failure to find anything to destroy in Scythia. B. N. Grakov
(1971, 151ff.) identifies the Chernoles and their eastern allies, the
Bondarykha, with the Neuri and Budini of Herodotos.

The Bondarykha tribes do not seem to have opposed the Chernoles
move east of the Dnieper. There had been trade between them for
90 centuries, but the arrangement at Belsk suggests that at first there was
little intermingling. An encircling rampart, dating probably to the turn
of the 6th–5th centuries and several times repaired or rebuilt,
incorporated two earlier east and west forts. In the well watered
intervening space there may have been wooden structures, but only a
few *zolniki* have been traced near the west fort. Shramko dates the west
fort to the mid-7th century and the eastern some fifty years later,
largely on the basis of Greek imports. Chernoles occupation of the west
fort is certain from the fine black polished local ware with knobbed
handles and geometric incised and encrusted decoration (Potapov
1929; Grakov 1971, 152). Six dugouts and several *zolniki* were
excavated, the latter containing hearth fragments, ash and refuse, as
well as many broken bronze, iron, silver, horn and clay artefacts.

The 6th-century level at the east fort has no *zolniki* and the dwellings are chiefly surface huts. No black polished ware or knobbed handled cups were found. The strong Srubnaya, Caucasian-influenced element of the Bondarykha group is here apparent from the abundant metallurgical finds – lumps of iron and bronze slag, iron ore, tin, copper and bronze ingots and a gold bar. Copper was imported and refined here, chemical analysis showing some ingots to be almost pure. Bronze was made with tin or, sometimes, lead as an alloy. Massive horsehoe-shaped clay bases and fragments of vaults of the bronze-smelting furnaces were found. Tools included part of a bronze matrix for small round gold appliqués and a saw for working soft metals, copper still adhering to its teeth.

Belsk, the largest known EIA fortified settlement in central and eastern Europe, illustrates the metallurgical primacy of the non-Thracian eastern tribes, but the opportunities offered by the Scythian market soon extended intensive production of arms, tools and ornaments to the Chernoles fortresses west of the Dnieper. Fragments of moulds as well as artefacts found in excavations include Scythian-type pedestalled cauldrons (using the *cire-perdu* technique), spear- and arrowheads, knives, handmirrors and stamps for the mass production of ornamental plaques (Shramko 1974). By the 5th century many forest-steppe workshops were competing with the Greek colonies for second-rank Scythian custom. Belsk, still an important industrial centre as well as importing Greek goods, lasted to the turn of the 4th century, adding a third fort, probably in the 4th century, to protect its Vorskla harbour.

In the 5th and most of the 4th centuries, Scyths, forest-steppe Thracians and Greek north Pontic cities achieved a highly profitable tri-partite association. The forest-steppe could supply the Scyths with agricultural produce, hides, cloth from hemp and its seed as a narcotic (Hdt IV, 75), also with metal artefacts – arms, especially arrow- and spearheads and scale armour; personal and bridle ornaments of gold, silver and bronze; horse gear; cauldrons and other vessels. The Greek cities, themselves skilled manufacturing centres and with access to others overseas and in the Caucasus, could satisfy the Scythian desire for luxury with plate, jewellery and other ornaments exquisitely made in precious metals, also with flamboyant Attic Kerch-style 'export' ware and with wine. The Scythian role was the congenial one of maintaining military control of the steppe, extorting payment in kind for granting a safe passage for the profitable trade between the forest-steppe and the Greek cities. They also supplied the Greeks with slaves, called 'Scythian' but most more likely Thracian.

Olbia's main trade route to the forest-steppe seems to have run due north up the Ingul valley to Smela and Cherkassy, but in the 6th century the Bug and Dniester route to Nemirov was also used (Grakov 1959). A bronze clover-leaf quiver ornament from Shumeiko in the Kiev region (Prushetskaya 1955, 331, Fig. 7) apparently came from the same mould as an electrum-plated one found in a late 6th century Thracian grave in Olbia. Another, from Opishlyanka on the Vorskla, is a cruder local adaptation. This form, unsuited to the Scythian gorytus, which held a bow as well as arrows, must have been designed for the

91 The influence of Olbian metalwork. 1 Bronze handmirror from Olbia. 2 Electrum-plated bronze quiver ornament from Olbia. 3 Bronze quiver ornament from Opishlyanka. Olbian metalwork was soon copied by the increasingly skilled forest-steppe Thracians and carried westwards (*see Ill. 82*).

forest-steppe trade and, duly copied, was carried by the Agathyrsi to Transylvania, Slovakia and Hungary. The Olbian handmirrors of bronze, iron or electrum were valued equally by noble Scythian and Thracian women and were as customary in their graves as weapons in men's; their gleaming circular form has suggested a cult use, which receives some support from one of the Letnitsa plaques. Other Olbian artefacts of the 6th–5th centuries which influenced not only the forest-steppe but also the Carpatho–Balkan area were costume appliqués, griffon-head bridle plaques (Petrenko 1967; Kozub 1974; Kaposhina 1956) and probably from the end of the 5th century, tetraskele horsehead bridle ornaments.

The Scythian drive to the lower Danube after the Persian invasion and their enmity towards the Agathyrsi in Transylvania and upper Moldavia affected Olbian trade, denying the city access to Transylvanian metals as well as to an otherwise convenient market. Transylvania and most of Moldavia were deprived of Greek contact, direct or indirect, until the late 4th century.

By the second half of the 5th century the Scyths, no longer purely nomadic, created a capital, their only fortified settlement, at Kamenka on the east bank of the lower Dnieper (Grakov 1954; 1971, 61ff.). Like the Chernoles fortresses a twin site, the acropolis-citadel of Znamenka was separated by an earth rampart from the rest of the partly naturally, partly artificially protected enclosure. Inside an empty refuge area another rampart guarded what by the 4th century was a metal-working centre, its wooden houses and semi-dugouts opening on to small yards containing slag and other rubbish. Here arrow- and spearheads, scale armour, harness equipment and a variety of tools were made. Iron was chiefly used, but also bronze and copper and, to a limited extent, gold. It is likely that many of the builders and smiths were Chernoles craftsmen, working willingly or otherwise, in the city whose foundation is attributed to King Ateas.

Detailed study of finds from new excavations outside Ordzhonikidze as well as others from such 19th-century ones as the Alexandropol tumulus (Lazarevsky 1895; Artamonov 1969, 59ff.) helps to identify 4th-century Thracian work for the Scythian market. A ceremonial gold collar in the primary burial of the unlooted Tolstaya Mogila tumulus (Mozolevsky 1972; Rolle 1972) surpasses in splendour and workmanship that from Great Bliznitsa (Artamonov 1969, Pl. 295), both perhaps ultimately deriving from such pectorals as the gold example from Ziwiye but probably Greco–Bosporan work. The smaller Homina Mogila, dated to the second half of the century, was the grave of a lesser Scyth warrior (Mozolevsky 1973). Although severely looted, two side niches were missed, each containing a horse burial with an iron bit and fine Thracian silver-gilt bridle ornaments. Stimulated by Greek art, Thracian craftsmen in the forest-steppe began to depict scenes of human life. Fragments of a plaque from the huge looted tumulus at Oguz of *c.* mid-4th century show some ritual act by human or partially-human figures in progress (Spitsyn 1906; Leskov 1974, 19ff.), but the crude modelling shows the Thracians had not mastered this new art.

Archaeologists at Cucuteni in the Moldavian forest-steppe found by chance in the village of Băiceni a gold treasure weighing some 2.5 kg.

Opposite.
92 *Above*: Olbian bridle ornaments were also copied and disseminated. *Left*: Bronze tetraskele bridle ornament from Olbia. *Centre*: Silver tetraskele bridle ornament from Oguz. *Right*: Lead tetraskele appliqué from Magdalenska Gora. Excavations at Magdalenska Gora, Stična and Toplica in Slovenia have shown that Thracian bridle ornaments were copied by Celts for dress appliqués, with a central hole instead of the metal loop for a bridle strap.

93 *Centre*: East Thracian bridle ornaments of cast silver covered with gold leaf from the Homina Mogila. 1 Frontlet. L. 10.3 cm. Ht of lion 4 cm. 2 Bridle-strap ornaments, 8 × 8 cm. 3 Bridle-strap ornaments, 14 × 7 cm. 4 Arrangements of ornaments on the bridle.

94 *Below*: East Thracian metalwork from Oguz (*see also Ill. 92.2*). 1 Fragment of silver-gilt plaque. Ht 12 cm. 2 Silver bridle-strap ornament, L. 7.2 cm. 3 Bridle frontlet depicting a bear cub. Max. W. 4.5 cm. 4 Bridle frontlet depicting a horsehead. Max. W. 4.5 cm; a similar frontlet was found in the Alexandropol burial.

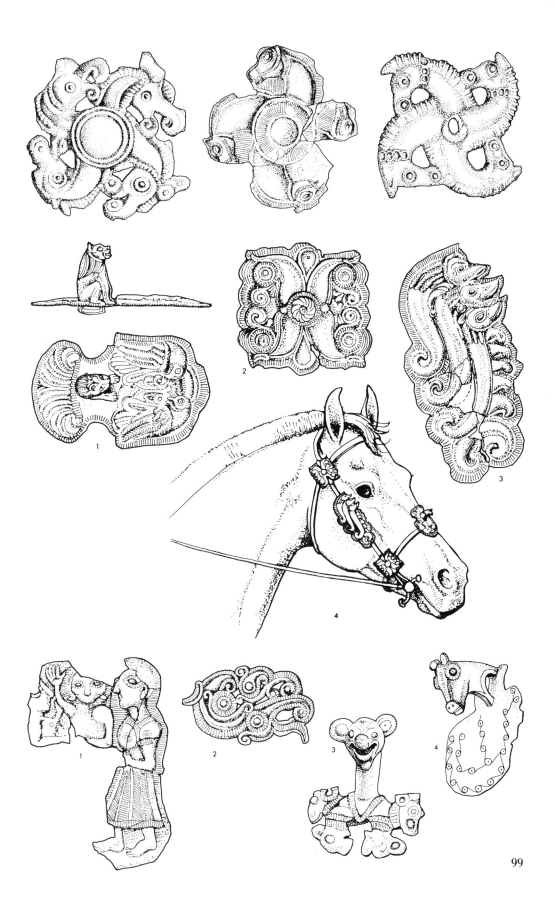

95 *Left*: Gold helmet from Băiceni. Ht 35 cm.

96 *Right*: The Băiceni helmet cheekpiece, showing a Thracian feasting.

Tentatively dated to *c*. 400, it may have come from a looted 4th-century tumulus near Cotnari or been hidden from some Scythian invasion (Petrescu-Dîmboviţa and Dinu 1975). The principal find was a gold

95 helmet, its high conical crown decorated with Otomani–Wietenberg flame symbols – not curls, for the Thracian mode appearing below and elsewhere is the customary straight hair – whilst the lower register,

96 cheek- and neck-guards have figural compositions. On the right cheek-guard a seated man, in profile, holds a bowl and a rhyton, the portrayal of his face identical with those on the Oguz plaque. On the back of his chair hangs a quiver, and a dragon-headed serpent is coiled below. On the neck-guard two winged horses, back to back, are standing, but give an impression of movement. The front and forehead-guard are missing, but a remaining fragment indicates that two eyes were represented. Among the other finds were bridle ornaments, a frontlet with an erect horse's head, four similar but not identical horsehead tetraskele bridle ornaments and another depicting a (?) dog fighting a mythical winged animal.

According to Herodotos (IV, 104) 'the Agathyrsi were a most luxurious people' and wore 'a profusion of gold'. A roughly contemporary gold helmet, a chance find at Coţofeneşti on the south-eastern edge of the Carpathians (D. Berciu 1969; 1974) also had a conical crown but this was covered with rosettes bordered by a line of running spirals and a rectangular forehead-guard from which stared

97 large expressive eyes – lost from the Băiceni helmet – above a line of triangles perhaps symbolizing flames. On either cheek-guard is an identical sacrificial scene. As on the Oguz plaque, the craftsmen could not depict the torso in profile; both arms emerge from one shoulder. On the upper register of the neck-guard are four winged creatures with human heads and long waving tails separated by a line of running spirals from the lower part, in which three fierce winged beasts seem to be devouring an animal already torn to pieces.

This new Thracian representational art was quickly overwhelmed by Hellenism, but these are among the earliest portrayals of Thracians by Thracians that we possess; they also provide a glimpse of the demonic world of their imagination.

97 Gold helmet from Coţofeneşti, detail showing forehead guard and cheekpiece.

The Persian occupation of South Thrace and the foundation of the Odrysian state

The Scyths continued to raid Persian lands over the Caucasus from the Pontic steppe. In 513–12 Darius decided to attack them from the west, perhaps also a first step in designs against Greece. The South Thracian tribes, fiercely hostile to the Greeks and impressed by Persian wealth and power, did not oppose him. But north of the Stara Planina the Getai, who enjoyed good or at least profitable relations with the Greek colonies, resisted Darius, an act which, although unsuccessful, perhaps earned them Herodotos' eulogy (IV, 93) as the noblest and most just of all the Thracians.

Darius' expedition was a failure; its only achievement was control for nearly half a century of Thrace south of the Danube, except for the lands of the Bessi and some western tribes. Even this was far from complete. About 495 a Scythian raid reached the Propontis. Mardonius, Darius' son-in-law, had to reconquer South Thrace before the Persian invasion of Greece in 492. Then, and also during Xerxes' invasion in 480, the South Thracians were on the side of Persia, but after the double failure and the Athenian counter-attack, resulting in the capture of Sestos in 478, Persian withdrawal from Europe was inevitable and a decade or so later was complete.

Their first encounter with a centralized autocratic power made a strong impression on the South Thracians. The satraps, Megabazus and Mardonius, are likely to have delegated considerable power to tribal chiefs, especially no doubt to the Odrysai who had not opposed the Persian arrival and were strategically placed at the eastern end of the Thracian Plain. The cultural impact of the occupation cannot be easily evaluated; Persian influences also infiltrated via the Ionian colonies. Yet grave goods in the Odrysian cemetery at Douvanli, near Plovdiv (Filow 1934), a splendid silver-gilt amphora, a gold twisted torque and some of the phialai, must be relics of the Persian period. The possibility that the mounted hunter, dog and lion, carved on a cliff at Madara, was Persian work, later adapted to honour a Bulgar khan, needs examination. The Persian concept of kingship linked with the

98 Gold pectoral from Bashova Mogila, Douvanli. L. 13.8 cm; Wt 19.6 gr. 5th century. The portrayal of a lion is exceptional and may be a relic of Persian influence. Gold pectorals were always of local workmanship. In many wealthy burials during their 5th–4th-century vogue they were the only precious metal objects not imported. Attached to a garment below the neck they were worn by the dead, if inhumed, as when alive.

supreme deity was easily capable of syncretization with the Thracian tradition of an heroic leader who developed into a semi-divine clan or tribal ancestor.

Persian influence is apparent, too, in the lion pectoral from the Bashova Mogila at Douvanli and in the general adoption of this symbolic ornament by the South Thracians. In the form of an oval or arc-shaped gold, occasionally silver, plaque fastened on the breast, it was an insignia of rank or power, male or female.

Within a decade or less of the Persian withdrawal, the Odrysai under King Teres I had formed the nucleus of a state, which must have emerged soon after Xerxes' defeat at Salamis in 480, extending from Aegean and Turkish Thrace to the Danube.

Scyths on the lower Danube

The Scyths gathered their forces to invade South Thrace after the Persian evacuation but by the time they appeared at the Danube Teres was ready to resist them. By a peace treaty he gave his daughter in marriage to the Scythian king Ariapithes, already married to a Histrian Greek, and relations remained reasonably friendly. But Sitalkes' succession to Teres sometime before 431 led his brother to seek asylum in Scythia. Here his Scythian cousin, Octamasades, raised a revolt against his half-brother Skyles, son of Ariapithes by his Histrian wife and his successor. Skyles, pursued by the Scythians, took refuge with the Odrysians. The two armies again met on the Danube but once more hostilities were avoided by Sitalkes' diplomatic suggestion of a mutual extradition of the two refugees (Hdt IV, 76–80).

Scythian influence was nevertheless felt. It appears in horse burials, harness fashions, the use of scale armour, especially in the north-east borderlands, and such ritual objects as the golden fish in the Koukova Mogila. But a negative aspect was more important. The lower Danube as far west as the river Argeş was a frontier between Thracians and Scyths for over two centuries. The Muntenian and Moldavian steppe between the Danube and Dniester, 'a desert and interminable tract' (Hdt V, 9–10) and 'largely waterless Getic desert' (Strabo, 7, 3, 14) was dangerous ground. Scythian relations with the west Moldavian Thracians, who included the Agathyrsi Bîrseşti group, were hostile. The Scythian enclave to the Danube blocked any contact between north Moldavia and Transylvania and the Greek cities. Excepting possibly some *c.* 4th-century fragments at Cernica (Bucharest), this

enclave has yielded only one Greek vase from this period, a mid-5th century Attic cup at Frumuşiţa in south Moldavia (P. Alexandrescu 1976).

The disruption of the links between the Getai on either side of the Danube effectively restricted the trade of Histria, Tomis and Kallatis to the immediate hinterland. Strabo's account (7, 4, 5) of the many who left 'Little Scythia' to cross the Dniester and Danube to settle in the Dobroudja, which then became known, too, as Little Scythia, and Pliny the Elder's reference to 'Scythian farmers and their settlements' (IV, 11 (18) 44) may refer to a 6th-century Agathyrsi migration, not, as often thought (Iliescu 1975), to Scyth nomads who suddenly became settled agriculturists. Thracian migration could account for the analogies between finds at Cernavoda and the cremation tumulus grave at Piatra Frecăţei and others at Bîrseşti and Ferigile (Simion 1976; Pippidi and D. Berciu 1965, 99).

Thracian pottery in the earliest levels of Histria reflect the immediate establishment of good relations with the local people and by the early 6th century Tariverde, 18 km south-west of Histria, was developing as a prosperous Thracian market for the exchange of Greek goods for local farming produce and, no doubt, slaves. Tariverde had the same carefully built, sometimes two-roomed dugouts as those found in Histria and Olbia, replaced for richer merchants during the 6th to mid-4th centuries by stone-built houses. The same prosperity enriched the whole coastal area, with 6th- and early 5th-century imported pottery in the Dobroudjan settlements of Corbu de Jos, Sarinasuf and Dolosman. Odessos, farther south, made similar contacts. A Getic settlement flourished at Galata, close to the city, and a 6th-century oinochoe was found in a grave at Dobrina, some 35 km away. The exchange of Greek ceramic and silverware, as well as oil, wine and textiles, for grain, hides, fish, fruit, honey and slaves continued. By about 400 BC grey wheelmade pottery, based on Greek or traditional forms, was a local industry.

This prosperity naturally attracted Scythian raiders. Finds of three Scyth-type 'kamenny baby' or rough stone statues, dated from about the mid-5th to early 4th century, suggest that, although not permanent, these incursions lasted long enough for a few ceremonial burials. More evidence comes from 5th-century bronze cauldrons found at Castelu and Scortariu, whilst a ritual bronze sword emblem at Medgidia, perhaps from a statue, recalls the short swords and scabbards worn by Sacian warriors on Persepolis reliefs.

99 Gold pectorals of Thracian design. *Left*: Golyamata Mogila, Douvanli. L. 38.5 cm; Wt 86.8 gr. The larger of two pectorals in a cremation burial, its overall punched decoration is common. 5th century. *Right*: Voinitsite, near Chirpan. L. 13.5 cm; Wt 7.26 gr. Again an overall punched design, but with the ancient horns symbol and sun symbols, the latter represented by circles with a central point. 4th century. The smaller Golyamata Mogila pectoral has the sun symbolized by tangented round punched bosses.

7

Southern and Danubian Thrace:
c. 5th–4th centuries BC

Odrysian relations with Athens
and the Macedonian conquest

Building on Teres' foundations, Sitalkes, who had succeeded him by
431, stabilized the southern flank of the Odrysian state by marrying the
sister of Nymphodoros, a leading Greek from Abdera. Ambitious and
extremely able, Sitalkes was courted by Athens and became her ally in
the Peloponnesian War. His son, Sadokos, became an Athenian citizen
and Nymphodoros was appointed Athenian delegate to Sitalkes and
Tereus, king, presumably, of the Asti tribe centred on Vize (Thuc. II,
xxix). For the first time we glimpse – through Greek eyes – South
Thracian rulers as historical figures on the (Greek) world stage.

Fragments of an Athenian decree or decrees of 430–29 refer to a
substantial Thracian population in Athens and especially in Piraeus
(Ferguson 1949), probably the result of the common Thracian practice
of selling their children as slaves. Some reached positions of influence;
Pericles appointed his Thracian slave Zopyros as tutor to Alcibiades
(Plutarch, *Alcib.* 1, 122). Athens, sorely beset by Sparta, even more by
the plague (Thuc. II, 47ff.), and her control of Delphi lost, took advice
from the Dodona oracle to inaugurate an official cult of the Thracian
goddess Bendis. Already a private cult, the Bendideia became a state
festival – its priest and priestess officials, a great public sacrifice of oxen,
a torch-race and procession – all unprecedented for a foreign deity.
Probably it was a desperate attempt to halt the plague, rather than to
ensure Sitalkes' military support.

Satisfactory relations established with Scythia and Athens, Sitalkes
then recognized the independence of such warlike border tribes as the
Paeonians, Dardanians, Agriani and Maidi, thus forming a buffer zone,
west of the Iskur and Strymon valleys and Pangaeus, between Odrysian
Thrace and Illyria, now developing into a formidable neighbour. The
Bessi also enjoyed virtual if not actual independence in the Rhodopes.
On the south-west border Macedonia, although militarily weak, was
dangerous. Its crafty king Perdikkas, initially hard-pressed in his
support of the Khalkidiki rising, persuaded Sitalkes to reconcile him to
Athens and refrain from helping his brother Philip, who had sought
refuge in Thrace, in his claim to the Macedonian throne. This
achieved, Perdikkas promptly abrogated the agreement. Joint
Athenian–Odrysian operations were planned. In 429 Sitalkes invaded
Macedonia at the head of a huge army which, swollen by followers
seeking loot, was said to number 150,000.

From Athens came envoys and gifts, but not the promised naval aid. Thucydides states that the Athenians did not believe that Sitalkes would mount the invasion. In view of its great, even if exaggerated size, ignorance of the event is hard to credit and the Athenian absence may have been due to a policy which Thucydides could hardly explicitly expose. Did Sitalkes' strength lead Athens, despite Herodotos' dictum on chronic Thracian disunity, to fear a future Thracian state impossible to manipulate and thus a threat to the coastal cities, access to timber for her ships and to the gold, silver and other resources essential to her power and even existence? If a loyal ally was a greater potential danger than a treacherous enemy, Athenian interests dictated that, by withholding support, her barbarian neighbours would weaken each other. Sitalkes' host spent 30 days ravaging the countryside but did little else. He finally retreated owing to lack of food, the onset of winter and the persuasions of his nephew and heir Seuthes, suborned by Perdikkas' offer of his sister Stratonike as a well-dowered bride (Thuc. II, xxix, xcv–ci).

For Athens the immediate result was successful; Sitalkes even remained an ally until his death in 424 during a campaign against the north-west Thracian Triballi tribes. G. Mihailov (1972, 61) points out an ambiguity in Thucydides' mention of Sitalkes' death, with the inference that Seuthes, his successor, and not the Triballi, was responsible; writing from his Thracian estates and probably of part-Thracian descent, again the historian was discreet. But Perdikkas' son and successor, Archelaos, built a road and fortification system, and Philip II and Alexander later achieved what, ironically, Athens may have feared from Thrace rather than Macedonia.

After the fiasco of Sitalkes' march Macedonia gradually encroached on south-west Thracian lands and Illyria, under Celtic pressures, added to the insecurity of the border zone. About the turn of the 5th century the Krakra fortress at Pernik was revived. This small peak above the plain inhabited, probably, by the Agriani tribe, was partly enclosed by a deep gorge of the upper Strymon, but now Greek craftsmen built a wall 3 m thick with a double facing of drystone dressed sandstone blocks and a compact fill of clay and broken stone, reinforced in places by a grill of wooden beams. Steps climbed the inner face, and a drain disposed of surplus rainwater. The buildings were used as a quarry, but drums and column-bases embedded in later constructions show it was not an ordinary Thracian settlement. Greek pottery was found, as well as grey hand- and wheelmade ware (Changova 1972).

About 410 Amadokos I succeeded Seuthes I. Seuthes II, vividly described by Xenophon (*Anab.* VII), was an insubordinate minor ruler in the south-east. Little is known about the next quarter-century, probably a time of weakness and confusion, but by 384/3 Kotys I, having liquidated his rivals, was reasserting Odrysian authority. Although cruel, hot-tempered, capricious and lascivious he succeeded by diplomacy in reuniting and strengthening the state to a stage where he could dispute control of the Propontic straits with Athens. But his support in 359 of a rival to Philip II led to his speedy assassination. Although Athens failed to depose his son Kersebleptes, Odrysian

Thrace was divided into three kingdoms and fell into chaos. Within two years all three kings made treaties with Athens, which was now reaping consequences which might have been averted by keeping faith with Sitalkes. By 385 Philip had captured Amphipolis and Krenides, renaming the latter Philippi, and gained control of the Pangaean mines now worked by the Pieres earlier expelled from the Vergina area. One by one, Thracian rulers submitted and in 342–1 a final campaign conquered all Thrace south of the Danube, where his army stopped. No doubt for the sake of good relations farther north, Meda, daughter of Kotelas, a north Getic tribal king, became one of his seven wives.

The impact of Hellenism

The Greeks paid highly for Odrysian co-operation. Cities on their land were forced to give gifts of equal value to the official tribute, or more, not only to the king but to his chiefs. 'It was impossible to accomplish anything without making gifts' (Thuc. II, xcvii). Some of the richest gifts were found in Odrysian graves at Douvanli, where the six main burials, under mounds 32 to 80 m in diameter are dated by Attic pottery to the last six decades of the 5th century (P. Alexandrescu 1976). Most of the grave goods are Greek – jewels, gold and silver plate from both Attica and the Bosporan cities and fine Athenian vases (Filow 1934; summarized Hoddinott 1975, 58ff.). A few pots, some 99 weapons and armour, and the gold pectorals alone are Thracian. In the female graves here and elsewhere, collections of pebbles, sherds, prehistoric artefacts such as miniature stone axes, shells and other oddments recall the deposit at Malko Kale and are thought to be the magic equipment of a priestess (Mikov 1958; Hoddinott 1975, 64).

Bronze corselets show Greek influence on the armour of Thracian nobles (Ognenova 1961). A breastplate of the second half of the 6th century, from Tatarevo east of Plovdiv, has simple linear breast and rib decoration, and a high collar reminiscent of an 8th century example from Argos (Snodgrass 1971, 271f.). In two with similar collars, from Turnichene near Kazanluk and Svetlen in north-east Bulgaria, dragon-headed serpents replaced the breast contours and palmettes ornamented the ribs; these were probably made for the Thracian market by craftsmen of Mesambria (Nesebur) or Odessos about the second quarter of the 5th century. The other three, from the Douvanli Bashova Mogila, the Dulboki tumulus near Stara Zagora and Rouets in north-east Bulgaria, are dated to the late 5th and first half of the 4th century. With plain chest contours and low necks, these were for use with such 100 collars as that from the early 4th century Mal-tepe tumulus at Mezek in 121 south-east Bulgaria (Filov 1937) and the fragments found at Yankovo and Vurbitsa in the north-east foothills of the Stara Planina. The corselets may be west Pontic work, but the collars, by analogy with the gold parade examples from Tolstaya Mogila and Great Bliznitsa, are more likely Bosporan. Probably the most popular helmet was a bronze version of the Thracian (or Phrygian) cap with cheekpieces, found at 101 Asenovgrad and Kovachevitsa in the north and south-west Rhodopes as well as outside Thracian lands, where they may sometimes have belonged to Thracian mercenaries (T. Ivanov 1948).

100 *Above*: An iron collar, its surface silvered with traces of gilding, from the Mal-tepe tumulus, Mezek. W. 29 cm. Probably of Bosporan manufacture, similar ones have been found elsewhere in east Bulgaria and in the Great Tumulus at Vergina (M. Andronikos, *Acta XI International Congress of Classical Archaeology*, London 1978 (1979)). See *p. 131*.

101 *Left*: A bronze helmet with cheekpieces, from Kovachevitsa, east of the upper Nestos valley. Ht overall 39 cm, helmet only 23.7 cm. The form follows the style of Thracian leather headgear, perhaps a legacy of the Otomani flame symbol.

The provenance and date of much 5th–4th century metalwork is obscure. A silver bridle frontlet from Sveshtari, near Shoumen, by reason of its well-proportioned head, is probably 5th century Olbian or Bosporan work. Some grave goods from a looted end 5th or early 4th century tumulus outside Brezovo, near Plovdiv, originate from Greece and possibly south Italy (Filov 1916–18), but a silver bridle frontlet depicting a lion too realistically to be local work may come from Olbia, the Bosporan kingdom or the Dnieper Thracian forest-steppe. The last is a likely provenance for four griffon-head bridle ornaments, with typically Thracian hatched edging and ear misplacement, for a square pair with a symmetrical design based on eight animal heads and a rounded plaque showing a stylized horse. It is very probable, although no workshops have yet been found, that forest-steppe fashions were

104

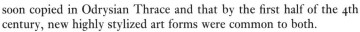

soon copied in Odrysian Thrace and that by the first half of the 4th century, new highly stylized art forms were common to both.

The Odrysian–Greek alliances perhaps encouraged the first South Thracian attempts at anthropomorphic art. Isolated early examples are hard to date; a silver belt-clasp from Lovets, south of Stara Zagora, may be 5th or early 4th century work and thus perhaps the earliest known pictorial example of the Thracian hero-hunter and his horse. The theme is further developed in a lively, less derivative style in a *c.* mid-4th century group of eight small silver-gilt plaques from a hoard at Letnitsa, near Lovech in north Bulgaria which present various aspects of the heroic life with an underlying religious significance. Other plaques in the hoard show a woman riding a hippocamp and a figure of

Opposite.

102 *Above*: Bronze bridle frontlet from Orizovo, near Chirpan. L. 4.8 cm; Ht 3 cm.

103 *Centre left*: Bridle strap ornament from Orizovo. L. 7 cm. The highly stylized zoomorphic decoration has the characteristic Thracian hatched outlines (*cf. Ill. 94.2*). With the frontlet, these may be forest-steppe or local work.

104 *Centre right*: Silver bridle strap ornament from Brezovo depicting a recumbent horse. Max. diam. 5 cm.

105 *Below*: Detail of the Lovets silver belt. Ht 4 cm. Overall L. 31 cm. Divided into three zones, both the outer zones portray a mounted hunter and attendant archer. A dog runs below one horse, a corresponding object shown here may be an animal's head. In the central zone two boars, one already speared, race towards a lotus tree of life. An early South Thracian attempt to use Greco-oriental models to depict a native theme.

indeterminate sex, with a mirror in hand of the type so common in graves, mastering a triple-headed serpent. There are three of fighting animals, one a winged griffon and all crudely but realistically depicted without 'Scythian' distortion. Others of finer work, symmetrical compositions of opposed fantastic animals, inviting comparisons with finds from the Alexandropol tumulus, and a triskele are probably Bosporan work, as may be some of the bridle ornaments from the largely unpublished hoard from Loukovit in the same area (D. P. Dimitrov 1957), a hoard richer and more varied in content, origins and dates of manufacture.

A wider if less spectacular impact was made by the introduction of the fast potter's wheel to produce what is known as 'Thracian grey' ware, perhaps inspired by imports to the coastal cities of grey 'Aeolian bucchero', recorded in 7th and early 6th century Troy VIII and elsewhere in the Troad, on Lesbos and Thasos and at Kavalla and Olynthos (P. Alexandrescu 1972). That these were all Thracian-populated regions may explain its popularity among Greco–Thracian potters in the Greek colonies and their hinterland. Storage and cooking

106 *Above*: Silver-gilt plaque from the Letnitsa hoard. Ht 5 cm. As on the Oguz plaque, the artist has difficulty in showing the – probably – male figure in profile. The scene is variously interpreted, but the resemblance to the combat between the hero and a demon, part man and part triple-headed monster, on the Hasanlu gold bowl may reflect Iranian influences on Thracian mythology received possibly during the Late Bronze Age.

107 One of four silver tetraskele bridle-strap ornaments from the Loukovit treasure. Ht 10.3 cm. Similar tetraskeles, with the characteristic Thracian hatching, occur in the Kaloyanovo burial and the 'Craiova treasure'.

pots continued to be made by hand, but the new wheelmade vessels whether deriving from Greek or local prototypes quickly became the indigenous fine ware (Chichikova 1963; P. Alexandrescu 1977). Its 5th century dissemination throughout Thrace south of the Danube was undoubtedly helped by trade rivalry among Aegean and Pontic colonies as well as the Odryso–Athenian relationship. From about 500, Doric Mesambria was competing with Miletan Apollonia for the agricultural wealth of the Thracian Plain, already exploited by North Aegean colonies.

Settlements and cemeteries

The influence of Odessos is seen in the second phase – later 5th and early 4th century – of the Ravna cremation cemetery, 45 km distant, where seventy-three pots were grey wheelmade ware and many of the fifty-six made by hand imitated Greek shapes. In the first phase here – late 6th and first half of the 5th century – incinerated remains with simple grave goods were laid in handmade high-necked biconical jars, often decorated with the horns symbol, in the earth. In the second, square or rectangular slab-roofed cists had an antechamber formed by projecting slabs. All were covered by low mounds (Mirchev 1962; Chichikova 1968 (with revised dating)). In the richer cemetery at nearby Dobrina, approximately contemporary with Ravna I, a few local wheelmade pots as well as Greek imports appeared (Mirchev 1965); further inland at Shoumen the 5th century settlement has similar ware (Antonova 1973).

In the late 5th century graves at Bailovo in the western Sredna Gora the same wheelmade ware appears. Through the Iskur gorge during the 5th century the products, followed by the wheel, reached Triballian and Getic lands. West of the Argeş and the Scythian enclave, the Danube was no real barrier, yet there is a paucity of contemporary finds: one high-handled cup at Gogoşu near the 'Iron Gates' (D. Berciu and E. Comşa 1956, 169, Figs 140–1) and two 'cauldron-bowls' at Grojdibrod west of Corabia (A. Vulpe 1959, Fig. 1) all, like similar finds on the south bank, approximately dated to the 5th or first half of the 4th century. Still farther north, there are early wheelmade fragments at Alexandria (Preda 1959, Figs 1–3), whilst others can be traced up the Olt valley from Bălăneşti to near the beginning of the Olt gap, where imported vessels at Gătejeşti-Govora (Petre 1971) and one fragment at Tigveni (A. Vulpe and E. Popescu 1972, Fig. 14/7) show they were copied by hand in late settlements of the Ferigile group.

Xenophon (Anab. VII) describes ordinary Thracian living conditions near Perinthos about 400 BC. A village consisted of scattered wooden huts inside small fenced enclosures for cattle. Hillforts were, as earlier and later, a refuge in time of danger. The tribesmen wore foxskin caps over their ears and long tunics against the cold; when riding, their cloaks reached their feet. Close-fitting trousers are shown on a 1st century BC relief from Abdera but were more common farther north.

Surveys (Dremsizova-Nelchinova 1972) and a few excavations in Getic north-east Bulgaria confirm and supplement Xenophon's

108 Late 6th or early 5th-century handmade clay urn from Dobrina. Ht 48.5 cm. With rounded biconical body, high cylindrical neck and everted mouth, it is a new version of an old Carpatho-Balkan form. Besides burnt human remains it contained bronze and shell ornaments. Offerings in a second urn nearby included a lightly burnt iron knife, suggesting a husband and wife burial.

account. Most settlements were open. Except on rocky land, dwellings were usually one-roomed rectangular semi-dugouts, about 3.5 m long and 3 m wide, but sometimes larger. The dugout base, 40–90 cm deep, was often stone-lined. The wattle and daub superstructure had a gabled or slanting roof of straw or branches mixed with mud or dung. Vinitsa, south-west of Shoumen, probably a typical village, comprised from twenty to twenty-five semi-dugouts (Dremsizova-Nelchinova 1967), each containing a hearth, usually in or near a corner, and an oven annexed to an outside wall and sometimes under a lean-to but with an opening into the hut. Surrounding post-holes remain from small fenced enclosures for stock. A few huts were built close together, perhaps for an increasing family without another plot of land. Most of the round pits near houses were to store grain; a few were rubbish dumps. Two huts were smithies with furnaces made of mud and broken rock; there was much wood ash and iron slag. Two hollows carved in a nearby rock were for tempering small objects like arrows or spearheads. Local deposits of clay account for pottery as another village industry. Other artefacts were few – some iron and bone implements, two small iron knives, some fibulae, a bracelet, a bead, and a few fragments of imported amphorae and black-glaze ware. Animal bones in quantity add cattlebreeding to agriculture as the basis of the economy. The absence of essential ironworking tools suggests that the inhabitants abandoned the settlement, taking their valuables with them. The pottery left dated the village to between end 5th and end 4th century BC. A contemporary village at Brestak, south-west of Tolbukhin (Mirchev 1969), with gabled surface huts and thatched roofs, had a more developed pottery industry, making pots from the local clay by wheel as well as by hand. Again, tools and other valuable objects were minimal.

Not all settlements in the south Getic hinterland were small or ephemeral. Near the Danube, Rousse, Slivo Pole and Stare Selo (Silistra district), Svalenik, on the middle reaches of the Malki Lom, and Shoumen were all inhabited continuously from the LBA. Double stone walls protected the strategically and commercially important Boba fortress on the Shoumen plateau; Rousse and Lovech also had stone fortifications. But Shoumen, like the villages, was deserted towards the end of the 4th century, the inhabitants taking all their valuables with them (Antonova 1973).

Sometimes a grave or cemetery can better illustrate the Thracian way of life in the Odrysian period. About halfway through the reign of Kotys I (387/359) a local chieftain was buried alone under a mound *c*. 50 m in diameter at Kaloyanovo, east of Sliven (Chichikova 1969). A roughly built entrance chamber containing a horse's skeleton with a rusted iron bit and four silver bridle ornaments, like the Loukovit tetraskeles, led to an anteroom and tomb chamber of dressed limestone slabs, lined with stucco bearing traces of painted and cord decoration and roofed by a gable of large tufa slabs laid on beams. On the skeleton's breast lay a lozenge-shaped gold pectoral 9.7 cm long with simple repoussé edging. Tiny, crudely stamped gold rosettes and palmettes must have been attached to a garment. A fragmented bronze helmet was probably of Khalkidian type. His weapons were an iron xyphos, or

109

107

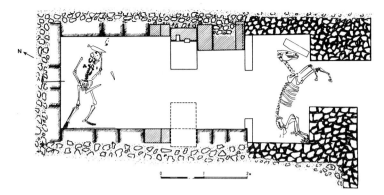

109 Ground plan of a
chief's tumulus burial at
Kaloyanovo.

short sword, placed above the head, two iron knives, one curved, a
hollow iron spear-butt, and in the anteroom some fourteen spearheads.
More significant than an iron candelabrum and a situla and other
bronze vessels in the chamber was an iron coulter, laid across the man's
left thigh. The spoon-shaped blade measured 10 cm long and 7 cm
wide, and the flat grip was 30 cm long. Such an early iron coulter in a
Thracian Plain burial shows that the dead warrior chieftain was a
landowner of unusual importance as well as a man of rank.

A slightly later – mid-4th to early 3rd century – cremation cemetery
at Branichevo, between Shoumen and Silistra, throws some light on the
customs of a small clan (Dremsizova 1965). There were ten small
tumuli 6–15 m in diameter, and one 41–45 m. The local chieftain was
buried in a quadrangular tomb of clay-mortared stones in the big
mound, in which a Scythian type catacomb grave was dug for his wife.
Like the Kaloyanovo chieftain, his tomb contained weapons and a
bronze helmet, also Scythian-influenced armour made of iron strips
linked by tiny rings and decorated with bosses and a small snake of
silver wire. The vessels included a small silver phiale with a short
inscription incorporating a Thracian name in Greek letters, a plain
bronze situla, the local copy of a Greek kantharos and amphorae, one
containing two bones and a gold pendant. In the wife's grave were a
91   bronze handmirror, gold, silver and bronze ornaments and a black-
glaze bowl. No horse bones were found, but it was common in all but
the richest Thracian burials for bridle ornaments – here a bronze horsehead triskele round a central boss and two silver bell pendants – to
symbolize the dead man's mount.

It is probable that three of the small tumuli also contained joint
burials. In one where the pyre was within the mound, the pair had been
dressed and equipped as in life. Sherds and animal bones from a
funerary feast were mingled with their ashes and placed with the
calcined bones in two urns, lidded by bowls and put with three small
jugs and a rough local cup in a pit by the pyre. In the man's urn were
two curved iron knives; in the woman's, beads, spindlewhorls and a
silver Apollonian coin. The other cremations had been carried out
elsewhere; in one mound the remains of both were distributed among
five bowls, one also containing three knives, a second a short sword and
a third five spindlewhorls. Another mound covered four separate
graves, perhaps of a family.

Thracian art in the lower Danube valley

Rich graves in two tumuli between the Stara Planina and the Danube, together with chance finds on both sides of the river, further illuminate burial ritual and the evolution of native art in the 4th century. Remains of a large tumulus in Vratsa contained three graves, the earliest dated by a Greek skyphos to the first quarter of the 4th century, but so thoroughly looted that the only other finds were a few bones and local wheelmade pots, one a copy of a Greek kylix. The second grave, collapsed but entire, dated to about the middle of the century, was a rough drystone rectangular construction roofed with beams (Venedikov 1975). In an outer compartment lay the skeletons of two horses, their iron bits in place, and killed still yoked to a heavy four-wheeled chariot that had perished but for the felloes and other iron parts. Nearer the tomb was a riding horse with a silver bit and many silver harness ornaments, four matching pairs with a frontlet from the bridle, the rest decorative buttons and miniature human heads such as were found in a contemporary cremation grave at Staroselka, near Shoumen (Tacheva-Hitova 1971) and in silver jewellery from Bukuovtsi, near Oryahovo (Venedikov and Gerasimov 1975, Pls 210–12). By the horse lay the contorted skeleton of a young woman, an iron 'Thracian' fibula at her shoulder, one iron spearhead between her ribs and eighteen more near by.

In the tomb chamber were the skeletons of a man aged about thirty and a woman about twenty. To his right were a fragmented bronze helmet, two iron knives, part of a *makhaira* or curved sword and scabbard, about eighty bronze trilobate arrowheads from a perished quiver and a silver-gilt greave. Farther away stood bronze jugs, situlae, a hydria, a flat dish and an iron candelabrum; also silver vessels, including a jug, a vase with fir-cone decoration and four phialai, one mesomphalos roughly pricked on the outer side: 'KOTYOS EΓBEOY'.* The name Kotys is inscribed on other phialai of this type.

*Published erroneously as KOTYOS ETBEOY.

110 *Left*: Silver bridle ornament from Vratsa. Diam. 8.5 cm. In an inscribed triskele of three animal heads around a central boss or sun-disc, three unidentifiable beasts fill the empty spaces. An oval pair from the same bridle combines these elements in a different manner. A third pair has a lion attacking another animal, heads simplified to jaw and eye but, unlike the Scythian taste, portrayed in natural attitudes.

111 *Right*: Silver bridle ornament from Vratsa, Diam. 7 cm. The most stylized of the four pairs, they are triskeles of rosette-like griffon heads. A less skilfully executed example, perhaps a copy, was found at Agighiol.

112

112 Silver-gilt greave
from Vratsa. Ht 46 cm.
The workmanship, at least
of the head, is Greek,
probably Bosporan. The
gilded bars across part
of the face are repeated
on a silver vase from
Mastyugin in the
Voronezh district
(Mantsevich 1959). The
zoomorphic decoration,
unquestionably Thracian
in spirit, may have been
executed by Bosporan
Thracians.

The woman's body lay where it had fallen, on the man's left, a knife still in her ribs. Among his accounts of the customs of some tribes in the interior, Herodotos (V, 5) describes the competition among widows and violent disputes among their friends as to which had been the husband's favourite. The one so judged, after due praise, was killed by her nearest relative at her husband's grave and buried with him, to the discomfiture and disgrace of the others. The Vratsa wife was indeed honoured. A gold laurel wreath encircled her skull, round which lay a pair of fine 'boat and disc' earrings, almost certainly Bosporan work and forty tiny gold rosettes and palmettes. On her neck was a satyr-like pendant of glass paste, and close by a collection of small ancient artefacts and oddments, including crude figurines, like those noted at Douvanli.

The same type of ceremonial greave was found at Agighiol and appears on one of the Letnitsa plaques. Unlike the plain Greek greaves found in the Thracian Plain and usual for Scythian and Macedonian warriors, this decoration offers further insight into Thracian demonology. Materials and workmanship, together with an analogous Medusa-head greave in a Kerch tomb suggest a possible Bosporan provenance.

The third burial, also a double inhumation in a similar grave, was outside the original mound and had been badly looted. Dated to about 325 by fragments of black-glaze ware (B. Nikolov 1967; 1970), seventy-three bronze trilobate arrowheads, a few pieces of gold jewellery, another collection of 'magic' objects, a small silver jug and a gold one remained. The body of the last bears a Greek-inspired scene of two men driving four-horse chariots. It is clearly Thracian work, using sheet gold hammered over a mould and finished with a finely pointed tool. Still barbarian by Greek standards, portrayal of the human face has improved during the century.

The Vratsa tumulus is in Triballi country, which probably extended into Oltenia and the Banat. Never conquered by the Odrysians, in 376 (within a few years of the first burial) a Triballi expedition said to number 30,000 men marched south and plundered Abdera before compelled, with Athenian help, to retreat (Diod. xv, 36). After Philip II had defeated the Getai, the Triballi refused him passage without the surrender of some of his booty. He won the fierce battle that followed, but only escaped death through the bravery of Alexander, who defeated the tribe again in 335. After more losses at the hands of the Illyrian Autariates and, in 295, the Celts, the Triballi gradually disappeared.

The second Vratsa burial is paralleled by a contemporary double inhumation in a tumulus at Agighiol in the north Dobroudja (P. Alexandrescu 1971; D. Berciu 1969; 1974). Here the man and woman were laid in adjoining rooms of dressed stone, roofed with beams and entered from a stone dromos. Looted and used as a quarry, only some finds recovered locally in the 1930s remain. A silver helmet is so like those of gold from Băiceni and Coţofeneşti that a common tradition must be assumed. The lower registers show four mounted Thracian chiefs. The Coţofeneşti perspective difficulty over the shoulders is repeated here. Two ceremonial silver greaves are less inspired and inferior work to the one at Vratsa. Both heads are apparently female,

113 A clay figurine, possibly prehistoric, in a collection of magical objects near the wife's skeleton in the second Vratsa grave. Ht 6.5 cm.

114 Small gold jug from the third Vratsa grave. Ht 9 cm. Considered to represent a double version of Apollo in his chariot, it illustrates Greek influence on Thracian work during the latter part of the 4th century.

with stylized curls in the Otomani flame-symbol form; one wears earrings, necklace and torque, the other has gilded bands across the whole face. On the side of the former a horseman resembling those on the helmet waves a bow; below, a seated man recalls the Băiceni cheekpiece.

Another Vratsa parallel is a silver phiale mesomphalos with an identical inscription. The other gold and silver pieces of jewellery and phialai show the original wealth of the tomb, which also contained silver bridle ornaments – three frontlets with heads of a griffon, a hyena and a bear cub; four strap ornaments also with the last motif, familiar from Oguz; a fragmented zoomorphic tetraskele and two highly stylized triskeles, as well as damaged fragments of the longer type.

Two silver beakers are ornamented in repoussé with stags, deer and predatory birds. The animals are in the tradition of Băiceni and Coțofeneşti, but with central European elements. The griffon with a limb in its jaws has an analogy in the lowest register of the *c.* 5th century Vače situla in Ljubljana; the extended antlers are a cruder version of those on the clasp from Zagorje, also in Slovenia. The way a pair of stag's legs are indicated might be a clumsy adaptation of the treatment on the *c.* 4th century Moritzing vase from the Tirol and the Arnoaldi situla at Bologna (Kastelić *et al.* 1965).

A silver helmet very much in the style of the one from Agighiol and reputedly found near the Danubian Iron Gates (Goldman 1963; D. Berciu 1969; Piggott 1965, Pl. XL b) has one cheekpiece repeating the eagle, fish and rabbit motif on the Agighiol beaker, the other apparently portrays a winged billy-goat.

These 4th-century zoomorphic representations show the emergence of a new Thracian animal art. The oriental inspiration appears in a bronze 5th–4th century matrix, found at Gurchinovo in north-east Bulgaria (Filow 1934b). If the stag and the baroque terminals of its antlers are 'Scythian', the striding lion shares a common ancestry with the 12th–9th century Iranian art of Hasanlu, Marlik and Gilan; even the triple-headed snake on a Letnitsa plaque may have an ancestor in the 12th–11th century Hasanlu gold bowl. Iranian influence may have entered Thracian myth as much as a millennium before it appeared as a Thracian art form in the 5th–4th century when the Achaemenid resurgence was reinforced by the orientalization of Greek art, the Persian occupation of South Thrace and the influences conveyed by the Scyths.

There are many other 4th-century silver bridle ornaments in the 'Craiova treasure', so-called from the Oltenian town where it was purchased, but probably loot from a burial (Schmidt 1927; Malkina 1928; D. Berciu 1969; 1974). A lion-headed frontlet links forest-steppe work with Agighiol; a group of six bull-head plaques are realistically modelled, except that all but one bear sun-symbols on their foreheads. Some of the zoomorphic tetraskeles and triskeles are more than usually stylized, contrasting with two simply represented lion and stag heads.

As already seen in the Vratsa gold jug and the Letnitsa plaques, during the end 5th and 4th centuries representation of the human figure

115 *Opposite above*: The cheekpiece, showing a mounted chief, of a partly gilded silver helmet from the Agighiol tumulus. Ht of helmet 27 cm.

116 *Opposite below*: Silver beaker from Agighiol. Ht 18 cm. The Agighiol beakers and another recovered near the Danubian Iron Gates illustrate the Thracian 'tooth and claw' view of the animal world although stags and goats are shown at peace. A traditional line of tangented circles outlines the bottom register of this and the Iron Gates beaker, but the top register of all three has the Otomani-Wietenberg running flame transformed into bird heads. This similarity with the Mecklenburg decoration (*Ill. 86.2*) suggests interaction of Thracian and Celtic influences along the lower Danube.

117 Bronze matrix from Gurchinovo. L. 29 cm. To decorate such objects as beakers, ceremonial helmets and plaques a matrix was hammered on to sheet metal.

118 Silver *rhyton* from Poroina. Ht 27 cm. As gold or silver *rhyta* were generally used by Thracians wealthy enough to obtain Greek imports, locally manufactured ones are rare. The stiff and formless figures present a strong contrast with Greek examples. The animal's horns are now missing, but on its forehead is a whirling sun-disc, identically repeated on bull-head bridle ornaments of the 'Craiova treasure'.

119 Silver plaque from Panagyurishte. Ht 27 cm. This waisted plaque and five round ones with similar beaded borders were recovered after the looting of a tumulus near Panagyurishte. In the upper register Herakles holds a tiny Nemean lion, in the lower a figure with claw feet and a bird- or fishtail carries a *kithara*. Possibly all decorations of a shield, three round plaques, diam. 8–9.5 cm, have vegetal ornament; two show affronted boars, between them a palmette, recalling the Lovets belt (*Ill. 105*), and behind them a bird.

gradually improved in Danubian Thrace, also in the Thracian Plain, Moldavia and the Dnieper forest-steppe. Thracian craftsmen working under Greek supervision in the coastal cities must have led the way, but that it was still fundamentally alien to them is shown by the inability to convey individuality, one example being the silver-gilt rhyton from Poroina in the Iron Gates region, a contrast with the Silenus on the silver rhyton from Rahmanli, now Rozovets, north-east of Plovdiv. The Herakles with the Nemean lion on the round silver plaque from Panagyurishte (Filov 1916–18) may be undistinguished Greek work, but the animals and lotus buds on the other plaques show the Thracian struggle to master Greek techniques, with a lack of success seen in a waisted plaque also showing Herakles and the lion, from Panagyurishte. The fact that South Thracians were as unsuccessful in this aspect of art as their Danubian and forest-steppe kinsmen in spite of their closer contact with the Greek is probably owing to the wide range of classical and Hellenistic Greek treasures – from the elegant refinement of the Douvanli incised silver-gilt vessels to the extravagant baroque of the Panagyurishte gold treasure – which were given to or extorted by the Odrysians and others. The few who could afford finely worked precious metal plate relied upon imports.

The Macedonian conquest of Odrysian Thrace ensured a gradual but wider and permanent degree of Hellenization. Settlers from Macedonia and the Khalkidiki were instrumental in the development of urbanization in the interior. Although not chosen for the purpose, the new colonists must have promoted the wider use of the potter's wheel, of ironworking, and of stone for building; they also broke the Thracian monopoly of internal trade. An even less premeditated result of the conquest was the destruction of the developing original, stylized, native Thracian art in favour of alien naturalism.

The Odrysian state:
c. 4th–1st centuries BC

The ashlar tholos tombs

Kotys failed to wrest control of the Propontis from Athens in the first
half of the 4th century. Instead, Byzantion took advantage of Athenian
decline and increased dependence on Black Sea grain. By the end of the
4th century and during the 3rd she was the leader of the Propontic
cities, her market for slaves and cattle drawn from Scythia, the south
Pontic coast and the south-east European hinterland becoming even
more important than that for grain. Her own labour force must have
been Thracian, but understandably Thraco–Byzantine relations were
hostile. Byzantion treated her Bithynian Thracian subjects as the
Spartans did their helots (Athenaeus, VI, 271 b). A perpetual struggle
was waged with the free South Thracians. Her fertile territory was so
vulnerable that her citizens were unhappy when a good harvest
promised, for it was certain that the local Thracians would descend,
destroy part of it and remove the rest. On the political level, there was
an equally insoluble difficulty, owing to the great number of local
dynasts. If one was successfully dealt with, three more would attack. By
paying tribute they were no better off, for by giving something to one,
five enemies would be acquired (Polybius IV, 45).

   In Propontic Thrace the innumerable tumuli on the crests of hills
or grouped in large cemeteries, especially round such tribal centres as
Vize and Kırklareli may reflect the prosperity derived from the growing
blackmail levied. The most impressive is Mal-tepe, covering a tholos or
beehive-shaped tomb, at this time a peculiarly Thracian form, in a great
cemetery dotted around Mezek, near Svilengrad and Bronze Age
Mihalich, where the Maritsa divides the Sakar and east Rhodope hills
(Filov 1937 a,b; I. Velkov 1937). Mal-tepe, its diameter some 90 m and
present height 14 m, is enclosed by a retaining wall 5 m thick and faced
with huge flagstones. An entrance of horizontally laid ashlar led to a

120 Mal-tepe tumulus
grave, Mezek. Section
showing the tholos tomb,
double antechamber and
dromos. Finds suggest
there was also a chariot
burial outside.

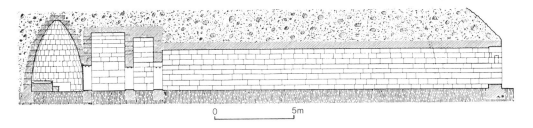

121 Maltepe tumulus, Mezek. Detail of the tholos tomb chamber, 4.3 m high, showing the finely worked drystone ashlar walls and the capstone. Diam. of chamber 3.3 m.

21.5 m-long dromos, two rectangular barrel-vaulted antechambers and the tholos tomb chamber.

The primary burial was an inhumation, the body on a monolithic bier opposite the door. Later the floor was raised and two square monolithic cremation urns inserted at each end. Still later, two female cremations were laid between the similarly raised floor and the earlier level of the antechambers. There are also signs of a 3rd-century Celtic phase. Looting caused disastrous disturbance and theft, except from the inter-floor burials, but objects retrieved reflect the magnificence of the tomb, probably built early in the 4th century for a Thracian ruler.
100   Except for the iron collar, B. D. Filov stresses the Greek character and workmanship as well as richness of all the finds. Among gold bridle ornaments are a pair like highly stylized examples from Craiova and Vratsa but using vegetal, not animal motifs, which, Filov suggests, are Greek attempts to imitate Thracian art.

A smaller Mezek tumulus with a tholos tomb, on the Kurt-kale peak, has no dromos and the single antechamber is vaulted by three rows of blocks placed cornerwise and capped by a single slab. The tomb chamber is similar in concept and workmanship to Mal-tepe. Looters left only amphora fragments and a bowl containing horse bones.

There are two more tholoi near Kırklareli 100 km east of Mezek. One, in the Eriklice locality, has a short passage from the entrance to the tholos, where the corbelled blocks, although finely worked, have concave faces giving a rippled effect. Intact when excavated in 1891, a man's skeleton lay on a marble bier, that of his horse near by. The silver and gilded bronze objects noted were all Greco–Hellenistic work; no bridle ornaments are mentioned (Hasluck 1910–11). Only the lower part was left of the second (Kırklareli B) tholos, in which a rectangular entrance-chamber opened directly into the tomb. The well-cut ashlar was evenly faced, as in Mal-tepe. No grave goods were recovered (Mansel 1943).

There were similar influences in Thracian Bithynia. At Kutluca, near Izmit (Nikomedeia), a ransacked tholos under a tumulus 55 m in diameter and 7 m high was encircled by a retaining wall. A dromos 9.75 m long led directly into the tholos, built of well cut ashlar with trimmed overhangs (Mansel 1974).

Apart from remains of two at Yankovo (Dremsizova 1955), there are other Thracian tholoi in the western half of the Thracian Plain. One, at Rahmanli, excavated in 1851, apparently consisted of dromos and tholos, with a single inhumation. Rich grave goods included a gold laurel wreath, a fragmented bronze helmet, an iron sword 50 cm long and silver vessels, among them a deer-head rhyton. Finds resembling bridle appliqués are mentioned, but objects described are all of Greek workmanship (Schkorpil 1898; Filow 1934). One more roughly worked, its diameter and height 3 m, in the Rhodope foothills at Lyaskovo, south of Plovdiv, had neither antechamber nor dromos (I. Velkov 1932). Others have been excavated in the southern foothills of the Sredna Gora, around Panagyurishte and on the north-west edge of the Thracian Plain. At Malko Belovo, west of Pazardjik, the lower rows of a ruined circular chamber 4.65 m in diameter, consisted of a double row of concentric ashlar with a rough stone fill. A bier stood opposite the doorway. Stones fallen from the roof indicated its tholos form. There was no antechamber or dromos (I. Velkov 1942).

East of Panagyurishte, the Zhaba tumulus at Strelcha is now being excavated. Brief preliminary reports, which also refer to many horse- and ram-head firedogs in the vicinity, describe a rectangular antechamber between the entrance and the tholos, 4.6 m in diameter and 2.5 m high, sited near the periphery of the large, still 20 m high mound. Thoroughly robbed, only fragments of Greek red-figure and local pots remain, with a heap of small clay prehistoric artefacts – to which had been added a small gilded lion head – indicating a noble female burial. Fine sculptural decoration of the façade and the interior is an unusual feature, clearly Greek work. Double doors had closed the entrance and the tomb was probably used several times. Later the entrance was sealed by a large slab. Outside were the remains of two horses with a four-wheeled chariot and of a riding horse. Fifty silver harness appliqués are mentioned but not described. (Kitov 1977 a,b; Tsonchev 1961; 1963). An exceptionally rich tomb, could it have contained the burial of Amadokos I (c. 410–386/5) who lived, Xenophon was told (*Anab.* VII. 3), 12 days' march from the Propontis?

V. Mikov (1942; 1955) has suggested that masonry tombs in south-east Thrace were a legacy of earlier rock-cut and megalithic chamber graves. They may have been contributory, but present evidence points to a continuance of the Mycenaean Greek tradition in Thessaly (Heurtley and Skeat 1930–1) as also an inspiration for the Thracian tholoi, with technical help from Byzantion and Macedonia. Why this form was used for some of the wealthiest burials of the 4th century, especially the first half, when Athenian power was yielding to Macedonia, is unknown. It co-existed with and, in the second half of the 4th century, was increasingly supplanted by the barrel-vaulted form popular in Macedonia and appearing in South Thrace as far apart as Varna, the environs of Plovdiv, and Iznik (Nicaea) in Bithynia.

Macedonian occupation and Odrysian revival

Although Philip's conquest of South Thrace and his three or more new cities in the interior – Philippopolis (Plovdiv), already inhabited in the

LBA, Kabyle, near Yambol, in course of excavation, and Beroe, very near Stara Zagora – made permanent changes in the material culture of the Thracians, they were still far from being subjugated. After Philip's death, a rising was quelled by Alexander in 335 during which he had to deal with the Triballi and with the Getai across the Danube. A year later, he left for Asia, taking with him Odrysian, Paeonian, Agriani and Triballi infantry and cavalry. Behind him, unruly Thracians and ambitious deputies renewed disorder. Memnon, instigating a Thracian revolt, was replaced by Zopyrion, who quelled a rising led by an Odrysian Seuthes, but was soundly defeated by the Getai in a planned march on Olbia. In 323, Lysimachos, to whom Macedonian Thrace fell in the division of Alexander's empire, faced another revolt led by Seuthes – commonly referred to as Seuthes III. Assuming that 'Seuthes III' was always the same Seuthes referred to intermittently in the sources for this period, Lysimachos' early victory was the beginning of a long struggle. In 313 Seuthes headed a revolt of Odrysai, Getai and Dobroudjan Scyths in league with Kallatis, Histria and Odessos, cities supported by Lysimachos' rival, Antigonos. Lysimachos' defeat of the alliance confirmed his possession of the Thracian province, but Seuthes remained an obstacle until some time before the end of the century when he achieved or was given virtual independence over part of the interior. Whether this extended north of the Stara Planina is uncertain.

Seuthopolis

The city of Seuthopolis, near Kazanluk, shows Seuthes' determination to revive a modernized Odrysian kingdom. Drawing on Greco–Macedonian experience, he planned and built a city which, following Macedonian precedents, he called Seuthopolis – the city of Seuthes (D. P. Dimitrov and M. Čičikova 1978). Whether it was founded before or after his assumed agreement with Lysimachos and whence his technical assistance came we have no means of telling. It was a small city, only 5 ha, on the site of an earlier settlement perhaps built round the *tyrsis*, or fortified residence, of a local chief. Mud brick curtain walls 2 m thick on a foundation of two rows of large stones followed natural defensive contours, and were reinforced by external towers at the corners and the more easily accessible north-west wall and gate.

The north corner was again occupied by a *tyrsis*. Separated from the rest of the city by a fortified wall with towers, a monumental entrance led to the main building, an imposing two-storeyed edifice 41 m wide and 18 m deep with a long, probably colonnaded portico. A spacious ceremonial hall or throne-room, with a large much-damaged hearth altar in the middle, occupied about half the ground floor; the rest was divided into three sets of rooms, all entered from the portico and containing a stairway. Painted stucco decorated the interior walls. Another hearth altar stood in the centre of a sanctuary adjoining the main hall; an inscription found here indicates that, although this was evidently Seuthes' palace, it was also a sanctuary of the Kabeiroi, the Great Gods of Samothrace, of whom the king was *ex officio* high priest.

122 The Seuthopolis excavation, photographed from the air before flooding by the Georgi Dimitrov dam. The tyrsis is in the north (*top left*) corner. The south-west and south-east sides were protected by the river Tundja.

123 Clay hearth altar in the sanctuary of the Kabeiroi, approx. 1 m square, at Seuthopolis. About thirty, variously decorated and all more or less square, were found in houses in the city.

The priest-king association may have been an Achaemenian legacy; among the Getai the functions were separate. In Seuthopolis the association apparently applied only to the Kabeiroi; Samothrace had been Thracian before its settlement and adoption by Greeks and Macedonians and probably had still a strong Thracian element. An inscription from the agora in Seuthopolis refers to 'Amaistas, son of Medistas, who was a priest of Dionysos'.

Of the 1200 coins found in the city and its environs, the earliest were silver tetradrachms of Philip II with the head of Zeus and, on the reverse, a horseman; but over two-thirds bore the name of Seuthes, another move towards civilized status. The opportunist Seuthes modelled his coins on Philip's, but the face assumed a new individuality. T. Gerasimov (1955) suggests that Seuthes substituted his own portrait, thus identifying himself with the supreme Greek god.

The houses were spacious, with many rooms and courtyards. Walls of sun-dried brick on stone foundations were faced with lath and plaster and roofed with tiles. In the centre of a main room in each stood a low clay hearth-altar with corded or incised geometric or vegetal decoration. Some were flat, others had a central bowl-shaped depression.

Seuthopolis was not a Greek polis, but the seat of a ruler and his court. The majority of the people lived outside. The basis of the economy was agriculture – a number of iron coulters were found – and stockbreeding, together with pottery, both hand- and wheelmade, and trade. Quantities of black-glaze ware are considered evidence for trade with Athens via the Toundja and Maritsa rivers and the coastal cities; two-thirds of the amphora stamps found were Thasian.

In 293, Lysimachos mounted an unprovoked attack on the Getai. He and his army were captured, but generously treated and freed by their king, Dromichaites. Thereafter, ruling Macedonia from 286 and coping with Illyrian and Celtic raids as well as political intrigues, he ceased to interfere with the Thracians.

The not fully published inscription identifying Seuthopolis (*IGB* 1731) was one of four copies of a treaty, which states that two were to be placed in Seuthopolis in the sanctuary of the Great Gods and in that of Dionysos in the agora, and two in the Phosphorion and agora of Kabyle. It recorded some undertaking by Seuthes' queen, Bereniki and her four sons, consequent on an act of Seuthes while he was in good health. Much is unclear, including the relationship with Kabyle, but the name of Bereniki suggests a late, diplomatic Macedonian marriage, perhaps part of a pact with Lysimachos.

Kazanluk and other brick tholos tombs

In the cemetery of Seuthopolis and its neighbourhood the tholos tomb was revived, using well fired brick instead of ashlar or mud brick as in the city. One was 20 m from a female cremation grave covered by a heap of stones in a slightly earlier tumulus dated *c*. 320 by virtue of its rich Greek offerings. The adjacent brick tholos, with a short dromos, was soon destroyed; its bricks, which had been specially moulded into trapezoidal segments to suit the beehive shape, were reused for two

124

124 Remains of a brick tholos tomb with antechamber and entrance in the Seuthopolis cemetery. Inner diam. of tholos at base 2.70 m. The stone jacket relieved the weight of the earth mound.

small rectangular tombs, each containing rich inhumation graves, in another part of the mound. A large flat-grave cremation cemetery with modest grave goods surrounded the two tumuli and served the ordinary inhabitants.

Though plundered and damaged, a second similar tholos tomb in the vicinity covered by a tumulus about 43 m in diameter, partly survived. The forequarters of a horse skeleton, the bit still in its mouth, lay outside the dromos; the mound also covered a pit containing a dog skeleton. The two brick tholos graves are dated to the late 4th, and the two rectangular tombs to the early 3rd century.

East of Seuthopolis, in the Kazanluk area, three other tumuli containing brick tombs had painted interiors. One (unpublished) at Krun, was very poorly preserved. A second, at Muglij (Tsanova and Getov 1975) had lost much of its decoration and been looted, but the complex structure was basically intact. A southern entrance room, flanked by side-chambers led into a dromos, which had been added to an earlier-built two-part dromos, leading to an anteroom and tomb-chamber. These were rectangular, built with well-mortared bricks and corbelled long sides evenly trimmed. Remains of a large bier and podium stood against the north wall and there had been something similar but smaller by the east side. Enough painted decoration remains to show its fine quality. The rest of the structure was built of rough stone and mortar, with timbered roofing.

The third tomb, in Kazanluk, terminated in a similarly corbelled tholos, almost identical in size to one outside Seuthopolis, entered from a rectangular gabled brick dromos and a roughly built entrance hall (Mikov 1954; Tsanova and Getov 1970; Verdiani 1945; Zhivkova 1974). Looting had not damaged the wall painting. Scenes on the dromos walls of battles between Thracians and unidentified adversaries contrast with the solemn composition on the tholos above a zone of bucrania and rosettes: opposite the door a man seated before a table   125 clasps the forearm of a woman on an elaborately decorated wooden

125 The funerary banquet of a deceased Thracian prince or noble. Detail from the Kazanluk painted tholos tomb showing the three principals.

throne. A woman standing on his other side offers him a bowl of fruit, including pomegranates, food of the dead. The remaining space is occupied by two female attendants of the enthroned woman, a cupbearer, two female trumpeters, a bodyguard and grooms, a four-horsed chariot and two riding horses, the humbler status of the retinue shown by their lesser size. Above, three chariots racing frenziedly round the capstone emphasize by contrast the peace below.

The painting is fine Greek work, not so distinguished in execution as, for instance, the Macedonian tombs of Vergina and Lefkadia, but outstandingly successful in the use of the tholos to present almost three-dimensionally and with great dignity the ritual passing of a Thracian chief from this life to the next, a ritual in which even the spectator is participating. The funerary banquet theme is differentiated by the importance of the enthroned woman and the presence of the subsidiary characters from the usual iconography on stelai. Thessalian tomb painting of the second half of the 4th century offers a closer, if simpler analogy in the pyramidal tomb at Krannon (Protonotariou 1960), but there are no real parallels. It remains a unique synthesis of Hellenistic art and Thracian ritual. The brief use of high quality fired brickwork solely for tombs was confined to this small area; its appearance has still to be explained.

Celts south of the Danube

The nascent Odrysian revival ended when the death of Lysimachos in 281 gave the Celts their chance to invade the Balkan peninsula. Seuthopolis fell and was put to flames, reoccupied partly by Celtic inhabitants, and then abandoned.

The boundaries of the Celtic kingdom, founded between 279 and 277 by Komontorios and existing for sixty years, are unknown, as is the site of its capital, Tylis. Although unable to capture the coastal cities, the Celts succeeded the Thracians in harassment of the countryside of Byzantion. First bought off by extortionate 'gifts' they then exacted an annual tribute of 80 talents. The last king, Kavaros, mediated for the city against an alliance of Rhodes and Prusias of Bithynia (Polybius IV, 45–46; 52). Salmydessos, Apollonia and Mesambria, weaker than Byzantion, probably also had to pay tribute (G. Katsarov 1919; G. Mihailov 1961). The Mal-tepe tumulus was reused for an unfortunately since looted important Celtic chariot burial (Jacobsthal 1944, nos. 164, 176), suggesting near-by Mezek, later a strategic Byzantine hill-fortress, as a possible site for Tylis. Another Celtic grave, believed to be a cremation, south of Turgovishte, contained an iron sword 98.7 cm long, bent double, a curved knive 44 cm long, a spearhead, shield umbo and bridle (Popov 1932–33, 349ff.). With other Celtic finds in the Lovech and Pleven areas they lend credence to G. Katsarov's belief (1919) that the kingdom stretched from the territory of Byzantion to the Danube, although other Celtic groups were advancing along the Danube valley (Todorović 1968).

126 Terracotta head from Seuthopolis. After its destruction during the Celtic invasions, Seuthopolis was briefly resettled. Celtic workmanship appears in this head, closely similar to others in southern France, notably one from Montsalier (Jacobsthal 1944, Pl. 7).

We do not know how numerous the Tylis Celts were, but their rule was harsh, probably leading many Thracians, including nobles, to become mercenaries. Some served with Antiochos II in his siege of Kypsela, whilst others were among the defenders. Polyaenus (*Strat.* IV, 16) relates that Antiochos provided his Thracian mercenaries with fine weapons and gold and silver ornaments; seeing these the Thracians on the other side came over to him. The last, statesmanlike King Kavaros, whose coins were found in the Sliven region and perhaps minted at Kabyle (Gerasimov 1959), was overthrown in 218 by a Thracian rising and the Celtic kingdom eliminated.

In the early 3rd century there was a substantial Celtic penetration unconnected with the Tylis kingdom (Gerov 1967). Skordiski groups entered north-west Bulgaria (B. Nikolov 1965) and others from the Morava valley took the 'Diagonal' route along the Nišava into the Sofia uplands, where the Serdi tribe settled, their centre Serdica (Sofia). The Skordiski and Serdi maintained their identity into the Christian era. Some groups went on to the upper Topolnitsa valley and the Panagyurishte area, perhaps as far as Plovdiv. The archaeological evidence is confused by lack of knowledge of the Tylis kingdom and by controversy over the dating and assignment of firedogs. Like hearth altars these were used at this period by both Thracians and Celts – Seuthopolis hearths and many Thracian firedogs are remarkably similar to Gallic examples, for instance at La Roque. Gerasimov's corpus of 'Celtic' firedogs found between the Strymon and the Sredna Gora (1960) undoubtedly includes Thracian specimens of various periods (Hänsel 1969; Gerasimov 1974). But any revised chronology needs verification by finds in controlled conditions.

63

South Thrace in the Late Hellenistic period

With the death of Lysimachos the north-west Pontic cities were free to take a more independent part in the growing complexity of the Late Hellenistic world. There was political disunion, occasional inter-city conflict and temporary allegiances such as that of Apollonia and Mesambria with Antiochos I Theos of Syria and the later more general alliance under Mithridates VI Eupator of Pontus against Rome. Yet, against this background, the cities shared the wide economic, cultural and religious interchanges of the period and transmitted their impact to the Thracian tribes within their sphere, thus easing a survival of Thracian values in the Roman period.

Mesambria's relations with a local ruler, Sadalas, were close and mutually profitable (*IGB* 307; Hoddinott 1975, 48). Third-century Thracian tumuli in its cemetery contained rich grave goods. From their beginning Greek relations with the coastal Getai had been generally good; but now, although Getic kinglets are recorded as helping Histria, inscriptions show constant anti-Greek revolts among the Getic work force, especially in the 2nd century (Condurachi 1954, 498ff.). In and near Odessos, leading Thracians were buried under tumuli with rich grave goods in sarcophagi decorated by incised bone panels depicting Dionysiac scenes and other motifs – a fashion in Panticapaeum whence no doubt they came.

Cults travelled as widely as coins and amphorae from the whole East Greek world. But the new gods admitted to the pantheon included Theos Megas, the Great (Thracian) God, with a temple depicted on Odessitan coins. In the 3rd century another was erected in his honour somewhere in the sacred enclosure at Histria – built of Thasian marble by a Thasian merchant. The cult, under the name of Darzalas and further syncretized, continued under Rome.

Byzantion's influence was especially strong in Odessos. N. Fıratlı (1964, 45) comments on the iconographical similarity between the funerary feast stelai of the two cities. Linking the likely origin of the iconography to the Cyzicus region (1964, 16) whence it was adopted by Byzantion, he suggests the Odessitan stelai as well as similar examples found in other coastal cities were made under the direct influence of Byzantion's workshops.

The earliest known mounted hunter reliefs from the Mysian south Propontic area had an especially important influence on Thracian religious art. Daskylion had been the seat of a Persian satrapy and part of its territory was ceded to Byzantion by Cyzicus in the 3rd century in return for help in driving out the Persians. A stele, dated *c.* 400, from Çavuşköy, shows a hunt and below it a banquet; an otherwise similar stele from Cyzicus reverses these positions. Their iconography and Persian attire identify them as probable Greek executions of Persian themes, in the view of T. Macridy (1913) the earthly activities of a Persian noble, hunting in his 'paradise' and feasting with his wives.

Three stelai depicting very similar hunting scenes were found, broken and badly battered, in a Thracian sanctuary at Galata, outside Odessos, which is thought to have existed in the 3rd century and been rebuilt in the 2nd century AD (Toncheva 1968). The stelai depict a hunter and one or more trees – one shows a stag in flight – but they are too mutilated to give more information. G. Toncheva dates them variously to the 3rd and 2nd–1st centuries BC. Although no analogous stelai have been found in Byzantion, this city, with its close links with Odessos, must surely have been the intermediary.

127 Greco-Persian stele from Çavuşköy, near Daskylion. Ht 1.08 m.

Roman intervention

A Ptolemaic occupation of North Aegean Thrace was ended by Philip V of Macedonia, aiming at control of the Aegean and thus inviting Thracian attacks and, more ominously, Roman intervention at the turn of the 3rd century. An invasion of Macedonia by the Thraco–Illyrian Dardanians failed and a Macedonian counter-attack ended in a heavy Dardanian defeat. Macedonian forays into the South Thracian interior included a brief re-occupation of Philippopolis and a mass deportation of Thracians to help rebuild their neighbour's depleted resources.

Perseus succeeded Philip in 179 and, with Thracian allies, made war on Rome. His defeat and death in 169 were the prelude to occupation of Macedonia in 167 and, following a revolt, to its incorporation in the Roman empire in 148. Now Thracian tribes were on the Roman frontier and usually hostile contacts led to constant raids and counter-raids. Thracians enlisted as auxiliaries in the Roman army and many others were taken as slaves; one, the gladiator Spartacus, led the great slave revolt in Italy in 73–71.

For another century Rome, having built the Via Egnatia from the Adriatic to Kypsela, tried to keep the peace by establishing client-kings, who usually behaved as treacherously among each other as with Rome. Mithridates exploited the situation by inciting independent Thracian tribes and the Skordiski to attack territory of Rome and her allies. During the First Mithridatean war (89–84), Macedonia was overrun, Dodona looted, and Delphi sacked by the Maidi and other tribes. A Roman expedition against the Maidi in the Strymon valley in error attacked a friendly tribe, the Dentheletai, who in revenge ravaged Macedonia and almost captured Thessalonica. Most of the Greek Pontic cities supported Mithridates and in consequence were objectives of a Roman punitive force in 72, when Apollonia was sacked and Mesambria and others obliged to maintain a Roman garrison. The Roman civil war after Julius Caesar's assassination placed the Thracian dynasts, anxious only to be on the winning side, in a dilemma. Two brothers, Raskos and Raskuporis, heading the Sapeian dynasty, solved the quandary at Philippi by taking opposite sides. Afterwards Raskos, who was with Octavius, asked for the return of his brother as a reward (Mihailov 1972, 81).

In 11 BC the intransigent Bessi rose against the Roman-supported Odrysians. Led by their priest Volosges, they killed the Odrysian king and caused much destruction. A Roman army restored order with difficulty and many Bessi were deported to the Dobroudja. By AD 6 the danger from Geto-Dacians and other peoples north of the lower Danube led Rome to establish the province of Moesia between the river and the Stara Planina, linking Pannonia to the Black Sea. This did not deter further risings in south Thrace in AD 11 and 26. Tacitus (*Annals*, IV, xlvi) describes a last stand in one of the Stara Planina hill forts during the latter. Excavation has recently uncovered a number of these drystone walled forts. One, at Chertigrad, on a peak in the upper Vit area on the north slopes, had a wall about 2.2 m wide and 3–3.5 m high, faced on both sides with well laid stones and a fill of small ones, to protect its only accessible side. It had been once rebuilt, using the same methods. Inside the wall a platform 2.4 by 1.4 m defended a narrow entrance, contrived between one end of the wall and the cliff, its access a ramp aligned along the wall's outer face. Remains of buildings showed that the fort was used for permanent habitation; it possessed a niche specially cut to receive the sun's first rays (V. Velkov and Z. Gocheva 1971; 1972). Dated by finds from the 5th–4th centuries BC, such forts continued to be occupied as needed before and after the Roman conquest until the 6th century AD. A number of others have been surveyed in the Botevgrad area east of the Iskur, some strategically sited for defensive warfare (Z. Gocheva and M. Domaradski 1976).

Vize (Bizye) may have been the last Thracian capital south of the Danube. One of a group of five tumuli in a large cemetery may be the grave of the last Sapeian king, Rhoemetalkes, who succeeded the Odryso–Astian dynasties as a reward for help in suppressing the revolt of AD 26. Nominated king of all Thrace in 38, he was killed in 45. Evidence for royal occupancy of the tomb is based solely on the wealth and date of its contents, such as four finely decorated deep silver drinking cups, 'probably a popular form of diplomatic present much in demand among friendly and client kings outside the frontiers' (Strong 1966, 136f.). A fine ashlar barrel-vaulted tomb-chamber with painted wall panels and white stars against a blue background in the vault and its stone sarcophagus painted to resemble a house, it is now in the Istanbul Archaeological Museum. Whether it is Rhoemetalkes' tomb or not, the night sky also symbolizes the end of South Thrace's twilight of chaos and division. In 46 the remaining Thracian lands south of Moesia were incorporated into a new Roman province of Thracia.

9

Danubian and East Thracians:
c. 4th–1st centuries BC

The end of the Scythian enclave

By the mid-4th century Danubian Thrace faced a double threat. In the west Celtic infiltration was increasing, but until the great invasion of 280–78, when the Triballi and Getai were defeated and much of the Banat, Oltenia and north-west Bulgaria were occupied by the Skordiski (Nicolăescu-Plopşor 1945–7; Todorović 1974; Zirra 1976), it was not alarming. In the east the Scyths, already on the Danube and under pressure from the Sarmatians, were more immediately dangerous for they had begun to cross into the Dobroudja despite resistance by an anonymous 'rex Histrianorum' (Pompeius Trogus in Justinus IX, 1–2). The Scythian king Ateas obtained a conditional promise of help from Philip II, busily assimilating Odrysian Thrace, which perhaps accounts for the Scythian gold gorytus and the gilded collar like the one from Mal-tepe at Mezek found by M. Andronikos in the royal tomb at Vergina; but the two fell out, Philip perhaps seeing the danger of a Scyth presence south of the Danube. The ensuing battle in 339 ended in the death of Ateas and a crushing defeat of the Scyths leading to the end of hegemony over the Pontic steppe and the immediate eradication of their Danube enclave. After two centuries the Getai regained freedom of movement across the Danube.

Zimnicea, a major Danube crossing, was resettled (Nestor 1949; 1950; A. D. Alexandrescu 1974). Its 4th-century tumulus cremation cemetery was found to contain moderately rich primary graves, with secondary burials of bowl-lidded urns in the mound-heap. A contemporary destruction level suggests Zimnicea as the feebly fortified city razed by Alexander (Arrian, *Alexander* I, 4, 4–5). Soon rebuilt but again destroyed, perhaps *c.* 300 by Lysimachos, it was resettled after an interval but not fortified, its importance more commercial than political. Wheelmade ware showed southern influences, but some of its handmade pots have Transylvanian analogies. By the end of the century it was probably Celtic-controlled. Cremation, adopted by the Celts, remained the burial ritual. Grave goods were poor; horse burials, either the complete skeleton or head and legs only, were separate from human burials. Fibulae in the 2nd century are all of Celtic type. The Celtic emphasis of this last phase could explain the city's destruction, attributed to Burebista, in the first half of the 1st century BC (A. D. Alexandrescu 1974).

East of Zimnicea recovery was slower but more stable. Dromichaites' defeat and capture of Lysimachos argues a sizeable Getic

128 Simplified 'Villanovan-type' handmade urn from Baraolt in south-east Transylvania dated to the 3rd century. Ht 35.6 cm. The same shape occurs south of the Danube at Pleven and Devetaki. It continued to influence Daco-Getic pottery and metalwork through the 1st century AD.

population in the Danubian plain following the Scythian expulsion. Disturbances south of the Danube led to the *c.* end 4th-century abandonment of many Getic settlements and the migration of their inhabitants to north of the river. Already using imported Greek or Greek-style pottery, often locally made near the Pontic colonies or in South Thrace, they would have introduced it, with wine and oil, especially the former, and, to a lesser extent, mass-produced bronze vessels and ornaments. In exchange there was grain from the plains; timber could be floated down the Danube tributaries, then carrying a far greater volume of water than today. Cattle, hides, furs, honey, beeswax and slaves were readily available, and salt was a peculiarly valuable commodity (Glodariu 1976).

Muntenian trade routes and settlements

Trade with the interior was a Getic monopoly. From Tariverde or other emporia dealing with Histria, they could cross the Danube at Hîrşova and follow the river Ialomiţa to Piscu Crăsani. Thence one route crossed the plain to Popeşti on the Argeş. Another, turning north-west, via Tinosu on the Prahova, reached Cetăţeni on the upper Dîmboviţa to gain the Bran pass into south-east Transylvania. Popeşti also was linked by road or river with Zimnicea.

The volume of trade from other Getic emporia trading with Odessos, Tomis and Kallatis was probably very large. As well as using the Danube as a highway, merchants crossed it from Silistra or Rousse to Călăraşi or Slobozia and then followed the Mostiştea and Argeş valleys under the protection of fortified trading posts. From Vlădiceasca (Trohani 1975; 1976), controlling the middle reaches of the Mostiştea, roads diverged to Cernica or north to Piscu Crăsani and beyond. The Argeş route branched either along the Dîmboviţa to Cernica, whence a road led to Tinosu, or continued to Popeşti and Cetăţeni. The same routes also provided Muntenian and Transylvanian links with Getai south of the Danube and with South Thrace, using Danube crossings at Svishtov-Zimnicea and Rousse-Slobozia.

The new trade network ended the isolation of the Muntenian plain. Whilst handmade pottery, often with the old horns symbol, was little 128 changed, the impact on local wheelmade ware was strong and, combined with Celtic influences, laid the foundation for the Geto–Dacian ware of the 1st century BC–1st century AD, with 'the same shapes made in the same techniques and decorated in the same way being found in Muntenia, Moldavia and Transylvania, ones that could even have been made by the same craftsmen' (Crişan 1969, 216).

Celtic craftsmanship was as important to the local artisan as that of the Hellenistic coast or South Thrace. Celts were mainly responsible for the introduction of ferrous technology and for initiating the manufacture of agricultural and other iron tools, all modelled on implements used in the Celtic regions of western central Europe. Celtic arms and armour, on the other hand, were not copied. Nor were they in Transylvania or South Thrace.

Near Ciolăneştii din Deal, north-west of Alexandria, a hoard of twenty-three black burnished handmade pots and innumerable sherds comes from an almost square well, its sides measuring just over 1.5 m and the lower part lined with interlocking oak beams, sunk 2.7 m below the then ground level, some 3 m from a stream. The pottery is attributed to the late 2nd or early 1st century BC, although some pots could be older. M. Petrescu-Dîmboviţa and S. Sanie (1972) stress the clearly votive nature of the well; it has many counterparts in Celtic western Europe.

Another possibly Celtic sanctuary was found near Conteşti, in the forested hills of the upper Argeş. An oval ashy area 13.5 by 8.5 m and 25–30 cm deep lay on sterile soil lacking any traces of burning (A. Vulpe and E. Popescu 1976). In the ashes were many tiny potsherds, mostly impossible to reconstruct, and some 3,000 bone fragments, mainly domestic animals but also birds and deer. All the finds had been exposed to fire, seemingly a deposit of ritually smashed relics of a feast held elsewhere. Beside and slightly overlapping the ashes a large pile of corroded but unburnt iron objects included forty-five arrowheads, twelve knives, five spurs, twelve large nails, five fibulae, one of the last lying just within the ashy area with a Celtic-type glass bracelet fragment and a silver coin of Dyrrachium, current from the late 3rd to the early 1st century but most common at the end of the 2nd, a date corresponding to the pottery. The excavators suggested this was a place of sacrifice, probably of a Getic tribe, but more recent soundings indicate the existence locally of Celtic graves (Dumitrescu 1975, 101).

The Muntenian settlement pattern was based on commerce. Most major settlements had good natural defences, usually on spurs, although at Tinosu, commanding a strategic ford over the Prahova, a ditch and rampart surmounted by a clay-plastered palisade were necessary (R. and E. Vulpe 1924). Popeşti, some 25 km south of Bucarest, developed as the major tribal centre between 200 and 150, perhaps succeeding Zimnicea (A. Vulpe 1976). From this time its ruler may have exercised authority over lesser chieftains in the region.

The only cemetery identified in the neighbourhood is a group of ten tumuli of which the four most prominent are dated by the excavator to the early 2nd century (A. Vulpe 1976). One was perhaps a cenotaph; the others, cremations, contained remnants of chain-mail; in one was also a Celtic sword, bent double, much other Celtic war equipment, and a sickle, but no handmade pottery. It is difficult not to conclude that these were graves of Celtic rulers.

Inside the citadel, earlier fired adobe walls the basis of its defences, were thatched wattle and daub huts and, immediately beneath a destruction level, a palace complex dating to the turn of the 2nd century, covering at least 815 m² and probably extending up to 2,000 m² (R. Vulpe 1957a; 1961; 1966). Also wattle and daub, but tile-roofed, large, symmetrically aligned rooms with narrow connecting corridors indicate Hellenistic influence. A two-roomed building was probably a shrine. The slightly apsidal inner room contained two square, carefully smoothed clay hearths, some 10–20 cm above floor level. One was plain, the other had mostly geometric cord-impressed decoration, bordered by the Otomani flame motif. In the outer room, a 129 plain hearth occupied the centre and a low clay stoup-like construction a corner, a hollow in the top designating it as a container for liquid. This

129 A hearth altar, 1.15 m square, from the upper level of an apsidal room in the palace at Popeşti. Closely related to those dated a century or so earlier at Seuthopolis, it retains links with the Otomani-Wietenberg culture.

building succeeded a smaller one, also with a plain square clay hearth. At Vlădiceasca an unusually large building contained three hearths and a similar stoup.

Other square hearths, plain or with simple linear ornament, were found at different levels elsewhere in the citadel. Whether they were domestic cult hearths or primarily a form of heating one cannot be sure but probably the two purposes cannot be entirely disassociated. Below the six superimposed levels of one was an offering pit containing broken hand- and wheelmade Getic pots, an intact Rhodian amphora, two sections of a rotatory handmill of imported tufa, an iron knife and other metal objects, a clay loomweight, carbonized beans, bones of domestic animals and fish. A similar pit is dated to the EIA by fragments of a polished black high-handled pot with characteristic horns and channelling. Among food offerings were two sucking pigs and cockleshells. Other pits had stored grain and had been filled up with ash and other hearth refuse. N. Conovici (1974) has pointed out the frequent presence in these Muntenian and contemporary Moldavian settlements of human, usually male, and animal figurines, roughly made even where, as at Piscu Crăsani and elsewhere, pottery skills are proven, and always associated with fire. Greek imports found in Popeşti included many amphorae, also bronze vessels and ornaments, the quantity perhaps due to the relatively extensive excavations, but also to the settlement's importance, which continued until early in the 1st century AD.

Cetăţeni was an important staging post (Rosetti 1962; Chîtescu 1976). More than 150 amphorae were found here, their contents presumably transferred to casks or skins which pack animals could carry more safely over the Bran pass to Transylvania (Glodariu 1976, 12). The settlement was defended by a powerful fortress dated to the 2nd century BC.

Rough stone-built dwellings, some probably warehouses and inns, dotted the rocky defile. A sanctuary was apsed and oriented as at Popeşti. Hellenistic gold jewellery, imported pottery and iron tools show the wealth of this remote mountain town. Its cemetery, containing cremated remains of adults accompanied by silver ornaments, iron weapons and chain-mail armour, demonstrates a sometime Celtic presence. Whether under Thracians or Celts, the inhabitants prospered until the point indicated by a thick burning layer in the fortress above a Roman coin of 88 BC which suggests its reduction as part of the liquidation of Celtic influence early in the 1st century BC.

Piscu Crăsani was closely linked through trade with the Dobroudja and strongly influenced by Hellenistic culture; and the few weapons and even fewer fibulae attributable to the Celts, especially of the 2nd century, suggest their presence was minimal. V. Pârvan (1926, 182ff.) found that although local potters used Celtic as well as Getic forms, the imports were Greek rather than Pontic colonial ware. Piscu Crăsani's end is uncertain, but a denarius of 80 BC in its final burning layer indicates an ending perhaps related to that of the Cetăţeni fortress (Babeş 1975, 139, n. 60).

Coinage was another Celtic introduction, only gradually adopted and still more gradually minted by the Danubian and North Thracians, the Celtic stylization contrasting interestingly with the Hellenistic coinage of South Thrace. C. Preda (1973) has suggested the existence of four main regional mints – Transylvania, central Muntenia, two Moldavian – striking Thracian coins by the mid-2nd century, implying the emergence of four main tribal regions.

Moldavian trade routes and settlements: 4th–3rd centuries BC

Histria was also the Greek end of an even more profitable and probably earlier developed trade route operated by the north Dobroudjan Getai with Moldavia. The first station was Barboşi, on the Siret near its confluence with the Danube, fortified to defend the plain against eastern raiders. Thence a road followed the Siret to Poiana, Răcătău and Brad, diverging from Poiana to settlements between the Bîrlad and the Prut, from Răcătău to important salt deposits at Tîrgu Ocna and over the Oituz pass into Transylvania. From Brad it also branched east to the Iaşi area and west to Bîtca Doamnei (Piatra Neamţ) and across the Carpathians.

In the early 4th century Poiana was a primitive village. Untouched by Hellenistic influences and unmolested by Scythian raiders, suddenly it was violently attacked. Huts were burnt, inside them unburied, often contorted skeletons, many of children; the debris contained numerous arrowheads. Yet later in the century and despite a burnt level attributed to the 3rd, Poiana was set on a long course of increasing prosperity (R. and E. Vulpe 1927–32; R. Vulpe et al. 1951;

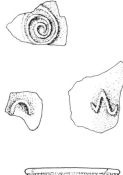

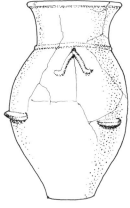

1952; R. Vulpe 1957b). Although remaining a huddle of clay-plastered wooden huts, the site's potentialities for trade and industry made it the chief tribal centre of south and central Moldavia west of the Prut.

Pottery developed on similar lines to Muntenian settlements, but a distribution analysis of Hellenistic and Roman pottery imports into Geto–Dacian lands north of the Danube shows that of the 90 per cent of the total found in modern Romania south and east of the Carpathians, Poiana, Răcătău and Brad accounted for 70 per cent, figures which exclude important unpublished finds at Pecica but indicate the relative volume of the Siret trade (Glodariu 1976, 19). Crucibles, iron and copper slag, many and varied iron tools, fine jewellers' implements, and many metal ornaments and plate, including some half-finished bronze and silver artefacts and some made from melted-down silver coins, testify to its metallurgical industry. Poiana minted coins in the 2nd century and a matrix for Roman Republican denarii shows these were also produced. As in Muntenia Celtic influence appears in metalwork.

No cult or public buildings have been identified, but four roughly rectangular clay hearths bordered with irregular incised lines and clay ram-head firedogs from uncertain find-spots are considered evidence of a hearth cult. Primitive figurines appeared in quantity at all levels. On handmade pottery spirals and 'horseshoe' and 'pointed omega' horns symbols continue to appear (R. and E. Vulpe 1927–32).

Răcătău, south of Bacău, was defended by a citadel with one ditch 6.7 m deep and another separating it from the settlement below (Căpitanu and Ursachi 1969; Căpitanu 1976). The modest 4th–3rd century settlement was replaced in the 3rd–2nd century by one reflecting the impact of trade. Thenceforward, the settlement pattern continues as at Poiana, haphazard, flimsy dwellings, usually of clay-plastered wooden beams, fastened with iron cramps and nails. Circular, presumed cult hearths have been found, and clay firedogs with ram protomes holding iron spits. Other cult objects included some twenty miniature vases of fine clay, twelve crude human figurines from 3.8 to 9.6 cm long and vessels with zoomorphic protomes.

There has been no report of any hiatus or destruction level within the Getic layer. The Roman approach on the lower Danube, far from affecting Răcătău's prosperity only extended the opportunities for trade until the settlement perished in the 2nd century AD.

Brad, about 40 km farther north (Ursachi 1968), was also defended by a citadel and a vast ditch, its period of prosperity from the 2nd century BC to the 2nd century AD. The find at nearby Negri of a large hoard of iron bars and other objects including flattened pieces of chain-mail, weighing in all about 275 kg, and another smaller similar hoard may indicate Celtic penetration either from Transylvania or from the Celto–Przewor group in Podolia. Probably from the late 3rd century the country north of Brad was occupied by the relatively backward Poieneşti–Lukashevka culture, of which the dominant elements are historically known as the Bastarnae.

Another trade route freed from Scythian interference by Philip II operated up the Dniester as far as the region of Kishinev (Melyukova 1969; 1971) from Tyras (Belgorod-Dnestrovsky) on the right bank of the estuary and Nikonia (probably Roksolany) on the left. Relations with the hinterland were good, although the extent of Getic integration in the Greek colonies can only be gauged by the fact that V. I. Kuzmenko and M. S. Sinitsyn (1963; 1966) note the proportion of Thracian handmade ware at Nikonia, decorated with the horns symbol and applied cordons, increased as the town's prosperity declined.

The Dniester estuary was jointly inhabited by Getai and the descendants of Sabatinovka tribes, one predominant on the right bank and the other on the left but with considerable intermixing. In the mid-4th century, Nadlimanskoe, 25 km north of Roksolany was a prosperous settlement fortified by a stone wall and ditch (Dzis-Raiko 1966). Forty well-made grain storage pots found in an area of 400 m² suggest it was a depot for corn from the Dniester valley. Nikolaevka, 5 km nearer Roksolany and unfortified, was equally prosperous.

On the right bank, Getic Pivdennoe, 17 km from Tyras was a wealthy open settlement. Besides semi-dugouts, there were surface houses with one or two rooms, the foundations of stone and the walls built of smaller stones with a lime and clay mortar. This type of construction, found also at Nadlimanskoe and Nikolaevka, was probably a Sabatinovka legacy strengthened by Hellenistic influence, another link with the past being the *zolniki* found on both sides of the estuary, although Melyukova (1971) notes the absence of specific cult objects. The unearthing at Pivdennoe of some 2,000 whole and fragmented amphorae (Salnikov 1966) throws light on the main import; relatively small amounts of fragmented Attic black-glaze ware were found. Wheelmade 'Thracian grey' pottery was common, its forms reflecting western and eastern influences, but local handmade Getic ware predominated.

Burial ritual reflected the mixed local traditions. Near Nikolaevka tumuli ringed by rough stone walls covered primary inhumation graves, both large stone-roofed rectangular pits and catacombs. Flat graves, also inhumations, were sometimes simply dug into the earth, even for the rich whose grave goods, besides meat, an amphora for wine and suitable vessels, included for the men bronze arrowheads, iron spearheads and swords, bronze, iron and silver ornaments; for the women bronze handmirrors, paste beads and other jewellery, and spindlewhorls. Some of the graves contained Thracian grey wheelmade ware. Another group, of twelve flat graves, had almost no grave goods except for remains of the funeral feast. In a cemetery farther north at Hanska-Luteria on the edge of the forest-steppe cremation predominated, the calcined bones, sometimes in a lidded urn, placed in a shallow pit. All graves contained the same few Getic pots. These settlements were short-lived; all disappeared in the second half of the 3rd century. Melyukova (1971) suggests their abandonment was caused by the same Celts who beset Olbia.

In the north of Moldavia a very different pattern emerges from the one enriching the Getai further south via the Dniester and the Siret. Soviet archaeologists have identified about thirty fortresses between the Dniester and Prut (Melyukova 1958; Zlatkovskaya and Polevoi 1969) and Romanian archaeologists about twenty between the Prut and Siret (A. C. Florescu 1971; Teodor 1973). Some are wholly or partly excavated, others only surveyed, none yet fully published.

Opposite:
130 Ancient symbols continue on 4th–3rd-century Moldavian pottery. *Above*: Potsherds from Poiana with horns and sun symbols. *Centre*: Urn from the Butucheny fortress on the Reut. Ht 61 cm.

131 *Below*: Clay figurine from Răcătău. Crude human figurines were common in Moldavian and Muntenian settlements.

Usually protected on accessible sides by one or more earth ramparts and ditches, these fortresses were generally smaller than those built to confront the Scyths. In a few cases, the same site was used, as at Stînceşti, but even here only the earlier was occupied. The two most northern, Lipnik and Rud, in the Mogilev–Podolsky area, could have been a protection against Celto–Przewor advance. Rud, on the Dniester, had four 5 m high earth ramparts, the outermost limestone-faced and with ditches 2 m deep; access was by a kind of barbican. As often, there was an open Getic settlement close by.

A group of fourteen, north and south of Rybnitsa are mostly on or near the Dniester west bank. Between this group and Kishinev, nine on the lower Reut link with a north-south string of four between Kishinev and the Prut. A parallel line west of the Prut extended from Arsura to Moşna and others in the Iaşi region, and north again to the re-fortified sites of Cotnari and Stînceşti. These could have been built to defend the Siret trade routes and incidentally the Danubian plain. By the end of the 3rd century all were apparently destroyed or abandoned.

The Bastarnae and the Poieneşti–Lukashevka culture

Described as Celtic or Germanic in the sources, the Bastarnae seem to have migrated from a mostly Germanic but partly north Celtic homeland, assimilating Baltic and other elements on their way (Teodor 1974; Babeş 1978). Trogus Pompeius (Justinus, *Epitome* XXXII, 3, 16) mentions a Getic king Oroles resisting them, but by the end of the 3rd century they reached the Danube delta. Polybius (XXVI, 9, 1) speaks of their courage in battle and many writers refer to them as mercenaries and to later raids across the Danube in alliance with the Dacians.

The Poieneşti–Lukashevka culture was basically a Geto–Bastarnae mix, although G. B. Fedorov (1960), excavator of Lukashevka II, considers the predominance of Getic artefacts there rendered the culture essentially Getic; M. A. Romanovskaya (1969) agrees. The people were settled farmers and stockbreeders living in open villages (Teodor 1974; Babeş 1978). Earlier fortifications were disregarded – at Arsura house remains were found between and outside the double rampart (Teodor 1975a). Graves, adults all cremated, were almost devoid of weapons. This is not conclusive, since the main German arm was a wooden spear, often without a bone or iron head. The few weapons found in graves or settlements are almost all unquestionably Celtic (Babeş 1978) and suggest military domination by a small Przewor element.

The Bastarnae could have been peaceful and industrious at home and yet fought well abroad, but they seem unlikely conquerors of the 4th–3rd century Moldavian fortresses. Excavations at Băiceni-Mlada (László 1969), Sorogari-Iaşi (Teodor 1969) and Cucorăni (Teodor 1974) where Poieneşti–Lukashevka levels succeed Getic ones of the 4th–3rd century show a continuity in handmade Getic ware only distinguished by the absence of developments taking place elsewhere. There was no wheelmade Getic ware. Boroseşti (Iaşi region) and Ghelăieşti (Neamţ region) have firedogs, at the former simple clay stands but at the latter most of a stylized zoomorphic pair were found and fragments of three others all judged to have north German and Danish analogies (M. Babeş and B. Mihăilescu-Bîrliba 1970–71).

The semi-dugouts, earlier universal, are mixed with surface huts in the 2nd century. It seems that, mingling with the intruders, the Getic majority lived in subjection with a lowered standard of living, whilst a small and scattered Przewor group had a disproportionate influence. A bronze squatting figurine from Lukashevka, undoubtedly Celtic, leads to the speculation that some, though not all, of A. Spitsyn's 'monstrous bronze statuettes' (1909a) had a Celt among their remote ancestors. But there is no evidence of Celtic or Celto–Germanic invasion on a scale sufficient to overpower the fortresses and the immigrants appear rather as settlers in an already ravaged territory.

One possible explanation could lie in inter-tribal warfare in the 3rd century after the retraction of Scythia. In this way a small group of invaders could find an impoverished but fertile area, its exhausted people isolated and easily dominated. Certainly the two groups mingled – no purely Bastarnian site has been found in west Moldavia (Teodor 1973b). Finds of imported amphorae show that a limited penetration of Greek products continued, probably using both the Siret and Dniester routes.

Thracian and Pontic luxury trade

The Scythian decline, at first a setback, showed Olbia's powers of resilience. The new Scythian capital at Neapolis in the Crimea was near enough for continued Scytho–Sarmatian control and patronage as well as support for the city against Zopyrion's attack. Olbia seems also to have continued for a time its traditional trade with the Dnieper and its prosperity is shown by public buildings of Late Hellenistic date uncovered in the city. Nevertheless, growing pressures from mainland tribes and the decline of the Dnieper market caused the city to strengthen its links with other colonies and their hinterlands.

Thracian handmade pottery found in both Olbia and Berezan and believed to be local suggests a possible small infiltration from South Thrace, a coin of Seuthes III also being found in Olbia (Marchenko 1974). Celts (Galatai) but not Getai are among the aggressive tribes listed in the Olbian decree in honour of Protogenas (*IOSPE* I², no. 32; Minns 1913) which T. N. Knipovich (1966) relates stylistically to one from Odessos (*IGB* 40) and dates to *c.* end 3rd century or possibly the beginning of the second. It is generally considered that these Celts were Celtic or Germano–Celtic migrants from the north and not survivors of the Tylis kingdom.

An interruption of Bosporan prosperity came with a new Sarmatian invasion from the east, which led the kingdom to seek the protection of Mithridates Eupator of Pontus. From his new base at Panticapaeum, Mithridates' opposition to Rome involved the more or less willing enlistment of Olbia and the other Greek cities of the north and west Black Sea coast, and even Cyzicus. That he planned to march up the Danube, sweeping the Balkan peoples into his army was 'credibly rumoured' (Cary and Scullard 1975, 254). It is likely that Mithridates'

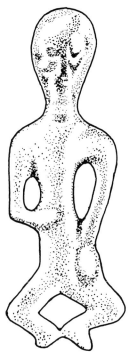

132 Celtic bronze figurine from the Lukashevka II settlement. Ht 7.5 cm.

133 *Left*: One of a hoard of 14 silver-gilt phalerae from Galiche. Diam. 12 cm. A repoussé hemispherical centre is edged by a flat band pricked with a running flame pattern and with four holes for attaching to a garment. The hoard also includes figural representations in high relief.

134 *Right*: One of a pair of silver-gilt phalera-fibulae from Herăstrău. Max. diam. 9.2 cm. The pin replaces the usual holes for attaching to a garment, but the general technique is similar to the figural phalerae from Galiche.

134

political and military activities temporarily brought a new stimulus to north Pontic trade with their Getic and South Thracian neighbours.

D. E. Strong (1966, 122) in considering that after about 350 it was no longer possible to identify the work of south Russian silversmiths – 'the plate is precisely like that found elsewhere in the Greek world' – emphasizes this stylistic interchange. There are technical as well as decorative analogies, including a characteristically Thracian emphasis on the 'running flame', between the Sîncrăeni hoard of silver vessels (D. Popescu 1958) and the types of silver or silver-gilt phalerae which are widespread in the Late Hellenistic period. Worn also by Celts (Polybius XXI, 6, 7) and Germans (Tacitus, *Germania* 15, 11), there are several related groups of phalerae found from the Kuban and north Pontic region (Spitsyn 1909 b) to Danubian and North Thrace (Fettich 1953). Others from the north Pontic region have closer analogies in the Thracian Plain, but all probably derive from intensified trade at this time in artefacts calculated to appeal mainly to Thracian tastes and probably often made by Thracian or Greco–Thracian craftsmen.

Hoards of phalerae dated to *c*. 2nd–1st centuries BC, usually circular with figural busts in high relief or vegetal ornament, have been found in Danubian Thrace at Yakimovo and Galiche, both in north-west Bulgaria, and at Herăstrău (Bucarest). In the Yakimovo hoard (Milchev 1973) one shows a bearded man, the other a barbaric winged goddess (a more classical Nike was found in a hoard at Yanchokrak, east of Nikopol on the Dnieper and one with a bust of Aphrodite in a 2nd-century grave at Apollonia (Mladenova 1963, Pl. 158a)). There are analogies at Herăstrău and to a goddess in one of the fourteen phalerae at Galiche.

Punched ornament fills the background of the figural plaques, both men and women wearing one or more heavy necklaces or torques, sometimes in almost Benin style. Most are convex and some almost hemispherical plaques with vegetal ornament from Galiche have analogies in the Taganrog and Starobelsk hoards from near Rostov on the Don and in the middle Donets basin (Spitsyn 1909b, Figs 51–57,

59–61) where the 'running flame' border was common. The Surcea
hoard in south-east Transylvania provides other links, with a griffon
head phalera resembling another in the Taganrog hoard. Then its oval
phalera with a dog below a rider and an eagle above his head, besides
comparability with a Galiche phalera depicting only a rider, could be
intended to represent a Celtic warrior wearing a helmet like that found
at Ciumeşti (Berciu 1967, Pl. 73). The Herăstrău face was skilfully
adapted to adorn a pair of fibulae found at Coada Malului in the Ploeşti
region, of which there is a crude local version from Bălăneşti in the
lower Olt valley (R. Florescu 1968, 44f.).

A different school is represented near Stara Zagora in a *c*. 1st century
BC tumulus grave containing four phalerae, three of them fragmentary.
Here finer work makes use of the circular shape to show real and
mythical animals, sometimes a combat like that of Herakles and the
lion. The fur is distinguished by the hatching used in 4th-century East
Thracian art; the subjects have a Greco-oriental tradition recalling the
4th-century South Thracian plaques from Panagyurishte and other
examples in south Russia. The distribution area is wide, perhaps
indicating Celtic use, a hoard of thirteen found on the island of Sark
being lost, but drawings of them happily preserved (Allen 1971);
another was found in a bog at Helden in Holland. One now in the
Bibliothèque Nationale, Paris, although of unknown provenance, has
special interest for the inscription recording its former ownership by a
king Mithridates, most likely, D. F. Allen considers, to be Mithridates
Eupator of Pontus. Allen suggests they found their way west with
Thracian auxiliaries and also points out that the subjects and treatment
of the Sark phalerae recall aspects of the Gundestrup cauldron, but are

135

135 Silver phalera from
near Stara Zagora. Diam.
17.8 cm. Another group of
phalerae, represented in a
Thracian tomb near Stara
Zagora and far afield,
makes greater use of real
and mythical animals.
Although the one
illustrated includes
Herakles and the Nemean
lion, the human figure is
rare in this type.

later and more debased. Further study may reconcile the cauldron's parallels with 4th-century Thracian art.

Other north Pontic finds, such as the Fedulov hoard, west of Novocherkassy on the lower Don (Spitsyn 1909b, Figs 47, 50) show yet more Greek influence. M. Rostovtseff (1922, 139) attributes these phalerae to a south Russian fusion of Sarmatian, Greco–Scythian, Celtic and Ionian art, but suggests that 'a few special traits may have been added by the native Thracian population'. More probably, Thracian craftsmen, trained for centuries in Greek cities to supply first a predominantly Scythian, then a Sarmatian market, adjusted successfully to changed patterns of trade, including for the Getic or Celtic noble a passable representation of himself.

The Dnieper Thracians

The gradual retraction of the Scythian state after the death of Ateas and under continuing Sarmatian pressure had grave consequences for the Thracians in the forest-steppe. With the loss of their Pontic Greek and Scythian markets, standards declined. Fewer people – or none – occupied the old fortified settlements and after the 3rd century there were only some secondary insertions in the great tumulus cemeteries such as Bobrintsy near Kiev (Petrenko 1961). The import of luxury goods declined sharply during the 3rd century and by the turn of the century even amphorae and the simplest Pontic wares no longer penetrated (Onaiko 1970).

In these circumstances there was probably little opposition to the arrival of groups of mixed Baltic, Germanic and Celtic peoples, and by the early 2nd century, if not before, a new cultural complex, the Zarubinets, had evolved in the middle Dnieper region and was to last until *c.* AD 100 (Tretyakov (ed.) 1959). Three main variants covered a wide area of the upper Dnieper and Pripet as well as the Kievan forest-steppe, where Thracian Chernoles traditions continued in its pottery (Sedov 1969) in both form and decoration, including the horns symbol. The Chernoles role in Zarubinets has been much debated in view of its possible contribution to the formation of the East Slavs. But the settlement pattern changed, the old sites being largely abandoned for smaller ones in naturally protected surroundings, and cremation and burial in flat-grave cemeteries became the predominant ritual. New pot forms appear and Celtic types of fibulae. It seems probable that the newcomers assimilated the demoralized Thracians. Like the Getic subjects of the 'Bastarnae', they became a substratum, although a large one. The forest-steppe Thracians, with now only a limited skill in ironworking (Voznesenskaya 1972), had no future independent ethnic role.

The Scyths, forced into an association with the early wave of Sarmatians which makes the term 'Scytho–Sarmatian' appropriate, concentrated their remaining resources in two areas separated by open steppe – the lower Dnieper and the Crimea. Kamenka did not lose its importance; rich burials continued. At the end of the 4th century a fortress was built at Belozerka at the mouth of the Dnieper (Pogrebova 1958). During the 3rd century trade with the coast was maintained, although no longer did fine works of art in precious metals come from the Bosporan or Olbian workshops (Onaiko 1970). In the 3rd or early 2nd centuries a chain of fortified settlements grew up south of Nikopol on the lower Dnieper, ten on the west bank and five on the east (Pogrebova 1958), mainly at crossing points and probably intended as defences or refuges from the second Sarmatian wave – the Roxolani – from the east and from Celto–Germanic migrants from the west. With stone walls, ramparts and ditches, and usually an additionally fortified citadel, they also provided shelter for open villages near by (Vyazmitina 1969a, b).

By the turn of the 3rd century BC the Scyths virtually abandoned the lower Dnieper for the Crimea. A late *c.* 2nd century Scythian warrior buried in the earth rampart at Kamenka had the then characteristic Scythian gold foil eye- and mouth-covers, a Megarian-type bowl and one of Zarubinets origin in his grave. The big industrial complex was abandoned, but life was maintained on the acropolis, Znamenka, its rampart strengthened by a stone wall and ditch. Left to themselves the settlements had a mixed rural economy, gradually augmented by a small-scale metal industry. They carried on barter trade with the coast and also had contact with Zarubinets groups, perhaps in the Tyasmin valley (Sedov 1969). At Gavrilovka, a late 3rd/2nd-century layer, with wattle and daub huts and imported amphorae as well as local pottery, was covered by a *c.* 1st-century BC burning layer, possibly associated with the sack of Olbia, although there is no reason to suppose the area came under Daco–Getic rule. The use of stone for housebuilding in later levels here and elsewhere shows coastal as well as Crimean Scyth influence.

The settlements continued to exist until about the 2nd century AD, when new Sarmatian invaders destroyed Znamenka and Goths, probably, the others, although some were later resettled by Chernyakhov-Sîntana-de Mureş elements. Their inhabitants constitute a remarkable ethnic mix, so far as limited excavation has been able to establish. M. I. Vyazmitina considers that Thracian influences predominate, including those exerted by Geto–Thracians from the Danube area. Nevertheless, in a 1st-century BC cemetery at Zolota Balka the burial ritual is largely Scythian and anthropological examination has identified many women as Sarmatian (Vyazmitina 1972).

Thracians here could have included Chernoles refugees from the Middle Dnieper, Getai from Moldavia or farther west, others fleeing from the Pontic coasts under Getic and Roman attacks, as well as a possible substratum of Sabatinovka descendants. Present evidence derives from pottery and cults for which many analogies exist at Poiana, Popeşti and elsewhere in the Getic world of the 2nd–1st centuries BC and earlier in Moldavia. Common features on pottery include applied finger-impressed cordons, symmetrically placed lug-handles, the Daco–Getic cup and the horns symbol as a decorative motif.

In the earlier level at Gavrilovka there are *zolniki* as much associated with the domestic hearth cult as a thousand years before (Pogrebova 1958). The clay cult hearth with its incised sun symbol at Zolota Balka has perhaps closer analogies in Danubian or South Thrace, which are

136 Jars from Zolota Balka. *Above*: Ht 24 cm. *Centre*: Ht 30 cm. *Below*: Ht 40 cm. Thracian presence on the lower Dnieper in the 3rd–2nd century is indicated by, *inter alia*, the horns symbol on pottery.

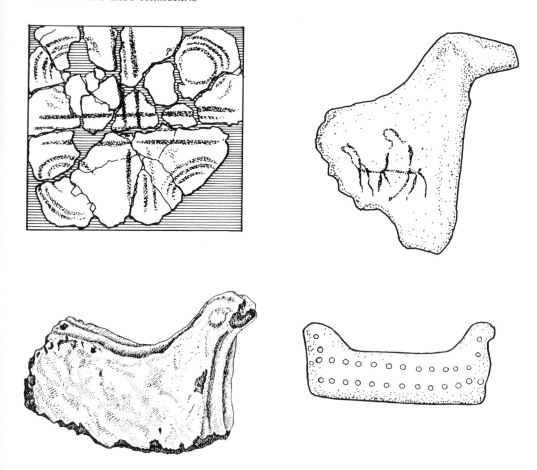

137 The sun-hearth cult in lower Dnieper fortresses. *Above left*: Hearth altar, Zolota Balka. *Above and below right*: Fragment of firedog with a horseman incised on the side, and a complete firedog, Zolota Balka. *Below left*: Firedog, Gavrilovka.

more nearly contemporary, than at Zhabotin, but the underlying kinship is clear. There are many firedogs, often in pairs, and, especially in the Zolota Balka settlement, with ram protomes and decorated with incised circles – one with a crudely incised horseman. Besides South Thracian and Moldavian analogies, the possibility of Celtic influence must also be considered. Although Celtic presence is not much in evidence here, stylistic resemblances with finds at La Roque in southern France and Hainaut in Belgium are very striking. While the Dnieper cults may be Thracian, they are also indications of a world coming briefly closer together.

Cult hearths and firedogs were found in shrines at Scythian Neapolis, where the culture is otherwise closer to the Greco–Roman. The 'great goddess' figurines of the north Pontic region, found from the 4th–3rd century onwards, are probably a Bosporan-transmitted oriental aspect of a general resurgence of the old sun-fire-hearth cult and its agriculture-fertility undertones, the latter exemplified by the local adoption of the cult of the dancing – often triple – nymphs. Carved on rough stone reliefs in the lower Dnieper area, sometimes with bull heads between, the nymphs persisted indefinitely to become part of popular decorative art (Gaidukevich and Kaposhina 1951).

153

10

The Geto–Dacian State
c. 1st century BC–AD 106

Celts in Transylvania and Oltenia

Thraco–Celtic relations in Transylvania from the earliest Celtic invasions until the emergence of the Dacian kingdom of Burebista in the 1st century BC are tantalizingly obscure and controversial. The view of V. Pârvan (1926; 1928, 110ff.) that the much superior Celtic culture enabled them to exercise a decisive influence on the Transylvanian and Danubian Thracians has since been disputed in varying degrees. The size of the migration is unknown and its distribution unclear, but V. Zirra (1971 a, b; 1976) has usefully summarized the available, if as yet incomplete evidence. There were several waves of Celtic invaders from various westerly directions, mostly during the 4th and 3rd centuries. Unlike the nomadic Cimmerians or Scyths, they came to settle, content to dominate the native population, levying tribute in goods and services. Military and cultural superiority ensured an easy conquest; a mass grave not in any cemetery at Berea, near Ciumeşti in north-west Romania, contains battered skeletons of twelve adults and four children, suggesting that resistance was met by severe repression (Zirra, n.d., 107, Pl. XXV/1). By the early 3rd, if not the late 4th century, they had established their domination over Slovakia, the middle and upper Tisza and the whole Transylvanian plateau (Zirra 1971; Crişan 1971).

The technological skills of the Celts and especially their introduction of iron agricultural, mining, metallurgical and domestic implements were an important factor in raising Transylvanian cultural and economic standards. Wheelmade pottery, although perhaps earlier introduced by Getic traders from the south, had not been locally manufactured. Under Celtic influence it came into general use. The traditional North Thracian handmade ware continued in use, but with the wheel new shapes which, partly traditionally Thracian and partly deriving from Celtic and Greek models, slowly evolved along new lines towards a distinctive blend that was to characterize subsequent Geto–Dacian ware.

Both Celts and Thracians believed in an afterlife possessing certain basic similarities. Although many of the earliest Celtic arrivals practised inhumation, by the mid-3rd century the two peoples used cremation. This followed a general trend and although we do not know how much it was influenced by Thracian custom, it was a move towards integration. Further evidence is found even in such heavily Celtic-

138 'Fruitstand' from Răcătău. The clay 'fruitstand' was a ubiquitous form of wheelmade ware in the Dacian period. It had appeared earlier in the Basarabi horizon.

populated areas as around Ciumeşti (Rusu 1969), where Thracian burials occur in Celtic cemeteries with no signs of discrimination. Artefacts of one race are often found in graves of the other (Zirra n.d.; Crişan 1966). Both had inherited sun-fire-hearth-heroic ancestor cults and the social structure – king, priesthood, warrior aristocracy and commoners – was natural to the Thracian temperament.

During the 3rd century BC, Transylvania became part of the vast Celtic *koine* which reached west to the Atlantic and south to territories dominated by Republican Rome, to Illyria and Macedonia and, for two-thirds of the century, through the kingdom of Tylis to Greece and Asia Minor. As a market open to the Mediterranean lands it had enormous possibilities. Besides a source of agricultural produce and ores it could offer an inexhaustible supply of slaves and mercenaries. A side-effect of trade relations and pay earned by Celtic mercenaries in the armies of nations fighting for supremacy or survival in the Mediterranean region was the adoption of coinage. Like the Odrysian king Seuthes III, the Transylvanian and Oltenian Celts modelled theirs on the silver tetradrachm of Philip II of Macedonia, but transmitting the symbolism of the head of Zeus and a horseman into a Celtic art form.

Burebista

> . . . another division of the country which has endured from early times, for some of the people are called Daci, whereas others are called Getae – Getae those who incline towards the Pontus and the east, and Daci, those who incline towards Germany and the sources of the Ister [Danube].
>
> (Strabo, *Geog.* 7, 3,12, transl. H. L. Jones).

Whilst the Getai emerge into history with Herodotos, under the name of Dacians they enter only at the approach of Rome, when Dacia gradually replaced Getica to denote the area from the Danube to and within the Carpathian arc.

By the beginning of the 1st century BC, Geto–Dacian recovery had almost been achieved. How far Celts had been assimilated is still debatable, especially in Transylvania where, as in Oltenia, they had adopted Getic cremation ritual. Whoever made them, Dacian iron tools were identical with those of central Europe, although the Dacians   141 did not copy Celtic arms and armour. The pottery is harder to classify owing to continuous inter-influences. Both the Celtic impact and degree of Geto–Dacian recovery are illustrated by issues of Dacian coins. Whether by co-existence or fusion, the Celtic contribution to Geto–Dacian culture had been absorbed.

The 1st century BC is dominated by one name – Burebista. Strabo (7, 3, 11, transl. H. L. Jones) says

> Boerebistas, a Getan, setting himself in authority over the tribe, restored the people, who had been reduced to an evil plight through numerous wars and raised them to such a height through training, sobriety and obedience to his commands that within only a few years he had established a great empire and subordinated to the Getae most of the neighbouring peoples.

How many of the settlements with a 1st century BC burning layer were destroyed in earlier wars, how many during Burebista's rise to power and how many in the confusion after his death it is impossible to say. The coinage of the four main Geto–Dacian groups ceased after the first decades, when Burebista forbade minting (I. Winkler 1968), presumably to assert his authority, possibly to diminish Celtic influence, and preferred to use Roman denarii, easily available through growing trade with the west or minted locally. Unless reliance is placed on Jordanes' (*Getica*, 67) reference to a 'king Buruista' in the time of Sulla (82–79 BC), his speedy consolidation of the Getic tribes and subjection of his neighbours probably began early in the 2nd quarter of the 1st century, although some scholars put the beginning of the latter to the mid-1st century (Móczy 1974, 18f.). First to be defeated were the Celtic Skordiski, later to be his allies in the westward drive against the Boii and Taurisci (Macrea 1956).

Next, it seems, came an eastern raid, ranging from Olbia in the north to Apollonia in the south, perhaps to keep his forces occupied and well rewarded away from home. Resisting cities, especially Olbia and Histria, suffered severe destruction and no doubt all were looted or paid heavy tribute to avoid worse. If epics of Bronze Age heroes had been told and transmitted down the centuries, Burebista must have appeared a worthy successor. Not since Sitalkes had any Thracian been a real threat to the outside world. Like Sitalkes he had his foreign adviser, Akornion of Dionysopolis, honoured by his city *c.* 48 BC (*IGB* 13) for protecting their interests. At home Decaeneus, called by Strabo (*Geog.* 7, 3, 11) 'coadjutor' and 'wizard', was apparently a priestly successor of Zalmoxis, the Getic divine or quasi-divine prophet. His powers of divination helped to secure the complete obedience of the Geto–Dacians; 'they were persuaded to cut down their vines and live without wine'. Decaeneus seems also to be linked by Strabo with the holy mountain of Koganaion, perhaps, but unproven, the Dacian civil and religious capital, Sarmizegetusa in the Orăştie mountains.

139 *Opposite above*: Daco-Getic cup from Poiana. The crude clay handmade Daco-Getic cup, usually 6–12 cm high, with one or two handles and either plain or with barbotine decoration, had some special significance for the Daco-Getic North Thracians. Some were used as lamps and they were ubiquitous grave offerings, even in rich burials. Outside Dacia they are found west to Budapest and east to the Dnieper. Usually locally made, a large pottery at Butovo, near Turnovo, also produced them, perhaps for the local Getic market, perhaps for export across the Danube.

As pursuit of the Celts was not pressed so far as Gaul, and Dacian troops were too late for the battle of Pharsalus, no confrontation with Roman forces took place. But in his last years Julius Caesar determined to remove the Dacian danger. The many coins from Histria found in the Transylvanian forts of Piatra Roşie and Costeşti suggest that Burebista, aware of Caesar's plans, strengthened his defences with technical help from the Greek cities (Macrea 1958). Then, in 44, came the almost simultaneous assassination of Julius Caesar and the death, natural or otherwise, of Burebista. The Dacian state disintegrated into tribal groups and it was nearly 150 years later that Dacian and Roman forces met in Transylvania.

Western and northern neighbours

The boundaries of the Dacian state were probably fluid at all times. In the west, it seems likely (Strabo, *Geog.* v, 1, 6; vii, 1, 3; vii, 5, 2) that Thracians inhabited both sides of the Tisza before the Boii arrival and again after Burebista had defeated them. They were subjugated and assimilated by the Roman-encouraged Sarmatian Iazyges (Sulimirski 1970, 171ff.) who reached the lower Tisza *c.* AD 20; thereafter settlements and cemeteries on both banks show Daco–Getic cups and other characteristic ware alongside Sarmatian bronze bells and chalcedony beads (Macrea 1968). A possible border town was Pecica on the Mureş, some 60 km from its confluence with the Tisza (Crişan 1964). Pottery in the 2nd century BC level here reflects Daco–Celtic fusion. A Dacian round sanctuary burnt down in the 1st century BC but immediately rebuilt remained until Trajan's final victory in AD 106. Both before and after its Roman occupation, first in AD 88, Pecica was probably virtually neutral and very prosperous as a trading centre, although until publication of its many Roman finds (Glodariu 1976, 19) no real assessment is possible. Smaller, open settlements continued in the Crişana as late as the 3rd or 4th century, but the balance between Getic and Roman is hard to define (Macrea 1969, 180; Bichir 1976, 306).

Elsewhere in the west, Daco–Getic cups found in the great Skordiski fortresses of Židovar, near Vršac (Gavela 1977) and Gomolava, near Sremska Mitrovica (Jovanović 1974) only show contact or a small infiltration after Burebista's campaign, just as sporadic finds of similar ware to Budapest and beyond are perhaps archaeological proof of his pursuit of the Boii and Taurisci, but no more.

Perhaps as the result of Burebista's victories, in Slovakia the Thracian element seems predominant in cremation cemeteries of the 1st century BC–1st century AD and in fortified settlements such as at Zemplin in east Slovakia (Benadik 1965). From the 1st century AD, Germanic Quadi elements infiltrated the largely Thracian Puchóv culture of west Slovakia (Crişan 1969; Neustupný 1961, 159) which was extinguished by *c.* 3rd century AD. In eastern Slovakia, Daco–Celtic coexistence continued until the general decline after the Marcomanni wars (Macrea 1968).

The Costoboci tribes on both slopes of the north Carpathians (Ptol., *Geog.* III, 5, 9; III, 8, 3) were a Thracian or Thraco–Celtic group

(Russu 1959) who formed the Lipica culture extending over Galicia and northern Moldavia (Sulimirski 1976; Bichir 1976, 288, n.14). Dated by M. Yu. Smishko (1952) from the 1st century BC, its flat-grave cremation cemeteries contain urn burials with poor grave goods. Farming communities lived in open settlements. Their wheelmade ware, evenly fired in closed furnaces, was decorated with polished geometric patterns, whilst coarse ware bore applied, finger-impressed or hatched cordons and conical or other protuberances.

Rome and Decebalus

The Roman frontier on the lower Danube was safeguarded by a clearance of the northern plain and deportation of some 50,000 Getai to Moesia. Farther north, the garrisons and traders of Pannonia and Moesia kept Transylvania quiet as long as commerce flourished. Little is known of Dacia during this period except that trade and Dacian raids into Roman territories continued until AD 85, when the king, Decebalus, invaded Moesia. He defeated and killed the Roman legate, probably in the Dobroudja, near Adamclise (Tropaeum Traiani) where the names of more than 3,000 Roman casualties were later inscribed on an altar. One counter-invasion of Dacia failed, but a second heavily defeated Decebalus at Tapae – which commanded the Transylvanian 'Iron Gates', a narrow gorge defending the western access to Sarmizegetusa. With trouble in Pannonia, Domitian wanted a quick peace; Decebalus by accepting Roman suzerainty kept his lands and even borrowed Roman engineers to improve his defences.

Trajan's two campaigns against Decebalus are illustrated on Trajan's Column in Rome and metopes on the Tropaeum Traiani (Rossi 1971; R. Florescu 1973). It is interesting to note the survival of Otomani motifs on some of the Dacian shields. In 101–2 he crossed the Danube and, with heavy losses, ejected the Dacians from Tapae. Then he attacked along the Apa Grădiştei valley in the Orăştie mountains, reducing several fortresses, and won a decisive victory near Sarmizegetusa. Decebalus surrendered but kept his kingdom by allowing Roman garrisons to occupy some fortresses and promising to dismantle

140 The strong Thracian element in the northern Lipica culture appears in its pottery. *Above*: Daco-Getic cup from the Zaleutsy settlement. Ht 8.5 cm. *Centre*: 'Fruitstand' from the Grinev cemetery. Ht 28 cm. *Below*: Wheelmade jug, also from Grinev. Ht 36 cm.

141 Iron agricultural implements from a smithy on one of the Sarmizegetusa terraces. A rake, W 46 cm; a grubbing hoe, L 22 cm; a hoe, L 23 cm; a coulter, L 26 cm; and a scythe.

142 Ornamental nails from Sarmizegetusa and Piatra Roşie. Diam. of heads 4–5.5 cm. Iron nails with finely worked heads using similar patterns to those on the vegetal phalerae (*see Ill. 133*) were used for sanctuaries.

the rest. Having thus bought time to recover, in 105 he again invaded Moesia, having eliminated the Roman garrisons. Trajan counter-attacked with twelve legions and after inflicting enormous losses, seized Sarmizegetusa in 106, Decebalus committing suicide to avoid capture. The booty – in gold, silver and captives – was immense. All the fortresses were destroyed. The temples received especially savage treatment, with every pillar decapitated. From the subsequent history of the Roman province of Dacia one infers a deliberate decision to destroy the native religion, testimony to the central place it held among the Geto–Dacians.

Sarmizegetusa and Dacian religion

The chronology of Dacian Sarmizegetusa (generally assumed to be modern Grădiştea Muncelului) is hard to establish since early 19th-century treasure-seekers of gold coin hoards continued the Roman destruction. The earliest remains probably belong to the beginning of the 1st century BC, after which were two main building phases. Both used wood and stone, limestone being characteristic of the earlier, about the middle or second quarter of the 1st century BC, whilst andesite came into use, especially for religious structures, in the later, dated from the second half of the 1st century AD until the destruction in 106. Continuity and common traditions are manifest in the general uniformity of the pottery of what has been termed the 'classic' Geto–Dacian phase. The horns symbols still frequently appear on clay handmade vessels, especially urns, unchanged since the EBA.

Sarmizegetusa was a large secular as well as sacred city. The settlement, built on tens of terraces of which few have been excavated, extended for about 3 km. A metalworking quarter on one terrace contained eight furnaces with bronze and copper slag, bronze ingots and sheets and spoilt artefacts. One shop contained a tonne of smelted iron ore shaped into round 'cakes'. On another terrace craftsmen

produced finished tools; the several hundred found included farming,   141
mining, woodworking and stone-cutting implements, as well as those
for metalworking and the iron nails, spikes, cramps and hinges used in
building. For the sanctuaries especially, even the nails were works of   142
art. Spearheads, curved daggers, straight swords and Dacian cutlasses
were also made. Metalworking on this scale was not uncommon in the
area with its wealth of iron and copper ore. Two other terraces were
part of the potters' quarter; depots of wheelmade pottery included
Dacian painted ware, portraying vegetal and animal motifs with
primitive realism and no trace of Celtic stylization.

A fortified enclosure of five terraces and some 3.5 ha in area was
chiefly a refuge, its 3.2 m thick 1st-century AD walls probably replacing
an earlier palisade but sheltering only scattered flimsy huts. The east
gate opened on to a 5 m wide stone-flagged road, bordered by parapets
and wooden watchtowers, which after about 100 m led to a small paved
courtyard skirted by stone channels carrying water from a spring. This
was the entrance to the sacred enclosure on terraces X and XI, where a
fine ashlar retaining wall probably carried architectural decoration.

There were rectangular and circular sanctuaries. H. Daicoviciu
(1972, 207ff.) has dated two of the former on terrace XI and one on
terrace X to the first phase. Another, assigned to an intermediate phase,
stood on an upper level of terrace XI. All but one were later wholly or
partially replaced by three of the same type on terrace XI and one on
terrace X. Orientation, where established, was approximately NE–SW.

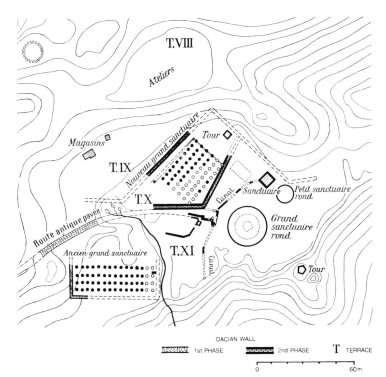

DACIAN WALL
▨▨▨ 1st PHASE   ▬▬▬ 2nd PHASE   **T** TERRACE

0   60m

143 Sarmizegetusa
(Grădiştea Muncelului),
plan of sacred area.

144 Sarmizegetusa. The unfinished great rectangular andesite sanctuary on Terrace X, planned to cover an area approximately 37.50 by 31.50 m.

The largest late sanctuary was built on an earlier one on Terrace X. Its six alignments of ten Ionic andesite bases were surmounted by andesite columns estimated to have been 1.2–1.5 m high. Whether they were to carry stone offering-vessels of burning spices, as H. Daicoviciu (1972, 210, Fig. XXVII) suggests, it is impossible to say. Trajan came before it was completed; bases and columns were found on the approach road.

Two round sanctuaries at the east end of terrace XI are assigned to the later phase. The smaller, a single ring 12 m in diameter, was made up of one hundred and fourteen andesite columns in thirteen groups. The taller columns were all decapitated.

145   Close by was the greatest circular temple known in Dacia, its external diameter approximately 29.4 m, almost exactly 100 Roman feet or a Greek *plethron*. Within a double outer andesite circle a ring of wooden columns enclosed a horseshoe-shaped structure. The outer circle consisted of one hundred and four closely fitting, curved blocks lined by thirty groups of six narrow, squared piers with small cubical tops and one wider pier, each being 12–13 cm apart. Sixty-eight

146   wooden columns, sunk 1.3–1.45 m into the earth, suggesting a height of some 3 m, and 36–40 cm apart, formed the inner circle, its diameter 20 m. Between the south-eastern of its four openings and the central structure, the clay-mortared pebble remains of a rectangular hearth 1.5 by 1.35 m were reddened but only slightly fired, perhaps due to the temple's brief life.

The central horseshoe structure had thirty-four similar but probably lower wooden columns, two stone thresholds roughly corresponding to the north-east and south-west entrances from the inner circle. On the same axis, just outside the whole sanctuary on the north-east, were burnt fragments of a square limestone pavement, its sides measuring 2.3 m.

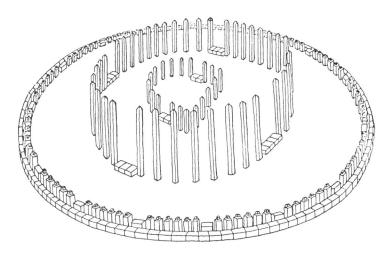

145 *Above*: Sarmizegetusa. The large circular andesite sanctuary on Terrace XI. External diam. approx. 29.50 m.

146 *Left*: Sarmizegetusa. Tentative reconstruction by H. Daicoviciu of the large circular sanctuary.

The theory that Dacian sanctuaries, open to the sky, served a urano-solar cult is supported by the excavation near this great sanctuary of an andesite disc from which ten segments, each 2.76 m long, radiated to form the top of a circular pavement-altar about 7 m in diameter, supported on stone blocks and a clay and rubble fill from which a channel led to a monolithic stone trough 1.03 m long.

Other similar rectangular sanctuaries are found in Dacia, some near Sarmizegetusa, others as far away as Bîtca Doamnei. Only two other circular buildings are believed to be temples, one, poorly preserved but possibly a ring of wood and stone columns in groups of 6 + 1 at Pecica (Crişan 1966 b), the other in even worse state at Feţele Albe, very near

Sarmizegetusa, 10.8 m in diameter, with a central hearth (H. Daicoviciu *et al.*, 1973). Other round buildings are regarded as secular prototypes. Yet also at Feţele Albe in an earlier Dacian level, separated by a sterile layer from one containing Celtic pottery, was a much damaged structure 11–11.5 m in diameter surrounded by a wide polished clay pavement decorated with close parallel and concentric linear incisions. Other, much cruder edifices, sometimes with an inner apsidal arrangement, have been found in groups on high mountain pastures above Sarmizegetusa, their wooden, unplastered walls on carefully chosen stone foundations sometimes without a hearth but with a wealth of pottery (250–300 pots) which suggest the summer courts of Dacian priests or nobles rather than early versions of modern shepherds' seasonal huts and sheepfolds. The pattern of evolution has still to be solved. The near-by site of Faţa Cetei, where rich surface finds have come from over forty terraces in four or five 'storeys' (H. Daicoviciu, 1972, 153) may even be a possible predecessor or counterpart to Grădiştea Muncelului-Sarmizegetusa.

There are many theories about the meaning of these sanctuaries. The frequency of the number six, their orientation and other factors have suggested a calendar for a 360-day, 12-month and 6-day week Dacian year; there are variations of this hypothesis, as well as suggestions regarding mathematical-astronomical purposes (H. Daicoviciu 1972, 241ff.). There are also many theories about Geto–Dacian religion and its *interpretatio graeca*. According to M. Eliade (1972, 24), 'The fact that Pythagoras was named as the source of Zalmoxis' religious doctrine indicates that the cult of the Getic god involved belief in the immortality of the soul and certain rites of the initiatory type . . . we divine that the cult had the character of a mystery religion.' But, as Eliade also points out, there could well be changes over the centuries. It must be remembered that the existing Dacian sanctuaries do not go back earlier than the 1st century BC and that oriental, Celtic, Greek and Roman ideas had all exerted influences on Dacia's fundamentally Thracian identity. The mystery still remains.

Dacian fortresses

Military architecture is Dacia's other major archaeological legacy, but, unlike the sanctuaries, it has predecessors as far back as the Later Bronze Age as well as points of resemblance in contemporary Europe. Dacian forts occupied hilltops, their slopes terraced as necessary. Piatra Craivii on a peak near Alba Iulia which dominated both the Mureş and the rich metalliferous slopes of the south Apuseni mountains was one of the earliest (I. Berciu *et al.* 1965; I. Berciu 1966). It occupied 11 long narrow terraces as well as many rock-cut platforms and balconies, some tiny, some as large as 65 by 30 m serving as outposts or refuges. One or two were perhaps linked to sun-worship, like the Chertigrad niche. Near one of two rectangular sanctuaries were five sacrificial pits, containing deposits of pottery, weapons, animal bones and cereal remains. This culture layer, preliminarily dated, without subdivision, from the end of the 3rd to the 1st century BC was shown by metal artefacts and other features to be partly Celtic, a reason for its likely

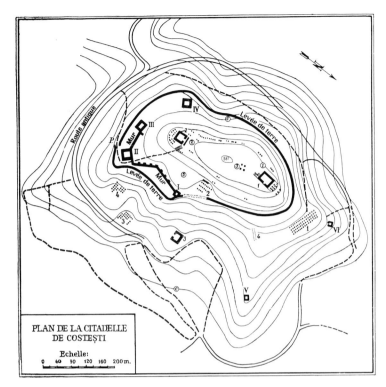

147 Costeşti, plan of fortress. An old tribal centre with several rectangular sanctuaries both inside and on terraces outside its powerful fortifications, Costeşti was an important link in the defences of Sarmizegetusa. One tower-house was approached by an imposing flight of wide stone steps.

PLAN DE LA CITADELLE
DE COSTEŞTI

Echelle:
0   40   80   120   160   200 m.

reduction by Burebista. The bare peak was not occupied or fortified until the main Geto–Dacian phase, to which belong most of the forts.

At this time Sarmizegetusa was protected by an irregular ring of forts, strategically sited to control all possible access points. Băniţa commanded the Jiu pass in the south, Piatra Roşie the Stingu and Luncani valleys in the west; the north route up the Apa Grădiştei valley was barred by Costeşti and Blidaru and the upper Mureş valley, north-eastwards, by Căpîlna and Tilişca. Some were old settlements, adapted; others were purpose-built. This, together with differences in terrain, lack of time or availability of foreign skills, and degrees of conservatism led to extraordinary variety within the general uniformity of site-type and construction materials.

Costeşti, a former tribal settlement, had a late 2nd-century BC palisade or rampart, destroyed in Trajan's first war and replaced by a new, but traditional rampart, 6–8 m wide at the base and today 2–2.5 m high. Wooden beams reinforced its interwoven wattle and daub framework and the ends overlapped to defend the gate. Inside, on the accessible south side a wall incorporated three bastions, and an isolated tower overlooked the west. Outside the rampart three similar towers guarded the valley and the paved road to Sarmizegetusa, 10 km away.

147

Piatra Roşie's first main building phase dates to c. mid-1st century BC, within the reign of Burebista. The curtain wall incorporating six interior towers enclosed an area largely occupied by a large and solidly built apsidal dwelling, the interior walls well plastered and partly

148 Blidaru. View from the south-west, showing the second fort built to reinforce the first, which lies behind.

148

painted. In an apsidal building outside the walls, perhaps a small replica of the Popeşti sanctuary, were found fragments of an unusually finely worked iron disc and other parts of a shield. When included in the defence system of Sarmizegetusa during Trajan's first war, a hastily built second enclosure was added to protect the rest of the settlement (C. Daicoviciu 1954).

Blidaru was a twin fort built to reinforce Costeşti, probably within the reign of Decebalus (C. and H. Daicoviciu 1963). The first fort, with four exterior towers, had one isolated tower inside and another outside. The second, only a little later, incorporated the outer tower but extended from the earlier west wall and corner towers of the first. With neighbouring entrances on the south, the forts were in fact semi-detached. The north-west and south-west walls were exceptionally strong, with a corner tower and eight casemates of alternating courses of limestone ashlar and uncut mica-schist blocks. Apart from their obvious uses, the casemates probably made a platform for some of the war engines on fortified mountains seized in Trajan's first war (Dio Cassius LXVIII, 9).

The walls here are fine specimens of the 1st century AD *murus dacicus*, a term used to distinguish it from its cousin *murus gallicus*. This development of BA Carpathian engineering linked inner and outer drystone ashlar faces with thick, horizontal beams laid in 'swallowtail' grooves which helped to withstand lateral pressure until the fill (of earth and stones but without mortar) had solidified. These grooves were probably adapted from a Hellenistic building technique found in walls at Histria (Preda and Doicescu 1966, 302ff. and Figs 68, 73, 74) though here, as in some Dacian forts, the beam did not fit into both faces, one end going only into the fill. The slope was levelled to build the first course; there were no foundations. The wall averaged 3 m thick and sometimes rose to a height of 3–4 m or, after two to five ashlar courses, was surmounted by mud bricks, protected from rain damage by tilted logs.

The same technique was used for building the isolated tower-houses found in most forts, the lower part used for storage and the upper storey, reached by wooden stairs, as a leader's dwelling. Sometimes, as in the small fort at Căpîlna, a bastion of the curtain wall was used for the same purpose (Macrea and I. Berciu 1965). One of the two at Costeşti was approached by an imposing stone staircase.

With the Geto–Dacian flat grave tradition it is hardly surprising that few burials have been traced in the mountainous area of the forts. At Tilişca, for instance, only two were found, although a rectangular cremation platform, like the one in the Celtic cremation cemetery at Apahida, showed signs of long use. The Tilişca graves, exceptionally, had a rich inventory of ritually broken silver ornaments. Silver-workers in the fortified settlement were well supplied, one workshop containing fourteen matrices for silver denarii (Lupu 1966). Elsewhere, precious metals were rarely found in graves, although in a cemetery with a similar rite on the Magura hill at Moigrad, the burials contained a wealth of pottery (Macrea et al. 1961; 1962).

Many more forts are being discovered elsewhere in Transylvania, often built purely in the local tradition and perhaps of purely local importance. Other forts were strategically sited to face an eastern danger. Sărăţel, near Bistriţa, was one of several built to hold the north-east Carpathian passes; here mortar was used and beams were thrust vertically as well as horizontally into the stone facings of walls and towers (H. Daicoviciu 1972, 142).

Beyond, on the eastern flanks of the Carpathians, Bîtca Doamnei was one of several forts protecting the Siret trade route (Gostar 1969, 9ff.). Here a destroyed 2nd-century BC palisade was replaced by a mortared clay wall 3.5 m thick and an estimated 4–5 m high, with an added wooden superstructure but no reinforcing beams within. Two rectangular sanctuaries here and another at Barboşi – where in the absence of stone, the drums were wooden – illustrate the uniformity of ritual over Decebalus' Dacia.

149 Căpîlna. View of the tower-house, its outer dimensions 9.50 m square. Finds suggest the fort was the home of local chiefs from the 1st century BC to the Roman conquest.

11

The end of the Thracian 'nation'

Thrace south of the Danube

An immediate effect of the creation in AD 6 of the Roman province of Moesia – initially a narrow zone bordering the south bank of the Danube and the Black Sea coast – was the thorough Romanization of the occupied area, only the Greek colonies generally maintaining their Hellenistic character. Tomis, the living conditions of which Ovid has described in his *Tristia*, retained its leading position and Odessos its civic autonomy. In Thracia, established in AD 46, Romanization was not attempted. Most of the province was subdivided into *strategiae*, based on whole or parts of tribal areas and administered by centrally chosen *strategi*, many of them Thracian (Lazarides 1953–54; Gaggero 1978). Greek was its main administrative language, and its culture Thraco–Hellenistic. The change to Roman rule brought no improvement to the impoverished Thracian economy.

As the century progressed, it was realized that the security of the *limes* necessitated Thracia's economic recovery. A policy of urbanization, developed strongly under Trajan and Hadrian, involved bringing immigrants from other provinces, especially Asia Minor, with the industrial, commercial and administrative skills which the Thracians lacked. This industrious new 'middle class' effectively provided the South Thracians with a modernized Hellenistic economic and social structure, influencing rural as well as urban areas.

The Thracian population was variously utilized. The Bessi were already known for their mining ability, and Roman mines at Malko Turnovo in the Strandja hills and elsewhere used Thracian labour. They produced grain and livestock for their Roman masters. Their martial qualities were fully exploited by the army and navy, but this and the continuing export of slaves seriously drained the population. Two plague epidemics, the first beginning in 162 and lasting up to twenty years, were especially severe in the Balkan peninsula. 'According to contemporaries almost half the people in the empire were killed' (D. Angelov 1971, 76 (transl.)). Living in open villages, Thracians, especially those north of the Stara Planina, were easy victims of Carpic and other trans-Danubian raiders, joined in the 3rd century by Goths. A major Gothic raid in 250–1 reached the Thracian Plain, sacked Philippopolis, took many of the population captive and amassed huge plunder. On their return they defeated and killed the Emperor Decius. The depopulation in rural areas made it impossible to produce the harvests required by Rome, leading to at least six mass settlements from outside the Empire in the last three decades of the 3rd century. Excepting some Romanized Dacians after Aurelian's evacuation of the province, this influx consisted of alien landworkers, permanently altering the racial composition of the rural population (D. Angelov 1971, 74ff.). In the following century more Gothic invasions, even a Gothic civil war which devastated Thracia, and a major Gothic immigration further impoverished and diluted the Thracian element.

Few villages of the Roman period have been excavated; probably most differed little from those recorded by Xenophon, except for new obligations. The inscription of AD 238 from Scaptopara in the middle Strymon valley (*IGB* 2236) details all the taxes to which they were liable, including the provision of free board and lodging for all military and civil personnel visiting a nearby popular resort; the result being the partial, perhaps total abandonment of the village. Confirmation of limited action to restore the rural economy comes from the AD 202 founding inscription of the emporium of Pizus east of Plovdiv (*IGB* 1690). The new settlers were declared immune from a long list of apparently normal military and civil exactions including the supply of corn and draught animals.

Erection of tumuli continued at first on both sides of the Stara Planina, declining after the end of the 2nd century as labour ceased to be available for building large mounds. Philippopolis was notably conservative and, until the Gothic sack, rich. Two 2nd/3rd-century tumuli were erected near the Hellenistic tomb at Filipovo, also another tumulus cemetery (Botoucharova 1962). With the building of fewer tumuli, secondary insertions increased; a total of fifty-three graves dated from the early 2nd to the mid-4th century were found in six mounds at Merichleri, near Pizus (Aladjov 1965). The use of tumuli for later burials is documented at least until the 14th century (Miyatev 1928–29; Djonova 1962). Possibly some ancestor or hero cult was later transferred to a saint or martyr believed buried there.

Epigraphic and archaeological evidence shows that not all Thracians were poor or were degraded to the peasantry. One, Maximinus Thrax, rose from the ranks and became emperor after the murder of Alexander Severus in 235, to be killed by his own troops in 238. Thracians and the offspring of mixed marriages (the mother almost always Thracian) held all manner of secular and religious office. The initial desirability of Roman citizenship was later equalled by the adoption of a Latin or Greek name, even in a village an advantage over a wholly Thracian-named candidate for an official post (Beshevliev 1965, 42ff.). A Romanized Thracian, Flavius Mestrianus, was wealthy enough to dedicate a silver drinking-set weighing 1.65 kg to the hero Pirou-miroula.

A Roman-period heroon near Lyublen in the Turgovishte area consisted of a tumulus 25 m in diameter and a small square sanctuary, both in a large courtyard enclosed by a stone wall and destroyed at the end of the 3rd century. In the tumulus were two rich cremation burials, male and female according to the grave goods, the former including surgical instruments and other objects of a medical nature. The head of a life-size male statue, stylistically dated to the second half of the 3rd

150 The Thracian Hero sanctuary at Daskalovo. The largest excavated, its use by Roman officials from Serdica as well as rich and poor Thracians is demonstrated by votive inscriptions, fine statues and well carved relief tablets (*see Ill. 165*).

century, was found in the remains of the sanctuary. D. Ovcharov (1974) suggests this was the cult-statue of a doctor, perhaps also a priest, whose tomb became a place of pilgrimage.

An outstanding example of a rich Thracian family's survival is provided by the *villa rustica* at Chatalka, near Stara Zagora, owned by Thracians from before the earliest of their rich tumulus graves with Roman Republican coins until its destruction in the 4th century (D. Nikolov 1976; D. Nikolov and H. Buyukliev 1967). The property included farms and a commercially viable pottery and the villa a domestic sanctuary of the Thracian Hero. Rich female burials may indicate priestesses. The wealthiest male grave at Chatalka contained a bronze helmet-mask, a gold wreath and other rich objects; but with them was still the ritual rough handmade jar. Such continuity is naturally more common in remoter and poorer areas. At Gela, high in the central Rhodopes, nineteen of twenty-five tumuli in a cemetery are dated to the 'Hallstatt'. The other six contain cremations dated by coins to the second half of the 2nd and the beginning of the 3rd century AD. Some of the latter's fragmented pots, used as offerings and to cover the remains, if not found *in situ*, says the excavator, would have been unhesitatingly dated by shape and composition to the 6th–4th centuries BC (Najdenova 1972).

The grave goods of the rich reflected the growing availability of luxury goods and there is a striking increase in the number of chariot burials found in or near the periphery of tumuli (Venedikov 1960). As earlier at Vratsa and elsewhere, chariots were buried with horses still harnessed. Assigned to the 2nd and 3rd centuries, possibly a little earlier, they are usually ornamented with silver or bronze figurines or plaques, the subject often related to the afterlife.

Paradoxically, shrines show even more clearly than burials both the degree to which Hellenistic influences had permeated Thracian culture and the underlying strength of Thracian continuity within the new

151 Monumental marble relief of the Thracian Hero. Ht 1.75 m. Found in Thessaloniki, it may have been the focal point of an important urban sanctuary.

framework. The custom of placing votive tablets in a sanctuary, hitherto almost entirely confined to the Greek colonies, now spread everywhere. The principal subject depicted was the Thracian Hero, mounted on his horse. Some two thousand reliefs of the Hero, often syncretized with such gods as Apollo and Asklepios, have been found in Bulgaria (Kazarów 1938) and in the Dobroudja (Scorpan 1967) and many more in Yugoslav Macedonia, Greek Thrace and Macedonia and Turkish Thrace, Bithynia and Mysia. Elsewhere, when found in former Thracian lands, as at Tyras and other places in south Russia, or in Transylvania, they are more likely to be evidence of South Thracian troops in the Roman garrison than of local cults.

B. Gerov (1968, 200 (transl.)) writes in relation to the territory of Serdica: 'The sanctuaries found so far are on heights or by springs, the votive plaques usually without inscription. In sanctuaries where the cult of other deities has been established – Asklepios, Apollo, Sabazios – it remains an open question whether these were not originally sanctuaries of the Horseman.' This comment is generally applicable, although in some places inscriptions are more frequent.

Where buildings have been excavated, they are usually simple, drystone-walled, rectangular structures, although numismatic evidence suggests the existence of a much more elaborate structure at Philippopolis, where the Horseman is associated with Apollo. At Daskalovo, between Sofia and Pernik, are impressive remains near a mineral spring and the site of a Roman road station. A rectangular walled enclosure c. 24 by 28 m was dated from the second half of the 2nd century AD to its destruction two hundred years later. In the centre a structure of huge well-dressed blocks was apparently a sacrificial altar in front of a simple edifice of cella and naos. The Thracian Horseman is here syncretized with Asklepios and Thracian, Greek and Roman names are among the dedicants of votive tablets (Lyubenova 1974). Near Kipia in the southern foothills of Pangaeus, the abundance of

150

165

152 At Lilyache a vigorous spring emerges from a natural limestone arch to form a whirlpool. Built remains of a shrine are barely visible today.

mainly 2nd-century AD Greek and Latin inscriptions found on the surface suggests an urban sanctuary of the Hero outside the city of Aulon (Koukouli 1969). The unusually large fragment – 90 by 47 cm – of an anepigraphic plaque of the Horseman found under the modern church of Alexander Nevsky in Sofia, outside the walls of Roman Serdica, may come from a sanctuary (Gerov 1968). A perhaps comparable but complete relief from Thessaloniki is dated to 1st century BC–1st century AD.

151

More impressive are natural Thracian sanctuaries such as mountain peaks and springs. At Glava Panega, in the Stara Planina foothills east of Vratsa, approached through a cave a great spring emerges below a platform open to the sky. Tablets of the Thracian Hero, often syncretized with Asklepios and other gods, were placed on the cave walls (*IGB* 510–586). Like the open sites of Daskalovo and of Lilyache in north-west Bulgaria (Venedikov 1952), where remains of a 4th-century BC wall exist, these shrines must long predate any archaeological evidence.

150, 152

Springs, especially warm mineral waters, are also associated with sanctuaries to the Three Nymphs, suggesting syncretization of a pre-Greco–Roman fertility cult. A rustic shrine at Burdapa, west of Plovdiv, contained in the usual simple building ninety-five tablets portraying the Three Nymphs, less than a third with inscriptions, suggesting a genuinely local cult (Dobrusky 1897). A spring at Bratsigovo, not far away, yielded a coin span of almost two millennia from 4th century BC to end 16th century AD (Mushmov 1928–29). Urban nymphaea, none yet excavated, probably had Greco–Roman

153

153 Votive tablet of the Three Nymphs from a shrine on Lesbos. Ht 27 cm. Their iconography entirely Greek, the Nymphs were often naked or lightly clothed but in less Hellenized areas the traditional long robes were often preferred. In South Thrace the number of their tablets is only exceeded by those of the Hero. Probably also through Greek influence, the cult was popular in the lower Dnieper region (p. 144).

architectural constructions. An edifice incorporating a triple spring at Kasnakovo, near Haskovo, was dedicated to the Nymphs by Thracian donors (Venedikov 1950; *IGB* 1714). Caves with springs, as at Madara, were also sanctuaries of the Nymphs, there associated with Herakles.

North of the Stara Planina, there is a contrast in the Popovo district west of Abritus (Razgrad) between a shrine at Lyublen to the Hero, frequented by Thracian villagers and auxiliaries (*IGB* 753–7), and a sanctuary of Artemis a few km away at Sadina, more favoured by Greeks and Romans (Gerov 1952–3; Ovcharov 1970). In this area Gerov notes Thracian names appearing in already Romanized Thracian families, which can only be a sign of growing emancipation during the 3rd century. Research has shown the continuance of the language and of Thracians in high places in the 4th century and after (V. Velkov 1958; 1959). But just when a South Thracian renascence within the framework of the Empire began to appear a possibility – one potentially of enormous importance with Constantine's 4th century transformation of Byzantion into the new imperial capital, Constantinopolis – an unending stream of alien invaders and settlers culminating in the 6th and 7th centuries with the Slavs, stifled any such revival for ever.

Roman Dacia: AD 106–274

Roman Dacia was both a bastion protruding into the barbarian world and a new source of wealth and manpower. Contact began early in the 2nd century BC, but the North Thracians had not undergone the South

Thracians' gradual acclimatization to the Greco–Roman world, and the intensive Romanization of the province surpassed that of Moesia and Thracia to an extent which makes it hard to find out what happened to the Dacians.

The province, based on a sector of the Danube *limes*, approximately comprised the Banat, Oltenia and most of Transylvania, the insecure eastern frontier beyond the Olt being retracted to this river about 245. A Roman garrison was installed in the ruins of Sarmizegetusa to forestall a possible revival, and a Roman sanctuary was created. A superficial semblance of continuity which, in effect, emphasized the break with the past, was subsequently provided by including Sarmizegetusa in the name of the new capital at Haţeg. Ten other *coloniae* or *municipia* were formed on Roman lines, all initially with an upper stratum of new settlers, many of Italic origin. Apulum (Alba Iulia) grew out of the *canabae* of Legio XIII Gemina. The rest were on earlier sites, Dierna, Drobeta and Sucidava (Celei) on the Danube, the last opposite Oescus and some 40 km north on the main north-south road was Romula. In the west, Tibiscum was on the road from Viminacium to Roman Sarmizegetusa. In the far north Porolissum (Moigrad) commanded the frontier defences; Napoca (Cluj), farther south, was an administrative sub-capital with a near-by legionary headquarters at Potaissa. Ampelum (Zlatna) was the administrative centre of the mining area. Besides these, forty-two forts have been identified (N. Gudea 1978).

The settlement pattern meant major displacements of the Dacians. They were dispossessed of the fertile Danubian plain and pushed into the forests and hills in the north. In Transylvania they were mainly driven into the eastern rural areas where land was poor and a string of forts guarded the frontier. A number of Dacians may well have fled immediately after Trajan's victory to join the free tribes outside (Macrea 1968). There were later transfers of Dacians into Moesia Inferior.

All known Dacian fortifications and temples were systematically destroyed and excavation has shown that the new towns and forts were built and administered on strictly Roman lines. The new population, besides the troops, were mainly first- or second-generation colonists from Noricum and Pannonia, later supplemented from more distant provinces.

The army soon began to recruit local auxiliaries. There is evidence for the presence of South Thracians, including four cohorts (Russu 1967), and for settlers from Hellenized Asia Minor. Latin was virtually the sole language for funerary and votive as well as official inscriptions; of some 3,000 found only thirty-five were in Greek (H. Daicoviciu 1975). The common practice of adopting imperial family names by Romanized natives was closely followed, probably to avoid prejudice. Only fifty-eight Thracian names appear in inscriptions, whether of North or South Thracians is uncertain. The name 'Decebalus' has not been found in Dacia (Macrea 1969, 268). It is thus impossible to assess what status Dacians achieved, but probably discrimination had lessened by the 3rd century when a locally recruited cohort shared in the defence of the province.

The same cloak of silence fell on earlier cults. It is very likely that some were hidden under Greco–Roman names or representations, but recognition is difficult and never certain (Macrea 1969, 378f.). It is possible that, as in South Thrace, the main healing springs were old cult centres, some turned into Roman spas. Băile Herculane (the baths of Hercules) is so named from the number of votive inscriptions to Hercules found there (Tudor 1968a, 24ff.). Some may have thus disguised an ancestral protector-hero. Germisara (Geoagiu) off the road from Apulum to Sarmizegetusa is considered a pre-Roman site; here is evidence of a cult of the Nymphs. About thirty Thracian Horseman tablets, mainly from Danubian or other cities, are stylistically similar to those in the south and there is no reason to suppose they were locally inspired (Russu 1967), nor similarly is a fragmentary tablet from Drobeta perhaps dedicated to Thracian Zbelsurdos (Tudor 1968b, Fig. 112). The votive tablets addressed to the twin 'Danubian Horsemen' are largely of oriental inspiration and unconnected with the South Thracian Hero.

Despite a large exodus – whether under duress into other Roman provinces or flight to freedom – Dacia was not, of course, depopulated. Handmade Getic pottery shows that, in however humble a position, native Dacians lived in and around all the Roman settlements. At Slimnic, north of Sibiu, a Geto–Dacian village is dated from the second half of the 3rd century BC with no hiatus to the late 3rd century AD, the same type of rectangular semi-dugout wattle and daub huts in use throughout and little, if any change in handmade ware (Glodariu 1972). The main developments were in grain-storage pits and wheelmade pottery; fruitstands and other Geto–Dacian pots of about 2nd century BC to 1st century AD were replaced in upper levels by common forms of Roman provincial ware.

Other villages were settled by those who had been forcibly moved north. Obreja, north-east of Alba Iulia, was on the territory of the legion stationed there and probably founded for its convenience. Here, exceptionally, grey wheelmade ware was more common than red, and Greco–Roman influence was limited chiefly to a 'Charon's obol' in graves. Obreja was inhabited until the arrival of the Huns (Protase 1973).

As in adjacent provinces, the output of wheelmade pottery was enormous, whether from city workshops or rural centres such as the *pagus* of Micia (Veţel) near Deva (Floca *et al.* 1970). Dacians must have worked alongside craftsmen of many nations, all using predominantly Roman techniques, forms and decoration. It is even questionable whether contemporary big wheelmade storage jars decorated with wavy horizontal incised lines derive from earlier Thraco–Getic types (Protase 1966, 66).

There was no interference with burial ritual; town and country continued either to use local rites or those practised by new arrivals. Cremation continued as the almost universal Dacian custom, whether at the grave or on an *ustrinum*, the remains placed in shallow pits or urns. At a *villa rustica* at Cinciş in south-west Transylvania cremation burials in stone-covered pits were near an inhumation in a brick sarcophagus, presumably of the Roman or Romanized proprietor (Protase 1971, 90f.).

With poor and sometimes non-existent grave goods, the flat-grave cemeteries are hard to date. The largest excavated, at Soporu de Cîmpie, west of Cluj, contained 193 graves; the few adult inhumations were dated to the 5th century, the rest by coins and fibulae from the mid-2nd century to the Roman withdrawal in 271–4 or perhaps a little later. Graves were not in rows as in a contemporary cemetery at Moreşti in the Mureş district, but in groups, yet although densely packed there was no overlapping, implying the use of some kind of grave marker. After cremation, always outside the grave, the remains, plus embers and a little ash, were placed in an urn with the poor grave goods, also showing signs of burning; the urn was usually an old household pot, whether Roman or handmade Dacian, often covered by a Daco–Getic cup, bowl or tureen, or a slab, on top of which was placed the inverted lower half of a grey jar (Protase 1966, 52ff.; 1971, 100ff.). Considered a local Dacian cemetery by D. Protase, silver filigree ornaments and other objects lead some scholars to believe it Carpic. Pending full publication one can only call it with G. Bichir (1976a, 156f.) 'a Daco–Roman cemetery with some Carpic elements', although whether the latter came through trade or a limited Carpic colonization in the second half of the 3rd century it is impossible to say.

Tumuli in the mining regions near Ampelum and Alburnus Maior (Roşia Montană) are almost certainly attributable to Illyro–Dalmatian miners known to have been brought here by the Romans (Protase 1966, 60ff.; 1971, 104ff.; Tudor 1968a, 183ff.), although the ritual was perhaps later adopted by Dacian fellow-workers (C. Daicoviciu 1958). A large 2nd-century tumulus cemetery as Caşolţ, near Sibiu, also containing cremations, but carried out at the grave in some kind of wooden construction, contains only wheelmade pottery, with varying analogies in Roman, Dacian and Celtic ware, the last including three-footed vessels common in Noricum and Pannonia. The lack of Getic handmade ware leaves the origin of the dead a matter of debate, as even if this cemetery was used by early colonists, another at Ighiu, near Alba Iulia, lacks the characteristic three-footed vessels (Macrea 1969, 262ff.; Protase 1971, 86ff., 92ff.). It may again be a case of Dacian adoption of foreign customs.

During Aurelian's phased evacuation of the province many Romanized Dacians, Roman settlers and other refugees were resettled in the newly created provinces of Dacia Ripensis and Dacia Mediterranea south of the Danube. Rome left reminders of her intensive colonization not only in monuments which decayed or were lost or destroyed, but in the everyday life of the Dacians, whose pottery and other artefacts were often imported as long as Rome stayed on the Danube and were certainly copied, along with their production techniques. Even the circulation of Roman currency continued.

Beyond the 'limes'

Outside the province, the 'free Dacians' were affected by the Roman presence in varying degrees. The Muntenian plain was at first as strongly romanized as the province itself. A typical village 15 km east of the *limes transalutanus*, Dulceanca, near the river Vedea, was an open farming settlement (Dolinescu-Ferche 1974). With easy access to clay, the inhabitants copied Roman provincial ware, whilst their coarse pottery, mainly big storage jars, was plain or decorated with alveolar relief cordons or the horns symbol. Dulceanca was destroyed or abandoned towards the end of the 3rd century.

In the Maramureş region of north-west Transylvania, Roman influence was also strong, although a Germanic Vandal element has been detected in a Thracian cremation cemetery at Medieşul Aurit, in the Satu Mare district, where thirteen pottery kilns have so far been uncovered in what must have been a big industrial settlement (Bichir 1976b; S. Dumitrescu and T. Bader 1967). The mass-produced wheelmade pottery, a developed version of earlier Geto–Dacian ware, was no doubt exported to neighbouring areas, including that of Porolissum within the province, from about the end of the 3rd century until some time in the 4th (Macrea 1968).

In the north-east the Costoboci people associated with the Lipica culture became known for their warlike qualities, especially for their invasion through Moesia Inferior and Thracia to Greece in 170 and destruction of Eleusis (Pausanias X, 34, 5). They also harried the north-east frontier of Dacia and were probably among Marcus Aurelius' opponents here in 174. Their remnant was gradually assimilated by the Carpi with whom they co-existed, especially in north Moldavia (Bichir 1976a, 161).

Apart from the dismantling of fortifications, south and central Moldavia were little disturbed by the Roman presence, Poiana continuing as a useful trading centre until overrun by invading tribes early in the 3rd century, and old settlements round Piatra Neamţ, Botoşani and Fedeleşeni remaining inhabited. Brad was destroyed and abandoned at the beginning of the 2nd century and Răcătău fell into decline. G. Bichir (1976a) believes that the original home of the tribes now generally identified with the historic Carpi was in a sub-Carpathian area of central Moldavia. Initially dominated by the Costoboci, the Carpic culture is dated from the early 2nd century to the first decades of the 4th. During the 2nd century groups moved to the steppe between the Danube delta and the Dniester, where they co-existed with the Sarmatians, making an unsuccessful attack on Tyras in 214 (*CIL* III 1441b), whilst in the north they soon mingled with Gothic and other tribes and formed an early Chernyakhov-Sîntana de Mureş horizon (Zelenchuk *et al.* 1974, 62). The great Gothic migrations reached the Siret, Prut and Dniester valleys about 200 and soon dominated the Pontic coast; by 250 Tyras, Olbia and Tanais had fallen.

Carpic settlements were much like those of the Lipica culture. In their flat-grave cremation cemeteries, poor burials were placed in a shallow pit, often with no pots, perhaps a single bead. Richer people used a lidded urn, usually with a fruitstand placed upside down and often a Daco–Getic cup inside or just by it. A potters' quarter at Butnăreşti, west of the Moldova and Siret confluence, used kilns capable of firing to both red and grey, but kilns and pots alike owed more to Geto–Dacian than Roman technology, although Roman as well as Sarmatian influence is apparent. Special wheelmade urns with Sarmatian-type zoomorphic handles were made for burials, and the

154 Carpic urn from Poieneşti. Ht 34.5 cm. The clay 'soup tureen', part of the Daco-Getic wheelmade repertoire by the 1st century AD, was adapted by the Carps as a burial urn. Sarmatian influence added naturalistic zoomorphic handles.

symbols incised on some pots are also adapted from Sarmatian magic. Almost all the Daco–Getic cups showed traces of smoke on the inside and are thought to have been used as lamps in settlements – where no other lamps have been found – and as incense-burners in cemeteries (Bichir 1976a, 51).

At Poiana-Dulceşti in the lower Moldova valley, cult pits have been found. One was cylindrical, 1.05 m in diameter and 0.95 m deep, containing seven new wheelmade jugs upside down in a semicircle at the bottom. The settlement had nine other pits, each with a single animal skeleton, either dog or hare; other pits held hearth fragments and broken firedogs. Damaged firedogs showing no trace of fire were also found in two semi-dugouts without hearths. Made of coarse clay and decorated with thumb-imprinted cordons, the protomes at either end are unidentifiable.

From the mid-2nd century onwards, Carps as well as Sarmatians began to penetrate the relatively empty but fertile Muntenian plain, their settlements distinguishable by the Sarmatian elements in their Dacian culture. They were possibly the attackers, by the early 3rd century if not before, of Callatis, Dionysopolis and Marcianopolis (Bichir 1976a, 167f.; *IGB* 24 *bis*); by 238 they were allied with the Goths in raids on Moesia Inferior, and in the wars of 245–7 forced the withdrawal of Rome's eastern frontier to the Olt, but in spite of continuing historical mentions increasing domination by the Goths and population transfers into the empire caused their virtual disappearance soon after.

With the cultural horizon known as Chernyakhov (USSR)-Sîntana de Mureş (Romania), North Thracians, whose racial unity had already undergone dilution from all quarters, ceased to be separately identifiable. The horizon has been noted from the Don in the east to Transylvania in the west. The eponymous cemetery at Chernyakhov, near Tripolye on the middle Dnieper, is dated by finds from the 2nd to the 5th century. In Muntenia its flowering, if not its whole existence, lies within the 4th century before the Hun arrival (Mitrea and Preda 1966). In Moldavia dating depends on how far the Carpic culture can be considered a separate entity after the Gothic arrival (Bichir 1976a, 144; Zelenchuk *et al.* 1974, 53ff.). There are striking pottery analogies from sites far distant from one another, but a recent analysis of non-ferrous metals distinguishes east and west zones (Chernykh 1972). Whether there is any overall ethnic basis for the horizon or whether it represents a varying amalgam of invaders and a Thracian or other substratum, all 'barbarians' but in different ways reflecting the influence of the Roman world, it is generally agreed that, at least west of the Dniester, a Thracian element remained to make its contribution (Rikman 1969).

The Hero in Thracian religion

The archaeological evidence for what may be considered Thracian religious beliefs, however little we understand them, has been a recurrent theme in this study as a means of tracing the national composition and continuity of the Thracian people. The individual components are rarely, if ever, peculiar to the Thracians alone, but as a whole they contribute substantially towards the Thracian identity, still only partly within our comprehension and consequently speculative.

The sun-fire-hearth cult manifest in the Carpatho–Balkans from the Neolithic period onwards – excepting an apparent hiatus in the EBA – was joined in the late Chalcolithic era by the horns symbol of a steppe stockbreeding cult. This symbol of power and potency, appearing in other forms elsewhere, as in Anatolia and Crete, continued to be used by the Thracians until the loss of their identity. Often dictating the form of personal ornaments and used especially as a 'decoration' on large storage jars, it seems to have had a protective function. By the end of the Bronze Age a very substantial degree of syncretism had been achieved between these two major cults; the Craiova bull heads and perhaps the Derroni coins show its continuance into the historic period. No doubt at different times in different regions the original meanings of the various symbols were forgotten, but continued as a superstition, stronger than but not unlike our lucky horseshoe.

From the EBA, when the Thracian identity begins to emerge, for several millennia their religion was virtually aniconic. The crude figurines which are a minor thread in the cult pattern appear at present as some lower form of magic, possibly stemming from Chalcolithic survivals. By the LBA the concept of the hero or tribal ancestor developed and was linked with beliefs in an afterlife; but he was not portrayed until an alien art evolved his iconography. The female fertility principle, never dominant after the Chalcolithic era, is even harder to trace because of its apparent lack of any specific symbol, although it, too, may be represented in the horns, a feature of male and female cattle, and be an indivisible part of the cults of the sun and of springs and rivers.

Thracian religion is further confused by the Greek viewpoint through which it was first and is still most commonly studied. The reported worship of Ares, Dionysos and Artemis (Hdt V, 7) only reflects on a superficial level a passion for fighting, drinking and hunting. The underlying implication of ecstasy, fertility and rebirth in the mention of Dionysos is almost certainly true of Thracian religion in

155 The obverse of this silver dekadrachm of the Derroni tribe, occupying land between the Vardar and Strymon, syncretizes the horned animal and solar cults by what may be Apollo in the sun chariot, the solar aspect emphasized by the rayed sun above the ox. Diam. 38 mm; Wt 40.51 gr.

156 Bendis, detail from an Attic stele.

its mystery aspect, but was not embodied in individual gods and goddesses. The Greeks of Histria and Odessos, where Greco–Thracian relations were close, acknowledged a Thracian supreme 'Great God', but this Greek interpretation did not necessarily mean the Thracians worshipped one they viewed in anthropomorphic terms. The abstract and aniconic nature of the Dacian sanctuaries also argues against any such personalization. The tribal ancestor-hero-protector may have been the highest personal concept in Thracian religion, corresponding approximately to a patron saint in Christianity or even to the supreme intercessor, the Virgin. As with early Christianity and Islam, what was higher could not be portrayed; we do not know how it was conceived. The Getai shooting their arrows at the sky during a thunderstorm to warn off an apparent enemy of their one god (Hdt. IV, 94) suggests, like 155 the Derroni coin, a continuance of solar worship (Gocheva 1978).

Among deities the Greeks regarded as Thracian, there is the riddle of the goddess Bendis, worshipped by Thracians in Attica, but documented in Thracian lands only in Hellenistic Bithynia and a small area of Roman Aegean Thrace – Philippi, Drama and Thasos (Collart 1937, 442, n.1). Bendis appears essentially as a healing deity quite unconnected with the mounted Thracian hero. Was she developed from the tradition of noble priestess-healer, of which evidence appears in rich South Thracian female burials, especially by the numerous Hellenized Thracian slaves from Bithynia and Aegean Thrace in Athens and Piraeus? It is possible. The official cult in Athens did not last long and was absorbed into that of Artemis; eventually, as they became Hellenized, among the Thracians of Attica too. In Hellenistic South Thrace, through the influence of Byzantion, her attributes as a saviour and healer were absorbed by Phosphoros or Hecate or by the

157 Local stone votive tablet of Diana, from Sandanski. Ht 38 cm. Relief carvings of Artemis-Diana appear on the rocky lower slopes of the acropolis of Philippi. The cult was carried, probably by Greek or Roman traders, up the Strymon valley and adopted along the middle reaches of the river by local Thracians.

more fundamentally Thracian Three Nymphs of the springs. At   153
Philippi it is Artemis-Diana, not Bendis, who was carved in relief on
rock faces (Collart and Ducrey 1975, 225) or, in the Strymon valley, on
stone tablets.   157

Zalmoxis is another riddle. Herodotos (IV, 94–6) draws him as
possibly a form of divine or semi-divine intercessor. We do not know
how representative this cult was, nor its relation to Orphic or other
Thracian mystery cults.

There are several versions of the legend of the life and death of
Rhesus, through the Iliad the earliest Thracian hero-ancestor known to
us. A late version (Philostratos, *Heroica*, 691) speaks of him as still
living, breeding horses, marching in armour and hunting, at a shrine in
the Rhodopes where wild animals offered themselves as a sacrifice
(Porter 1929, xxv). Early this century a similar legend was current near
Pirdop on the south foothills of the Stara Planina of stags offering
themselves at the shrine of St Elia, a mountain saint of clearly pagan
ancestry (Mutafchiev 1915). Rhesus was also said to ward off plague
from his frontiers, embodying the apotropaic aspect of the hero.

One of the earliest examples of Greco–Thracian art, the 6th-century
Derroni coin, is replete with Thracian symbolism. Later, as Greek   155
ideas of anthropomorphic art spread among the South Thracian rulers,
the Thracian Hero appeared in the form of Herakles, a mortal who was   119
admitted to the Olympian pantheon after superhuman labours and who
also fathered peoples. By about the mid-4th century Thracian art had
sufficiently mastered the new style to depict an authentic Thracian
rather than Greek hero on the Letnitsa plaques – as a great hunter and
master of wild animals, a mighty warrior, the possessor of many horses,   158–162
the chief of a numerous tribe and as fathering a progeny.

158–162 Aspects of the Thracian Hero depicted on the Letnitsa plaques (p. 108). A rounded plaque shows him as a mighty hunter, spearing a boar, a dead wolf beneath his horse's hooves. Others use a symbol, usually inserted into the space at the Hero's back, to indicate the range of his powers, perhaps further emphasized by the horns motif edging. Hts 5 cm.

158 With a cup in hand and a bear behind, he is shown as a great drinker and the master of wild animals. 159 His power in battle is demonstrated by brandishing a spear with a bow behind. 160 A horse's head tells of his wealth and possession of many horses. 161 One of two plaques on which he appears with a man's head, another showing a woman's, to indicate his numerous tribe. 162 His ancestral role of tribal progenitor.

During the late Hellenistic period the iconography of the Hero began to crystallize into the forms so widespread in South Thrace in the Roman period. By far the commonest art form was a carving in relief on a stone tablet, normally 30–40 by 20–30 cm. G. Katsarov (1938) identified three main groups, with many subdivisions. In one the mounted hero rides slowly towards a woman, an altar or a tree round which a serpent is coiled. In a second the hero with his dog gallops to attack a boar emerging from a similar tree, sometimes preceded or replaced by an altar. In a third, effectively a variant of the second, he is returning from the hunt, holding up a deer. Other figures appear on some tablets and there are many variations; the boar, for instance, may be replaced by a lion.

The iconography of the first is unquestionably Greek. The second has a probably Greco–Persian ancestry in the *c.* 400 BC stelai of the Daskylion satrapy, reaching the north Aegean and west Pontic coasts via Byzantion, but its analogies with the Letnitsa plaques and wide popularity in the Roman period show the correspondence to Thracian ideology. There are difficulties of interpretation in both. The hero is mounted, as he was since the LBA, but whether the horse has a chthonic significance as well as being a symbol of rank and power we do not know. The boar was a hero's quarry in Greek eyes with its

163–165 G. Katsarov identified three main iconographical groups of the Thracian Hero:

163 Riding towards an unidentified woman. Ht 51 cm. From a sanctuary in Odessos. 2nd–1st century BC.

164 The Hero gallops with his dog to spear a boar emerging from behind a tree round which a serpent is coiled. Ht 19 cm. Amphipolis, 2nd century AD.

165 The Hero-Hunter holds up a deer at which his dogs snatch. Fragment from Daskalovo (*Ill. 150*). First half of 3rd century AD.

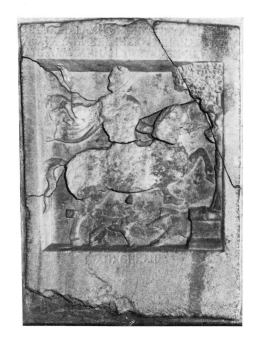

166 *Left*: Family funerary stele from Piperitsa, middle Strymon valley. The appearance of the Thracian Hero on funerary stelai in the 2nd to 3rd century, either representing or accompanying Roman-style portraits of the newly dead, symbolized their heroization, thus achieving immortality and a position to benefit the living.

167 *Right*: Mutilated Hero stele from Galata. Ht 77 cm. After Theodosius' Edict of Thessalonica the Hero *Karabazmos* sanctuary at Galata, like many others, was destroyed and a Christian basilica built on its ruins. Excavation has shown that tablets dedicated to the Hero were taken before the altar, defaced and then reused upside down as paving stones.

Herakleian and Calydonian associations; it was also sacred to Artemis and generally a chthonic beast among all Indo–European peoples. The tree must be a tree of life and symbol of fertility. The serpent may symbolize immortality since it is neither attacked nor feared by the Hero and may incorporate or have the apotropaic aspect which, apart from its Asklepian association, led to its representation on storage vessels and which the Balkan house-snake still has today. The woman in the first group derives from a goddess but in Thracian eyes may have symbolized the Hero's homecoming to effect the continuance of the tribe or dynasty, a concept more explicitly rendered at Letnitsa.

These votive tablets were made in their thousands by the same craftsmen who portrayed the Greco–Roman pantheon for their customers. Many anepigraphic, they may also be addressed to the Hero with or without a Thracian epithet of local or wider application, notably Pirmeroula, variously spelled and recorded from Danubian Thrace to the Mesta valley, or simply to the god with whom the Hero was syncretized – chiefly Asklepios or Apollo the Healer but also Dionysos, Sabazios and others. When funerary stelai became common in South Thrace in the Roman period the dead man was often depicted as the mounted hero to symbolize his immortality as a 'new hero' who might exert a beneficent influence on the living. The majority are dated stylistically to the 2nd–3rd century, but there was continuity from their first appearances until the Edict of Thessalonica in 380, after which the Christians savagely destroyed the richer and more accessible shrines and broke the tablets. Ironically, after the Slavs had completed the Roman and Gothic work of destroying the Thracian people and a representation of an heroic ancestor of an extinct tribe or family had lost all its original meaning, the mediaeval acceptance of Christianity caused many surviving tablets to be considered icons of Christian saints, notably St George and St Demetrius to whose original

iconography they may have contributed. At Glava Panega, un-
discovered during the early Christian onslaught on paganism, the
tablets dedicated to Asklepios and the Hero became identified with St
George and as late as 1907 peasants still made pilgrimages to seek cures
at the Hero's shrine on St George's Day (Vulić 1941–8). Other
instances include: one tablet used as an icon in a private house in
Plovdiv (*IGB* 973); another built in the belltower of the church of St
George at Izvorovo, some 50 km east of Plovdiv (Kazarow 1958); a
third in the wall near the main gateway to the mediaeval citadel at Ainos
(Casson 1926, Fig. 98; Erzen 1973, Fig. 2). In 1968 I saw one fixed to
the outer wall of the metropolis of Kalambaka in Thessaly.

Whether as Prince Marko or as St George, a mounted hero
continued to be revered and Byzantium carried the iconography as well
as Old Church Slavonic to the early Russian church. Mediaeval
Christianity syncretized the mounted Hero with St George slaying the   168
dragon; the tree and serpent had unacceptable associations but the boar
simply received a new image. In time there came another change. In
1974 in a once Thracian area of the Ukraine a display of modern
ceramics included a plaque depicting the mounted Hero spearing a
dragon, the Hero, unmistakably identified by the hammer and sickle
on his army helmet. The Thracian legacy to European culture has still
to be comprehended and assessed.

168 18th-century icon of
St George from Turnovo.
In official Christianity
Greco-Thracian heroes
were replaced by saints, in
the case of St George with
a basically similar but
suitably amended
iconography. In later
times, even into the
present century, surviving
tablets came to be
regarded as icons of St
George.

Abbreviations

AAA	Archaeologika Analekta ex Athenon	*IOSPE*	*Inscriptiones orae Septentrionalis Ponti Euxini*
AAP(A)	*Acta antiqua Philippopolitana (studia archaeologica)*, ed. D. P. Dimitrov *et al*, Sofia 1963	*IVAD*	Izvestiya na Varnenskoto arheologichesko Drujestvo
ABSA	Annual of the British School at Athens	*Iz. Dechev*	*Izsledvaniya v chest na Akad. D. Dechev*, ed. B. Beshevliev and V. Georgiev, Sofia 1958
AJA	American Journal of Archaeology		
AMN	Acta Musei Napocensis (Cluj)	*KSIAK*	Kratkie soobshcheniya Instituta arkheologii (Kiev)
AO	Arkheologicheskie Otkritiya		
AR	Archeologické Rozhledy	*KSIAM*	Kratkie soobshcheniya Instituta arkheologii (Moscow)
Arch. Iug.	Archaeologia Iugoslavica		
Arh.	Arheologiya (Sofia)	*KSIIMK*	Kratkie soobshcheniya Instituta istorii materialnoi kultury
Arh. Mold.	Arheologia Moldovei (Iaşi)		
AS	Anatolian Studies	*KSOGAM*	Kratkie soobshcheniya . . . Odesskogo gosudarstvennogo arkheologicheskogo muzeya
ASPR	American School of Prehistoric Research		
Baden Symposium	*Symposium über die Enstehung und Chronologie der Badener Kultur*, ed. B. Chropovský, Bratislava 1973	*MASP*	Materialy po arkheologii Severnogo Prichernomorya (Odessa)
BASEE	Bulletin d'archéologie sud-est européenne	*MCA*	Materiale şi Cercetări Arheologice
		Megalitite	Trakiiski Pametnitsi I : *Megalitite v Trakiya*, ed. I. Venedikov and A. Fol, Sofia 1976
BRGK	Bericht der Römische-Germanische Kommission		
CIL	*Corpus Inscriptionum Latinarum*	*Mem. Ant.*	Memoria Antiquatis (Piatra Neamţ)
ESA	Eurasia Septentrionalis Antiqua	*MIA*	Materialy i Issledovaniya po Arkheologii SSSR
European Community	*The European Community in Later Prehistory : studies in honour of C. F. C. Hawkes*, ed. J. Boardman *et al.*, London 1971	*MPK*	Muzei i Pametnitsi na Kulturata
		Nitra Commission	*Kommission für das Aeneolithikum und die ältere Bronzezeit in Nitra*, ed. A. Točik, Bratislava 1961
GNBMP	Godishnik na Narodnata biblioteka i muzei v Plovdiv		
GSU	Godishnik na Sofiiskiya Universitet	*Pulpudeva*	Pulpudeva : semaines philippopolitaines de l'histoire et de la culture thrace (Sofia)
Hallstatt Symposium	*Symposium zu Problemen der jüngeren Hallstattzeit in Mitteleuropa*, ed. B. Chropovský, Bratislava 1974		
		PZ	Prähistorische Zeitschrift
		SA	Sovetskaya Arkheologiya
IBAD	Izvestiya Bulgarskoto Arheologichesko Drujestvo	*SAI*	Svod arkheologicheskikh istochnikov Arkheologiya SSSR
IBAI	Izvestiya na Bulgarskiya Arheologicheski Institut	*SCIV(A)*	Studii şi cercetări de istorie veche (1974–) şi arheologie
IBID	Izvestiya na Bulgarskoto Istorichesko Drujestvo	*Slov. Arch.*	Slovenská Archeológia
		Thraco–Dacica	*Recueil d'études à l'occasion du II*[e] *Cong. Internat. de Thracologie*, ed. C. Preda *et al.* Bucarest 1976
IGB	*Inscriptiones Graecae in Bulgaria repertae*		
IIAK	Izvestiya Imperatorskoi Arkheologicheskoi kommissii	*VDI*	Vestnik drevnei istorii
		1st Balkan Congress	*Actes du 1*[er] *Congrès International des études balkaniques et sud-est européennes*, vol. 2, Sofia 1969.
INMV	Izvestiya na Narodniya muzei, Varna		

Bibliographical references

Major general works of reference such as the Cambridge Ancient History and Pauly-Wissowa are additional to the following, as are T. Sulimirski's invaluable guides to recent Soviet archaeological literature in Bulletins 6–11 (1966–74) of the Institute of Archaeology of the University of London. J. Wiesner, *Die Thraker*, Stuttgart 1963, is only partly outdated and remains a valuable contribution.

References to Greek and Latin sources are in the text.

Where known, a later western-language version of a book earlier written in a south-east European one has been substituted.

The preponderance of recent publications selected partly reflects increased interest in Thracian studies, but most have full references to earlier works to facilitate more detailed research.

References to sites and cultures appearing in more than one chapter are usually limited to the first mention.

It must be emphasized that many of the books as well as a number of articles cover much wider aspects than the reference implies.

Chapter 1 (Pages 14–21)

ARTEMENKO, I. I. 1974. *SA* 1974/4, 12ff.
BIBIKOV, S. N. 1953. *MIA* 38.
CHERNYKH (ČERNYCH), E. N. 1966. *MIA* 132. –1974. *Thracia* 3, 379ff. –1978. *Proc. Prehist. Soc.* 44, 203ff.
DUMITRESCU, H. 1961. *Dacia n.s.* 5, 69ff.
GAUL, J. H. 1948 *The Neolithic Period in Bulgaria*, *ASPR* 16, Cambridge, Mass.
GEORGIEV, G. I. 1967. *Arch. Aust.* 42, 90ff.
IONESCU, B. 1974. *SCIV* 25/1, 115ff.
KLEIN, L. S. 1968. *Problemy Arkheologii* 1, Leningrad, 5ff.
MERPERT, N. YA. AND E. N. CHERNYKH 1972. *AO* 1971, Moscow, 553f.–1974. *Voprosy Istorii* 1974/6, 208ff.
NIKOLOV, B. and V. I. GEORGIEV 1970. *Arh.* 12/3, 1ff.
PASSEK, T. S. 1949. *MIA* 10.
PIGGOTT, S. 1965. *Ancient Europe*, Edinburgh.
RADUNTSCHEVA, A. n.d. (*c.* 1975). *Die prähistorische Kunst in Bulgarien*, Sofia.
RENFREW, C. 1969. *Proc. Prehist. Soc.* 35, 12ff.

SERGEEV, G. P. 1963. *SA* 1963/1, 135ff.
TODOROVA, H. 1973. *MPK* 1973/4, 5ff. –1976. *MPK* 1976/2, 12ff.
TRINGHAM, R. 1971. *Hunters, Fishers and Farmers of Eastern Europe*, London.

Chapter 2 (Pages 22–39)

ANGELOV, N. 1958 in *Iz. Dechev*, 389ff.
BERCIU, D. 1961. *Dacia n.s.* 5, 123ff. –1962. *Dacia n.s.* 6, 397ff.
BERNABÒ-BREA, L. 1964. *Poliochni* I, Rome.
BICHIR, G. 1964. *Dacia n.s.* 8, 67ff.
BLEGEN, C. W. 1963. *Troy and the Trojans*, London.
BLEGEN, C. W. *et al.* 1950–58. *Troy* I–IV, Princeton, N.J.
BOGNÁR-KUTZIÁN, I. 1963. *The Copper Age Cemetery of Tiszapolgár-Basatanya*, Budapest. –1972. *The Early Copper Age Tiszapolgár Culture in the Carpathian Basin*, Budapest. –1973 in *Baden Symposium*, 31ff.
BONEV, A. G. 1977. *Arh.* 19/4, 11ff.
CHERNYKH, E. N. 1974. *Thracia* 3, 379ff.
DENNELL, R. W. and D. WEBLEY 1975. *Palaeoeconomy*, ed. E. S. Higgs, Cambridge, 97ff.
DJAMBAZOV, N. and R. KATINCHAROV 1974. *IBAI* 34, 107ff.
DUMITRESCU, V. 1957. *Dacia n.s.1*, 90ff. –1974. *Arte preistorică în România*, Bucarest.
DUMITRESCU, V. *et al.* 1954. *Hăbăşeşti*, Bucarest.
FLORESCU, M. 1965. *Dacia n.s.* 9, 69ff.
FLORESCU, M. and C. BUZDUGAN 1972. *Arh. Mold.* 7, 103ff.
FRENZEL, B. 1967 in *World Climate from 8000 to 0 BC*, ed. J. S. Sawyer, London, 99ff.
GEORGIEV, G. I. 1963. *IBAI* 26, 157ff.
GEORGIEV, G. I. and N. ANGELOV 1957. *IBAI* 21, 41ff.
GEORGIEV, G. I. *et al.* (ed.) 1978. *Studia Praehistorica* 1–2, Sofia.
HÁJEK, L. 1961 in *Nitra Commission*, 59ff.
IVANOV, I. 1974. *MPK* 1974/2–3, 44ff. –1975. *INMV* 11(26), 1ff.
KALICZ, N. 1968. *Die Frühbronzezeit in Nord-Ost Ungarn*, Budapest.
KATINCHAROV, R. 1974. *Arh.* 16/1, 1ff.
KOZLOVSKA, V. 1926 in *Tripilska kultura na Ukraini*, ed. V. Kozlovska and P. Kurinny, Kiev.

LAMB, W. 1936. *Excavations at Thermi in Lesbos*, Cambridge.

LEAHU, V. 1966. *Cultura Tei*, Bucharest.

MAKARENKO, M. 1926. in *Tripilska kultura na Ukraini*, ed. V. Kozlovska and P. Kurinny, Kiev.

MARGOS, A. 1961. *IVAD* 12, 128ff.–1965a. *INMV* 1 (16), 59ff.–1965 b. *Arh.* 7/1, 57ff.

MARGOS, A. and G. TONCHEVA 1962. *IVAD* 13, 1ff.

MERPERT, N. Ya. 1969. *1st Balkan Congress*, 235ff.

MIKOV, V. 1948 *Razkopki i Prouchvaniya* 1, 7ff. –1958. *Zlatnoto sukrovishte ot Vulchi Trun*, Sofia.

MIKOV, V. and N. DJAMBAZOV 1960. *Devetashkata Peshtera*, Sofia.

MORINTZ, S. and P. ROMAN. 1973. in *Baden Symposium*, 259ff.

MOZSOLICS, A. 1965–66. *BRGK* 46–47, 1ff.

NESTOR, I. 1927–32. *Dacia* 3–4, 226ff. –1953. *SCIV* 4/1–2, 69ff. –1955. *SCIV* 6/4, 497ff.

NIKOLOV, B. 1976. *Arh.* 18/3, 38ff.

PASSEK, T. S. 1949. *MIA* 10.

PETKOV, N. 1964. *Arh.* 6/1, 48ff.

POPOV, R. 1930–31. *IBAI* 6, 89ff.

RENFREW, C. 1971. *Antiquity* 45, 276.

ROMAN, P. 1976. *Cultura Coţofeni*, Bucarest. –1977. *The Late Copper Age Coţofeni Culture of South-East Europe, BAR(S)* 32, Oxford.

SCHLIEMANN, H. 1880. *Ilios*, London.

SHMAGLY, N. M. and I. T. CHERNYAKOV 1970. *MASP* 6, 5ff.

SPERLING, J. W. 1976. *Hesperia* 45/4, 305ff.

TELEGIN, A. Ya. 1973. *Seredno-Stogivska kultura epoha midi*, Kiev.

THEOCHARIS, D. 1971. *Prehistory of Eastern Macedonia and Thrace*, Athens.

TODOROVIĆ, J. 1973. *Arch. Iug. 4, 23ff.*

TONCHEVA, G. 1973. in *Baden Symposium*, 471ff.

VULPE, A. 1960. *Dacia n.s.* 4, 319ff. –1961. *Dacia n.s.* 5, 105ff. –1964. *Arh. Mold.* 2–3, 127ff.

ZBENOVICH, V. G. 1973 in *Baden Symposium*, 513ff.

ZIRRA, V. 1960. *MIA po arkheologii Yugo-Zapada SSSR i Rumynskoi NR*, Kishinev, 97ff.

Ezero, the Dipsis tell – main references consulted:

GEORGIEV, G. I. 1961 in *L' Europe à la fin de l'âge de pierre*, ed. J. Böhm and S. J. De Laet, Prague, 45ff. –1966. *Arh.* 8/3 10ff.–1967. *Arch. Aust.* 42, 90ff.

GEORGIEV, G. I. AND N. Ya. MERPERT 1965. *IBAI* 28, 129ff. –1966. *Antiquity* 40, 33ff.

KATINCHAROV, R. 1974. *Arh.* 16/1, 1ff. –1975. *Arh.* 17/2, 1ff.

MERPERT, N. Ya. 1963. *KSIAM* 93, 24ff. –1965. *KSIAM* 100, 19ff. –1966. *Sborník Národniho muzea*, Prague, 20–A. 1–2, 109ff. –1969 in *1st Balkan Congress*, 235ff. –1970. *AO* 1969, Moscow, 440ff. –1972 in *Novoe v Arkheologii*, Moscow, 49ff. –1976. *SA* 1976/3, 341.

MERPERT, N. Ya. and E. N. CHERNYKH 1972. *AO* 1971, Moscow, 553ff. –1973. *AO* 1972, Moscow, 500f. –1974. *Voprosy Istorii* 1974/6, 208ff.

MERPERT, N. Ya. and G. I. GEORGIEV 1973 in *Baden Symposium*, 215ff.

Chapter 3 (Pages 40–60)

ALEXANDRESCU, A. D. 1966. *Dacia n.s.* 10, 119ff.

ARTEMENKO, I. I. 1965. *MIA* 130, 110ff. –1967. *MIA* 148.

BADER, T. 1972. *SCIV* 23/4, 509ff.

BALAGURI, E. A. 1969. *SA* 1969/2, 147ff.

BALKANSKI, I. 1976. *Pulpudeva* 1, 168ff.

BERCIU, D. and E. COMŞA 1956. *MCA* 2, 7ff.

BEREZANSKAYA, S. S. 1972. *Sredny period bronzogo veka v severnoi Ukraine*, Kiev.

BICHIR, G. 1964. *Dacia n.s.* 8, 67ff.

BLEGEN, C. W. *et al.* 1950–58. *Troy*, Princeton, N.J.

BOGNÁR-KUTZIÁN, I. 1972. *The Early Copper Age Tiszapolgár Culture in the Carpathian Basin*, Budapest.

CASSON, S. 1926. *Macedonia, Thrace and Illyria*, Oxford.

CHERNYKH, E. N. 1974. *Thracia* 3, 379ff.

CHICHIKOVA (ČIČIKOVA), M. 1972. *Thracia* 1, 79ff.

CHIDIOŞAN, N. 1968. *Dacia n.s.* 12, 155ff.

COLES J. M. and A. F. HARDING 1979. *The Bronze Age in Europe*, London.

CRIŞAN, I. H. 1961. *MCA* 7.

DETEV, P. 1968. *Apulum* 7/1, 61ff.

DJAMBAZOV, N. and R. KATINCHAROV 1974. *IBAI* 34, 107ff.

DUMITRESCU, V. 1961. *Necropola de incineraţie din epoca bronzului de la Cîrna*, Bucarest. –1971. *BASEE* 2, 108.

FLORESCU, M. *et al.* 1971. *Mem. Ant.* 3, 157ff.

FRENCH, D. H. 1965. *AS* 15, 34.

GIMBUTAS, M. 1957. *Proc. Prehist. Soc.* 22, 143ff. –1965. *Bronze Age Cultures in Central and Eastern Europe*, The Hague.

GIZDOVA, N. 1974. *Thracia* 3, 115ff.

HÁJEK, L. 1961. *Nitra Commission*, 59ff.

HÄNSEL, B. 1968. *Beiträge zur Chronologie der mittleren Bronzezeit im Karpatenbecken*, Bonn.

HOREDT, K. 1960. *Dacia n.s.* 4, 107ff.

HOREDT, K. and C. SERAPHIN 1971. *Die prähistorische Siedlung auf dem Wietenberg bei Sighisoara-Schassburg*, Bonn.

KACSÓ, C. 1975. *Dacia n.s.* 19, 45ff.

KARAIOTOV, I. 1978. reported at Bulg. Nat. Arch. Conf. in *Arh.* 20/1, 57.

KATINCHAROV, R. 1972. *Thracia* 1, 43ff.

LAZAROV, M. 1974. *Thracia* 3, 107ff. –1975. *Potunalata flotiliya*, Varna.

MACQUEEN, J. G. 1968. *AS* 18, 169ff.

MELLAART, J. 1968. *AS* 18, 187ff.

MERHARDT, G. von 1952. *Festschrift des Römisch-Germanischen Zentralmuseum in Mainz* II, 1ff.

MIHAILOV, G. 1972. *Trakite*, Sofia.

MIKOV, V. 1928–29. *IBAI* 5, 330f. –1937–39. *GPNBM*, 55ff. –1970. *Arh.* 12/3, 48ff.

MIKOV, V. and N. DJAMBAZOV 1960. *Devetashkata Peshtera*, Sofia.

MOZSOLICS, A. 1965–66. *BRGK* 46–47, 1ff. –1967. *Bronzefunde des Karpatenbeckens*, Budapest. –1973. *Bronze- und Goldfunde des Karpatenbeckens*, Budapest.

NAIDENOVA, V. 1977. *Arh.* 19/1, 56.
NESTOR, I. 1955. *SCIV* 6/3–4, 497ff.
ORDENTLICH, I. 1963. *Dacia n.s.* 7, 125ff.
ORDENTLICH, I. and C. KACSÓ 1970. *SCIV* 21/1, 49ff.
PETRESCU-DÎMBOVIŢA, M. 1977. *Depozitele de bronzuri din România*, Bucarest.
POLLA, B. 1958. *AR* 10, 511ff.
RADUNCHEVA, A. 1970. *IBID* 27, 213ff.
RENFREW, C. 1970. *Antiquity* 44, 131ff.
RUSU, M. 1963. *Dacia n.s.* 7, 184ff.
SAFRONOV, V. A. 1968. *Problemy Arkheologii* 1, Leningrad, 75ff.
SANDARS, N. K. 1971 in *European Community*, 3ff.
STOYANOVA–SERAFIMOVA, D. 1970. *Arh.* 12/2, 69ff.
SULIMIRSKI, T. 1968. *Corded Ware and Globular Amphorae NE of the Carpathians*, London. –1970. *Prehistoric Russia*, London.
SVESHNIKOV, I. K. 1965. *MIA* 130, 86ff.
SZÉKELY, Z. 1955. *SCIV* 6, 854ff.
TASIĆ, N. 1974. in *Praistorija Vojvodine*, B. Brukner *et al.*, Novi Sad, 185ff.
VLADÁR, J. 1973. *Slov. Arch.* 21/2, 253ff.
VULPE, A. 1975. *Dacia n.s.* 19, 69ff.

Chapter 4 (Pages 61–75)

AKHANOV, I. I. 1961. *SA* 1961/1, 139ff.
ALADJOV, D. 1969. *Arh.* 11/4, 63ff.
ALEXANDRESCU, A. D. 1973. *Dacia n.s.* 17, 77ff. –1974. *Thracia* 3, 47ff.
BERCIU, D. and E. COMŞA 1956. *MCA* 2, 7ff.
BLEGEN, C. W. 1963. *Troy and the Trojans*, London.
CHERNYAKOV, I. T. 1964. *KSIAM* 102, 18ff. –1966. *KSIAM* 106, 99ff.
CHICHIKOVA (ČIČIKOVA), M. 1972. *Thracia* 1, 79ff.
DELEV, P. 1975. *Studentski Prouchvaniya* 3, Sofia, 81ff.
DERGACHEV, V. A. 1975. *Bronzovye predmety XIII–VIII vv. do n.e. iz Dnestrovskogo Prutskogo mezhdunarechya*, Kishinev.
DETEV, P. 1964. *Arh.* 6/4, 66ff. –1968. *Apulum* 7, 61ff.
DUMITRESCU, V. 1961. *Necropola ... de la Cîrna*, Bucarest.
FLORESCU, A. C. 1964. *Arh. Mold.* 2–3, 143ff.
FLORESCU, M. 1961. *Arh. Mold.* 1, 115ff.
FLORESCU, M. *et al.* 1971. *Mem. Ant.* 3, 157ff.
FOL, A. and I. VENEDIKOV (eds) 1976. *Megalitite*, Sofia.
FRENZEL, B. 1967. in *World Climate from 8000 to 0 BC*, ed. J. S. Sawyer, London, 99ff.
GEORGIEV, G. I. and N. ANGELOV 1957. *IBAI* 22, 45ff.
GRAKOV, B. N. 1971. *Skify*. Moscow.
HÄNSEL, B. 1976. *Beiträge zum regionalen und chronologischen Gliederung der älteren Hallstattzeit an der unteren Donau*, Bonn.
HOREDT, K. 1974. *Hallstatt Symposium*, 205ff.
JEFFERY, L. H. 1976. *Archaic Greece*, London.
KANSU, Ş. A. 1963. *Belleten* 27, 491ff. –1964. *Belleten* 28, 327ff. –1969 *Belleten* 33, 577ff.
KARAIOTOV, V. 1976. *Trakiya* 3, Plovdiv, 74.
KÖYLÜOĞLU, N. 1976. personal communication.
KRIVTSOVA-GRAKOVA, O. A. 1955. *MIA* 46.

KRUPNOV, E. I. 1949. *KSIIMK* 24, 27ff.
LÁSZLÓ, A. 1973. *SCIV* 24/4, 595ff.
LAZAROV, M. 1974. *Thracia* 3, 107ff. –1975. *Potunalata flotiliya*, Varna.
LESKOV, A. M. 1971. *MIA* 177, 75ff.
MARKOVIN, V. I. 1973. *SA* 1973/1, 3ff.
MELYUKOVA, A. I. 1961. *MIA* 96, 5ff.
MERHART, G. von 1956. *Jahrbuch des Röm.-Germ. Zentralmuseums Mainz* 3, 28ff.
MIKOV, V. 1955. *IBAI* 19, 15ff.
MIKOV, V. and N. DJAMBAZOV 1960. *Devetashkata Peshtera*, Sofia.
MORINTZ, S. 1964. *Dacia n.s.* 8. 101ff.
MORINTZ, S. and N. ANGHELESCU 1970. *SCIV* 21/3, 373ff.
MORINTZ, S. 1964. *Dacia n.s.* 8. 101ff.
MOZSOLICS, A. 1973. *Bronze- und Goldfunde des Karpatenbeckens*, Budapest.
NIKOLOV, B. 1964. *Arh.* 6/2, 75ff.
NOVIKOVA, L. A. 1976. *SA* 1976/3, 25ff.
PETRESCU-DÎMBOVIŢA, M. 1953. *MCA* 1, 132ff. –1964. *Arh. Mold.* 2–3, 251ff. –1966. *Arh. Mold.* 4, 345ff. –1977. *Depozitele de bronzuri din România*, Bucarest.
PETRESCU-DÎMBOVIŢA, M. *et al.* 1954. *SCIV* 5/1, 19ff.
POGREBOVA, N. N. 1960. *SA* 1960/4, 76ff.
RUSU, M. 1963. *Dacia n.s.* 7, 184ff.
SHARAFUTDINOVA, I. N. 1968. *SA* 1968/3, 16ff.
SHRAMKO, B. A. 1957. *SA* 1957/1, 178ff.
SMIRNOVA, G. I. 1969. *MIA* 150, 7ff. –1974. *SCIV* 25/3, 359ff.
SNODGRASS, A. M. 1971 in *European Community*, 33ff.
SULIMIRSKI, T. 1970. *Prehistoric Russia*, London.
TALLGREN, A. M. 1934. *ESA* 19, 1ff.
TERENOZHKIN, A. I. 1961. *Predskifsky period na Dneprom pravoberezhe*, Kiev. –1976. *Kimmeritsy*, Kiev.
TODOROVA, H. 1972a. *Thracia* 1, 67ff. –1972b. *Arh.* 14/2, 17ff.
TRIANDAPHYLLOS, D. 1973. *AAA* 6, 241ff.
VENEDIKOV, I. and D. ALADJOV 1976 in *Megalitite*, 52ff.
VENEDIKOV, I. *et al.* 1976 in *Megalitite*, 128ff.
ZAHARIA, E. 1965. *Dacia n.s.* 9, 83ff.

Chapter 5 (Pages 76–87)

ANDRONIKOS, M. 1969. *Vergina* I. Athens.
BERNARD, P. 1964. *Bull. corr. hell.* 88, 77ff.
BOARDMAN, J. 1964. *The Greeks Overseas*, London.
CASSON, S. 1926. *Macedonia, Thrace and Illyria*, Oxford.
DESBOROUGH, V. R. d'A. 1972. *The Greek Dark Ages*, London.
DUŠEK, M. 1974 in *Hallstatt Symposium*, 127ff.
DZIS-RAIKO, G. O. 1963. *MASP*, 2, 36ff.
GALLUS, S. and T. HORVATH 1939. *Un peuple cavalier pré-scythique en Hongrie*, Budapest.
GERGOVA, D. 1977. *Vekove* 1977/1, 47ff.
GOLOBKO, I. D. *et al.* 1965. *KSOGAM* 1963, 68ff.
HASLUCK, F. W. 1910. *Cyzicus*, Cambridge.
HENCKEN, H. 1968a. *Tarquinia, Villanovans and Early*

Etruscans, ASPR 23, Cambridge, Mass. –1968b. *Tarquinia and Etruscan Origins*, London.

HOREDT, K. 1974 in *Hallstatt Symposium*, 205ff.

KAPOSHINA, S. N. 1956. *MIA* 50, 154ff.

KHANENKO, B. I. 1899, 1900. *Drevnosti Pridneprovya* II, III, Kiev.

KOLEV, B. 1965. *Vesti Nar. Muzei Haskovo* 1, 205ff.

KOVPANENKO, G. T. 1971. *MIA* 177, 115ff.

MANTSEVICH (MANZEWITSCH), A. P. 1959. *Acta Arch. Hung.* 9, 315ff.

MELYUKOVA, A. I. 1958. *MIA* 64, 5ff. –1961. *MIA* 96, 5ff. –1972. *SA* 1972/1, 57ff.

MIKOV, V. 1930–31. *IBAI* 6, 153ff. –1940–41. *GPNBM*, 19ff. –1955. *IBAI* 19, 15ff.

MILCHEV, A. 1955. *IBAI* 19, 359ff. –1958 in *Iz. Dechev*, 415ff.

PATEK, E. 1974. in *Hallstatt Symposium*, 337ff.

POPOV, R. 1921. *IBAI* 1, 68ff. –1930–31. *IBAI* 6, 89ff.

SNODGRASS, A. M. 1971. *The Dark Age of Greece*, Edinburgh.

SULIMIRSKI, T. 1959. *Bull. Inst. Arch. London* 2, 45ff.

SZÉKELY, Z. 1966, *Dacia n.s.* 10, 207ff.

TASIĆ, N. 1974 in *Praistorija Vojvodine*, B. Brukner *et al.*, Novi Sad.

TERENOZHKIN, A. I. 1961. *Predskifsky period na Dneprom pravoberezhe*, Kiev.

THOMAS, E. 1956. ed. *Archaeologische Funde in Ungarn*, Budapest.

TONCHEVA, G. 1975. *Studia Thracica* 1, 45ff.

TSONCHEV (CONČEV), D. 1965. *AAP(A)*, 121ff.

VELKOV, I. 1952. *Festschrift R. Egger* I, Klagenfurt, 28ff.

VENEDIKOV, I. and V. BIHODTSEVKI 1972. *IBID* 28, 5ff.

VENEDIKOV, I. and T. GERASIMOV 1975. *Thracian Art Treasures*, London.

VENEDIKOV, I. *et al.* 1976 in *Megalitite*, 128ff.

VULPE, A. 1965. *Dacia n.s.* 9, 107ff. –1970. *Mem. Ant.* 2, 182ff.

Chapter 6 (Pages 88–103)

ALEXANDRESCU, P. 1976. *Thraco-Dacica*, 117ff.

ARTAMONOV, M. I. 1969. *Treasures from Scythian Tombs*, London.

BERCIU, D. 1969. *Arta traco-getică*, Bucarest. –1974. *Contribution à l'étude de l'art thraco-gète*, Bucarest.

BLAVATSKAYA, T. V. 1959. *Ocherki politicheskoi istorii Bospora v V–IV vv. do n.e.*, Moscow.

CRIŞAN, I. H. 1965. *Dacia n.s.* 9, 133ff.

DUŠEK, M. 1966. *Thrakisches Gräberfeld der Hallstattzeit im Chotín*, Bratislava. –1978. *Die Thraker im Karpatenbecken*, Amsterdam.

DZIS-RAIKO, G. A. 1959. *MASP* 2, 36ff.

FILOV (FILOW), B. D. 1934. *Die Grabhügelnekropole bei Duvanlij*, Sofia.

FLORESCU, A. C. 1971. *Cercetări istorice* 2, Iaşi, 103ff.

GERASIMOV, T. 1962. *IBAI* 25, 89ff.

GRAKOV, B. N. 1954. *MIA* 36. –1959. *SA* 1959/1, 259ff. –1971. *Skify*, Moscow.

HÄNSEL, B. 1969. *Germania* 47, 62ff.

ILIESCU, V. 1975 in *Relations between Autochtonous and Migratory Populations in Romania*, ed. M. Constantinescu *et al.*, Bucarest 13ff.

JACOBSTHAL, P. 1944. *Early Celtic Art*, Oxford.

JOVANOVIĆ, B. 1976. *Starinar* 27, 19ff.

KAPOSHINA, S. I. 1956. *MIA* 50, 154ff.

KILIAN-DIRLMEIER, I. 1969. *BRGK* 50, 97ff.

KLINDT-JENSEN, O. 1950. *Acta Arch.* 20, Copenhagen, 119ff. –1953. *Bronzekedelen fra Brå*, Aarhus.

KOVPANENKO, G. T. *MIA* 177, 115ff.

KOZUB, Yu. I. 1974. *Nekropol Olvii V–IV st. do n.e.*, Kiev.

LAZAREVSKY, Ya. 1895. *Zapiski Imp. Russ. Arkh. Obshch.* n.s. 7, 24ff.

LESKOV, A. M. (O.) 1974. *Skarbi kurganiv Khersonshchini*, Kiev.

MAKARENKO, N. 1930. *ESA* 5, 22ff.

MEDOVIĆ, P. 1978. *Naselja starijeg gvozdenog doba u jugoslovenskom podunavlju*, Belgrade.

MONGAIT, A. L. *Archaeology in the USSR*, Harmondsworth.

MORINTZ, S. 1957. *Dacia n.s.* 1, 117ff.

MOZOLEVSKY, B. N. 1972. *SA* 1972/3, 268ff. –1973. in *Skifskie drevnosti*, ed. V. A. Ilinskaya *et al.*, Kiev, 208ff.

NEUSTUPNÝ, E. and J. 1961. *Czechoslovakia*, London.

PÁRDUCZ, M. 1974 in *Hallstatt Symposium*, 311ff.

PÂRVAN, V. 1926. *Getica*, Budapest.

PETRENKO, V. G. 1967 *SAI* D1–4.

PETRESCU-DÎMBOVIŢA, M. and M. DINU. 1975. *Dacia n.s.* 19, 103ff.

PIGGOTT, S. 1965. *Ancient Europe*, Edinburgh.

PIPPIDI, D. M. and D. BERCIU 1965. *Din Istoria Dobrogei* I, Bucarest.

POKROVSKAYA, E. F. 1962. *KSIAK* 12, 73ff. –1973. *SA* 1973/4, 169ff.

POTAPOV, A. 1929. *ESA* 4, 162ff.

POWELL, T. G. E. 1971. in *European Community*, 181ff.

PRUSHEVSKAYA, E. O. 1955 in *Antichniye goroda severnogo Prichernomorya*, ed. V. F. Gaidukevich and M. I. Maksimova, Moscow, 325ff.

ROLLE, R. 1972. *PZ* 47, 59ff.

SANDARS, N. K. 1968 *Prehistoric Art in Europe*, Harmondsworth.

SCHMIDT, H. 1927. *PZ* 18, 1ff.

SHRAMKO (ŠRAMKO), B. A. 1973 in *Skifskie drevnosti*, ed. V. A. Ilinskaya *et al.*, Kiev, 82ff. –1974 in *Hallstatt Symposium*, 469ff.

SPITSYN, A. A. 1906. *IIAK* 19, 157ff.

SPROCKHOFF, E. 1954. *Jahrbuch des Röm.-Germ. Zentralmuseums Mainz* 1, 28ff.

SULIMIRSKI, T. 1970a. *The Sarmatians*, London. –1970b. *Prehistoric Russia*, London.

SVESHNIKOV, I. K. 1968. *SA* 1968/1, 10ff.

SZLANKÓWNA, A. 1936–37. *Swiatowit* 17, 293ff.

TEKHOV, B. V. 1963. *SA* 1963/1, 162ff.

TEODOR, S. 1973. *MCA* 10, 53ff.

TERENOZHKIN, A. I. 1965. *MIA* 130, 211ff.

VASIĆ, R. 1971. *Arch Iug.* 12, 1ff.

VULPE, A. 1967. *Necropole Hallstattiana de la Ferigile*, Bucarest. –1977. *Dacia n.s.* 21, 81ff.

Chapter 7 (Pages 104–118)

ALEXANDRESCU, P. 1971. *SCIV* 22/4, 66off. –1972. *Dacia n.s.* 16, 113ff. –1976 in *Thraco-Dacica*, 117ff. –1977. *Dacia n.s.* 21, 113ff.

ANTONOVA, V. 1973, *Arh.* 15/3, 31ff.

BERCIU, D. 1969. *BRGK* 50, 209ff. –1974. *Contribution à l'étude de l'art thraco-gète*, Bucarest.

BERCIU, D. and E. COMŞA 1956. *MCA* 2, 7ff.

CHANGOVA, J. 1972. *Arh.* 14/4, 33ff.

CHICHIKOVA, M. 1963. *AAP(A)*, 35ff. –1968. *Arh.* 10/4, 22ff. –1969. *IBAI* 31, 45ff.

DANOV, C. M. 1976. *Altthrakien*, Berlin and New York.

DIMITROV, D. P. 1957 in *Arheologicheski otkritiya v Bulgaria*, Sofia, 64ff.

DREMSIZOVA, TS. 1965. *IBAI* 25, 165ff.

DREMSIZOVA-NELCHINOVA, TS. 1967. *Izvestiya Nar. Muzei Shoumen* 4, 57ff. –1972. *I Kongres Bulg. Ist. Drujestvo* I, Sofia, 335ff.

FERGUSON, W. S. 1949. *Hesperia*, supp. 8, 130ff.

FILOV, B. D. 1916–18. *IBAD* 6, 1ff. –1934a. *Die Grabhügelnekropole bei Duvanlij* –1934b. *ESA* 9, 197ff. –1937. *IBAI* 11, 1ff.

GOLDMAN, B. 1963. *Bull. Detroit Inst. Arts* 42/4, 63ff.

HODDINOTT, R. F. 1975. *Bulgaria in Antiquity*, London.

IVANOV, T. 1948. *Razkopki i prouchvaniya* I, 99ff.

KASTELIĆ, J. *et al.* 1965. *Situla art*, Belgrade.

MALKINA, K. 1928. *PZ* 19, 152ff.

MIHAILOV, G. 1972. *Trakite*, Sofia.

MIKOV, V. 1958. *Iz. Dechev*, 668ff.

MIRCHEV, M. 1962. *IBAI* 25, 97ff.–1965. *INMV* 1(16), 33ff. –1969. *INMV* 5(20), 95ff.

NIKOLOV, B. 1967. *Arh.* 9/1, 11ff. –1970. *Obzor* 1970–2, 76ff.

OGNENOVA, L. 1961. *Bull. corr. hell.* 85, 501ff.

PETRE, G. I. 1971. *SCIV* 22/4, 557ff.

PIGGOTT, S. 1965. *Ancient Europe*, Edinburgh.

PREDA, C. 1959. *Dacia n.s.* 3, 179ff.

SCHMIDT, H. 1927. *PZ* 18, 1ff.

SNODGRASS, A. M. *The Dark Age of Greece*, Edinburgh.

TACHEVA-HITOVA, M. 1971. *Arh.* 13/4, 42ff.

VENEDIKOV, I. 1975. *Skrobishteto ot Vratsa*, Sofia.

VENEDIKOV, I. and T. GERASIMOV 1975. *Thracian Art Treasures*, London.

VULPE, A. 1959. *MCA* 5, 363ff.

VULPE, A. and E. POPESCU 1972. *Dacia n.s.* 16, 75ff.

Chapter 8 (Pages 119–130)

CONDURACHI, E. 1954. ed. *Histria* I, Bucarest.

DIMITROV, D. P. and M. ČIČIKOVA 1978. *The Thracian City of Seuthopolis, BAR(S)* 38, Oxford.

DREMSIZOVA, TS. 1955. *IBAI* 19, 61ff.

FILOV (FILOW), B. D. 1934. *Die Grabhügelnekropole bei Duvanlij*, Sofia. –1937a. *IBAI* 11, 1ff. –1937b. *Antiquity* 11, 300ff.

FIRATLI, N. 1964. *Les stèles funéraires de Byzance greco-romaine*, Paris.

GERASIMOV, T. 1955. *IBAI* 19, 123ff. –1959. *IBAI* 22,

111ff. –1960. *IBAI* 23, 165ff. (catalogue also publ. in *Latomus* 3, 1972). –1974. *IBAI* 34, 1ff.

GEROV, B. 1967. *GSU Fakultet Zapadni Filologii* 61/1, 3ff.

GOCHEVA, Z. and M. DOMARADSKI 1976. *Acta Arch. Carpathica* 16, 117ff.

HÄNSEL, B. 1969. *Germania* 47/1–2, 62ff.

HASLUCK, F. W. 1910–11. *ABSA* 17, 76ff.

HEURTLEY, W. A. and T. C. SKEAT 1930–31. *ABSA* 17, 31ff.

HODDINOTT, R. F. 1975. *Bulgaria in Antiquity*, London.

JACOBSTHAL, P. 1944. *Early Celtic Art*, Oxford.

JIVKOVA, L. 1974. *Le tombeau de Kazanlăk*, Sofia and Recklinghausen.

KATSAROV, G. I. 1919. *Spisanie Bulg. Akad. Nauk. (klon. ist. fil.)* 18, 41ff.

KITOV, V. 1977a. *Vekove* 1, 12ff. –1977b. *Obzor* 39, 85ff.

MACRIDY, T, 1913. *Bull. corr. hell.* 37, 355ff.

MANSEL, A. M. 1943. *Türk Tarih Kurumu Yayrilarindan* 6/2, 37ff. –1974. *Thracia* 3, 207ff.

MIHAILOV, G. 1961. *Athenaeum n.s.* 39/1–2, 33ff. –1972. *Trakite*, Sofia.

NIKOLOV, B. 1965. *IBAI* 28, 174ff.

OGNENOVA, L. 1977. *Thracia* 4, 1977ff.

POPOV, R. 1932–33. *IBAI* 7, 349ff.

PROTONOTARIOU, E. 1960. *Thessalika* 3, 29ff.

SCHKORPIL (SKORPIL), H. and K. 1898. *Mogili* Plovdiv.

STRONG, D. E. 1966. *Greek and Roman Gold and Silver Plate*, London.

TODOROVIĆ, J. 1968. *Kelti u jugoistoćnoj Evropi*, Belgrade.

TONCHEVA, G. 1968. *INMV* 4(19), 17ff.

TSANOVA, G. and L. GETOV 1970. *Trakiskata grobnitsa pri Kazanluk*, Sofia. –1975. *Arh.* 15/2, 15ff.

TSONCHEV, D. 1961. *Arh.* 3/4, 44ff. –1963. *Arheologicheski pametnitsi po yujnite sklonove na Panagyurska Sredna Gora*, Sofia.

VELKOV, I. 1932. *Bulgarska Misl* 7, 418. –1937. *IBAI* 11, 117ff. –1942. *Godishnik Nar. Muzei* 7, 37ff.

VELKOV, V. and Z. GOCHEVA 1971. *Arh.* 13/4, 52ff. –1972. *Thracia* 1, 121ff.

VERDIANI, C. 1945. *AJA* 44, 402ff.

Chapter 9 (131–144)

ALEXANDRESCU, A. D. 1974. *Thracia* 3, 56ff.

ALLEN, D. F. 1971. *Archaeologia* 103, 1ff.

BABEŞ, M. 1975. *Dacia n.s.* 19, 125ff. –1978. *Moldova centraleşi de nord în sect. II–I î.e.n.*, Bucarest.

BABEŞ, M. and V. MIHĂILESCU-BÎRLIBA 1970–71. *BRGK* 51–52. 176ff.

BERCIU, D. 1967. *Romania*, London.

CĂPITANU, V. 1976. *Carpica* 8, 49ff.

CĂPITANU, V. and V. URSACHI 1969. *Carpica* 2, 93ff.

CARY, M. and H. SCULLARD 1975. *A History of Rome*, 3rd edn, London.

CHÎTESCU, L. 1976. *Cercetări Arheologice* 2, 155ff.

CONOVICI, N. 1974. *SCIV* 25/2, 295ff.

CRIŞAN, I. H. 1969. *Ceramica Daco-Getica*, Bucarest.

DUMITRESCU, V. 1975. *BASEE* 3, 101.
DZIS-RAIKO, G. A. 1966. *MASP* 5, 163ff.
FEDOROV, G. B. 1960. *MIA* 89, 17ff.
FETTICH, N. 1953. *Acta Arch. Hung.* 3, 127ff.
FLORESCU, A. C. 1971. *Cercetări Istorice*, Iaşi, 2, 103ff.
FLORESCU, R. 1968. *L'art des Daces*, Bucarest.
GAIDUKEVICH, V. F. and S. A. KAPOSHINA 1951. *SA* 1951, 162ff.
GLODARIU, I. 1976. *Dacian Trade with the Hellenistic and Roman World*, *BAR(S)* 8, Oxford.
KNIPOVICH, T. N. 1966. *VDI* 1966/2, 142ff.
KUZMENKO, V. I. and M. S. SINITSYN 1963. *KSOGAM* 79ff. –1966. *MASP* 5, 56ff.
LÁSZLÓ, A. 1969. *Arh. Mold.* 6, 65ff.
MARCHENKO, K. K. 1974. *VDI* 1974/2, 149ff.
MELYUKOVA, A. I. 1958. *MIA* 64, 90ff. –1969. *MIA* 150, 61ff. –1971. *MIA* 177. 39ff.
MILCHEV, A. 1973. *Arh.* 15/1, 1ff.
MINNS, E. H. 1913. *Scythians and Greeks*, Cambridge.
MLADENOVA, Ya. 1963 in *Apoloniya*, ed. I. Venedikov, Sofia, 293ff.
NESTOR, I. 1949. *Studii* 2/1, Bucarest, 116ff. –1950. *SCIV* 1, 93ff.
NICOLĂESCU-PLOPŞOR, C. S. 1945–47. *Dacia* 11–12, 17ff.
ONAIKO, N. A. 1970. *SAI* D1–27.
PÂRVAN, V. 1926. *Getica*, Bucarest.
PETRENKO, V. G. 1961. *MIA* 196, 53ff.
PETRESCU-DÎMBOVIŢA, M. and S. SANIE 1972. *Arh. Mold.* 7, 24ff.
POGREBOVA, N. N. 1958. *MIA* 64, 234ff.
POPESCU, D. 1958. *Dacia n.s.* 2, 157ff.
PREDA, C. 1973. *Monedele Geto-Dacilor*, Bucarest.
ROMANOVSKAYA, M. A. 1969. *MIA* 150, 81ff.
ROSETTI, D. V. 1962. *MCA* 8, 73ff.
ROSTOVTSEFF, M. 1922. *Iranians and Greeks in South Russia*, Oxford.
SALNIKOV, A. G. *MASP* 5, 176ff.
SEDOV, V. V. 1964. *MIA* 163.
SPITSYN, A. A. 1909a. *IIAK* 29, 142ff. –1909b. *ibid.* 18ff.
STRONG, D. E. 1966. *Greek and Roman Gold and Silver Plate*, London.
TEODOR, S. 1969. *Arh. Mold.* 6, 321ff. –1973a. *MCA* 10, 53ff. –1973b. *Studii şi Materiale (Istorie)* 3, Suceava, 37ff. –1974. *Thracia* 3, 151ff.
TODOROVIĆ, J. 1974. *Skordisci*, Novi Sad and Belgrade.
TRETYAKOV, P. N. 1970. ed. *MIA* 70.
TROHANI, G. 1975. *Cercetări Arheologice* 1, 151ff. –1976. *Cercetări Arheologice* 2, 87ff.
URSACHI, V. 1968. *Carpica* 1, 171ff.
VOZNESENSKAYA, G. A. 1972. *MIA* 187, 31ff.
VULPE, A. 1976 in *Thraco-Dacica*, 193ff.
VULPE, A. and E. POPESCU 1976 in *Thraco-Dacica*, 217ff.
VULPE, R. 1957a. *MCA* 3, 227ff. –1957b. *Dacia n.s.* 1, 143ff. 1961. *MCA* 7, 323ff. –1966. *Aşezări Getice din Muntenia*, Bucarest.
VULPE, R. and E. 1924. *Dacia* 1, 166ff. –1927–32. *Dacia* 3–4, 253ff.
VULPE, R. *et al.* 1951. *SCIV* 2/1, 177ff. –1952. *SCIV* 3, 191ff.
VYAZMITINA, M. I. 1969a. *SA* 1969/4, 62ff. –1969b. *MIA* 150, 119ff. –1972. *Zoloto-Balkovsky mogilnik*, Kiev.
ZIRRA, V. 1976 IN *Thraco-Dacica*, 175ff.
ZLATKOVSKAYA, T. D. AND L. L. POLEVOI 1969. *MIA* 150, 39ff.

Chapter 10 (Pages 145–157)

BENADIK, B. 1965. *Germania* 43, 63ff.
BERCIU, I. 1966 in *Cetăţi dacice din sudul Transilvaniei*, M. Macrea *et al.*, Bucarest, 45ff.
BERCIU, I. *et al.* 1965. *Celticum* 20, 115ff.
BICHIR, G. 1976. *Archaeology and History of the Carpi*, *BAR(S)* 16, Oxford.
CRIŞAN, I. H. 1964. *Apulum* 5, 127ff. –1966a. *Materiale dacice din necropola şi aşezarea de la Ciumeşti . . .*, Baia Mare. –1966b. *AMN* 3, 91ff. –1969. *Arh. Mold.* 6, 91ff. –1971. *SCIV* 22/2, 149ff.
DAICOVICIU, C. 1954. *Cetatea dacică de la Piatra Roşie*, Bucarest.
DAICOVICIU, C. and H. 1963. *Sarmizegethusa*, Bucarest.
DAICOVICIU, H. 1972. *Dacia de la Burebista la cucerirea romană*, Cluj.
DAICOVICIU, H. *et al.* 1973. *AMN* 10, 65ff.
ELIADE, M. 1972. *Zalmoxis: The Vanishing God*, Chicago.
FLORESCU, R. 1973. *Adamclisi*, Bucarest.
GAVELA, B. 1977 in *Symposium: Ausklang der Latène-Zivilisation . . .*, ed. B. Chropovský, Bratislava, 47ff.
GLODARIU, I. 1976. *Dacian Trade with the Hellenistic and Roman World*, *BAR(S)* 8, Oxford.
GOSTAR, N. 1969. *Cetăţi dacice din Moldova*, Bucarest.
JOVANOVIĆ, B. 1974 in *Praistorija Vojvodine*, B. Brukner *et al.*, Novi Sad and Belgrade, 277ff.
LUPU, N. 1966 in *Cetăţi dacice din sudul Transilvaniei*, M. Macrea *et al.*, Bucarest, 34ff.
MACREA, M. 1956. *SCIV* 7/1, 119ff. –1958. *Dacia n.s.* 2, 351ff. –1968. *Apulum* 7/1, 171ff. –1969. *Viaţa în Dacia romană*, Bucarest.
MACREA, M. and I. BERCIU 1965. *Dacia n.s.* 9, 201ff.
MACREA, M. *et al.* 1961. *MCA* 7, 362ff. –1962. *MCA* 8, 485ff.
MÓCZY, A. 1974. *Pannonia and Upper Moesia*, London.
NEUSTUPNÝ, E. and J. 1961. *Czechoslovakia*, London.
PÂRVAN, V. 1926. *Getica*, Bucarest. –1928. *Dacia*, Cambridge.
PREDA, C. and A. DOICESCU 1966 in *Histria* II, ed. E. Condurachi.
ROSSI, L. 1971. *Trajan's Column and the Dacian Wars*, London.
RUSSU, I. I. 1959. *Dacia n.s.* 3, 341ff.
RUSU, M. 1969. *BRGK* 50, 267ff.
SMISHKO, M. Yu. 1952. *KSIIMK* 44, 67ff.
SULIMIRSKI, T. 1970. *The Sarmatians*, London. –1976. *Bonner hefte zur Vorgeschichte* 11, 131ff.
WINKLER, I. 1968. *Apulum* 7/1, 207ff.
ZIRRA, V. 1971A. *AR* 23/5, 529ff. –1971b. *Dacia n.s.*

15, 171ff. -1976. *Thraco-Dacica* 175ff.-n.d. *Un cimitir celtic în nord-vestul României*, Baia Mare.

Chapter 11 (Pages 158–168)

ALADJOV, D. 1965. *IBAI* 28, 77ff.

ANGELOV, D. 1971. *Obrazouvane na Bulgarskata narodnost*, Sofia.

BESHEVLIEV, V. 1965. *Prouchvaniye vurhu lichnite imena u Trakite*, Sofia.

BICHIR, G. 1976a. *Archaeology and History of the Carpi, BAR(S)* 16, Oxford. -1976b in *Thraco-Dacica*, 287ff.

BOTOUCHAROVA, L. 1962. *Hommages à Albert Grenier*, ed. M. Renard, Brussels, 317ff.

CHERNYKH, E. N. 1972. *MIA* 187, 66ff.

DAICOVICIU, C. 1958. *Dacia n.s.* 2, 265, n.2.

DAICOVICIU, H. 1975 in *Relations between autochtonous and migratory populations in Romania*, ed. M. Constantinescu *et al.*, Bucarest, 35ff.

DJONOVA, D. 1962. *Arh.* 4/3, 30ff.

DOBRUSKY, V. A. 1897. *Bull. corr. hell.* 21, 119ff.

DOLINESCU-FERCHE, S. 1974. *Aşezări din sec. III şi VI e.n. în sud-vestul Munteniei*, Bucarest.

DUMITRESCU, S. and T. BADER 1967. *AMN* 4, 121ff.

FLOCA, O. *et al.* 1970. *Micia: grupul de cuptoare romane*, Deva.

GAGGERO, G. 1978. *Pulpudeva* 2, 260ff.

GEROV, B. 1952–53. *GSU Filofsko-Istoricheski Fakultet* 47, 1ff. -1968. *GSU Fakultet Zapadni Filologii* 66/2, 121ff.

GLODARIU, I. 1972. *AMN* 9, 119ff.

GUDEA, N. 1978. paper read to 11th Int. Congr. Class. Arch., London.

KAZAROW, G. 1938. *Die Denkmäler des Thrakischen Reitergottes in Bulgarien*, Budapest.

KOUKOULI, Ch. 1969. *AAA* 2, 191ff.

LAZARIDES, D. 1953–54. *Arch. Ephemeris* 1953–54, 235ff.

LYUBENOVA, V. 1974. *Thracia* 3, 369ff.

MACREA, M. 1968. *Apulum* 7/1, 171ff. -1969. *Viaţa în Dacia romană*, Bucarest.

MITREA, B. and C. PREDA 1966. *Necropole din sec. al IV-lea în Muntenia*, Bucarest.

MIYATEV, K. 1928–29. *IBAI* 5, 34ff.

MUSHMOV, N. A. 1928–29. *IBAI* 5, 328ff.

NAJDENOVA, V. 1972. *Thracia* 1, 145ff.

NIKOLOV, D. 1976. *Roman Villa at Chatalka. BAR(S)* 17, Oxford.

NIKOLOV, D. and H. BUYUKLIEV 1967. *Arh.* 9/1, 19ff; *Arh.* 9/3, 10ff.

OVCHAROV, D. 1970. *MPK* 1970/1, 8ff. -1974. *Thracia* 3, 345ff.

PROTASE, D. 1966. *Problema continuăţii în Dacia . . .*, Bucarest. -1971. *Riturile funerare la Daci şi Daco–Romani*, Bucarest. -1973. *Acts of 8th Pre- and Protohist. Congr.*, Belgrade, III, 214ff.

RIKMAN, E. A. 1969. *MIA* 150, 178ff.

RUSSU, I. I. 1967. *AMN* 4, 85ff.

SCORPAN, C. 1967. *Cavalerul trac*, Constanza.

TUDOR, D. 1968a. *Oraşe, tîrguri şi sate în Dacia romană*, Bucarest. -1968b. *Oltenia romană*, Bucarest.

VELKOV, V. 1958 in *Iz. Dechev*, 731ff. -1959. *Gradut v Trakiya i Dakiya prez kusnata antichnost*, Sofia.

VENEDIKOV, I. 1950. *IBAI* 17, 105ff. -1952. *IBAI* 18, 195ff. -1960. *Trakiiskata kolesnitsa*, Sofia.

ZELENCHUK, V. Z. *et al.* 1974. *Drevnyaya Moldaviya*, Kishinev.

Chapter 12 (Pages 169–175)

CASSON, S. 1926. *Macedonia, Thrace and Illyria*, Oxford.

COLLART, P. 1937. *Philippes, ville de Macédoine*, Paris.

COLLART, P. and P. DUCREY 1975. *Philippes I: les reliefs rupestres*, Paris.

ERZEN, A. 1973. *Türk Arkeoloji Dergisi* 20/2, 29ff.

GOCHEVA, Z. 1978. *Pulpudeva* 2, 343ff.

KAZAROW, G. 1938. *Die Denkmäler des Thrakischen Reitergottes in Bulgarien*, Budapest. -1958. *Iz. Dechev*, 521ff.

MUTAFCHIEV, P. 1915. *IBAD* 5, 20ff.

PORTER, W. H. 1929. ed. *Euripideş: Rhesus* (2nd edn), Cambridge.

VULIĆ, N. 1941–48. *Spomenik* 98, 281ff.

List of illustrations

Index

General index

Index of sites and findspots